Maker Innovations Series

I0016808

Jump start your path to discovery with the Apress Maker Innovations series! From the basics of electricity and components through to the most advanced options in robotics and Machine Learning, you'll forge a path to building ingenious hardware and controlling it with cutting-edge software. All while gaining new skills and experience with common toolsets you can take to new projects or even into a whole new career.

The Apress Maker Innovations series offers projects-based learning, while keeping theory and best processes front and center. So you get hands-on experience while also learning the terms of the trade and how entrepreneurs, inventors, and engineers think through creating and executing hardware projects. You can learn to design circuits, program AI, create IoT systems for your home or even city, and so much more!

Whether you're a beginning hobbyist or a seasoned entrepreneur working out of your basement or garage, you'll scale up your skillset to become a hardware design and engineering pro. And often using low-cost and open-source software such as the Raspberry Pi, Arduino, PIC microcontroller, and Robot Operating System (ROS). Programmers and software engineers have great opportunities to learn, too, as many projects and control environments are based in popular languages and operating systems, such as Python and Linux.

If you want to build a robot, set up a smart home, tackle assembling a weather-ready meteorology system, or create a brand-new circuit using breadboards and circuit design software, this series has all that and more! Written by creative and seasoned Makers, every book in the series tackles both tested and leading-edge approaches and technologies for bringing your visions and projects to life.

More information about this series at https://link.springer.com/bookseries/17311.

Creating MakerSpaces

For Electronics, Arts, Engineering, and More

Sevile G. Mannickarottu
Michael G. Patterson
Carolyne Godon

Apress®

Creating MakerSpaces: For Electronics, Arts, Engineering, and More

Sevile G. Mannickarottu
Ambler, PA, USA

Michael G. Patterson
Southampton PA, USA

Carolyne Godon
Brookline MA, USA

ISBN-13 (pbk): 979-8-8688-1308-5
https://doi.org/10.1007/979-8-8688-1309-2

ISBN-13 (electronic): 979-8-8688-1309-2

Managing Director, Apress Media LLC: Welmoed Spahr
Acquisitions Editor: Miriam Haidara
Development Editor: James Markham
Editorial Assistant: Jessica Vakili

Cover designed by eStudioCalamar

Distributed to the book trade worldwide by Springer Science+Business Media New York, 1 New York Plaza, New York, NY 10004. Phone 1-800-SPRINGER, fax (201) 348-4505, e-mail orders-ny@springer-sbm.com, or visit www.springeronline.com. Apress Media, LLC is a Delaware LLC and the sole member (owner) is Springer Science + Business Media Finance Inc (SSBM Finance Inc). SSBM Finance Inc is a **Delaware** corporation.

For information on translations, please e-mail booktranslations@springernature.com; for reprint, paperback, or audio rights, please e-mail bookpermissions@springernature.com.

Apress titles may be purchased in bulk for academic, corporate, or promotional use. eBook versions and licenses are also available for most titles. For more information, reference our Print and eBook Bulk Sales web page at http://www.apress.com/bulk-sales.

Any source code or other supplementary material referenced by the author in this book is available to readers on GitHub. For more detailed information, please visit https://www.apress.com/gp/services/source-code.

If disposing of this product, please recycle the paper

This book is dedicated to our families and friends, whose encouragement and support sustain us through every challenge.

To the students, faculty, and staff of Penn Engineering, who inspire us with their ingenuity and dedication to pushing the boundaries of what is possible.

To all the Makers who pursue creativity, curiosity, and collaboration.

Table of Contents

About the Authors

Sevile G. Mannickarottu worked as a design engineer before taking over management of the University of Pennsylvania's Bioengineering Educational Laboratories. Seeing the need for an open space for "making" and learning through making, Sevile turned the lab into Penn's first open MakerSpace and one of the few Bio-MakerSpaces in the world. Students from across the University have used the space to work on projects and launch successful startups in a variety of fields. Sevile currently serves as the Director for Technological Innovation & Entrepreneurship at Penn's School of Engineering and Applied Science.

Michael G. Patterson has worked in the University of Pennsylvania's Bioengineering Educational Laboratory for nearly a decade, moving from undergraduate to full-time staff member. Michael worked closely with Sevile to transition the Educational Lab into a thriving Bio-MakerSpace and was instrumental in the creation of lab automations. Michael currently serves as the Director of the Bioengineering Educational Labs.

ABOUT THE AUTHORS

Carolyne Godon worked as a graduate student at the University of Pennsylvania's Bioengineering Educational Laboratories and was instrumental in establishing the lab as a Bio-MakerSpace.

About the Technical Reviewer

Farzin Asadi received his B.Sc. in Electronics Engineering, his M.Sc. in Control Engineering, and his Ph.D. in Mechatronics Engineering. Currently, he is with the Department of Computer Engineering at the OSTIM Technical University, Ankara, Türkiye. Dr. Asadi has published more than 40 international papers and 30 books. His research interests include switching converters, control theory, robust control of power electronics converters, and robotics.

Acknowledgments

This book would not have been possible without the support, dedication, and contributions of many individuals and institutions.

First and foremost, we extend our deepest gratitude to our friends and families, whose unwavering encouragement and patience have been a source of strength throughout this endeavor. Your support fuels our passion for innovation and learning.

We are profoundly grateful to the University of Pennsylvania and Penn Engineering for fostering an environment that champions creativity, collaboration, and hands-on learning. A special thanks to the George H. Stephenson Foundation Bio-MakerSpace, which has been an essential hub for exploration and discovery, empowering students to bring their ideas to life.

We would also like to thank Penn Engineering's Department of Bioengineering, whose commitment to interdisciplinary innovation has helped shape the foundation of this work. We also wish to recognize the faculty, staff, student employees, and students who have generously shared their expertise, excitement, and encouragement, ensuring that the vision of this MakerSpace continues to thrive.

To all who have contributed—whether through teaching, advising, or simply inspiring the next generation of makers—thank you. Your dedication makes this journey possible.

Introduction

This book will serve as a guide to MakerSpaces, with the primary audience being individuals and organizations who run a MakerSpace, but suitable for anyone who is curious about MakerSpaces and wants to know more about what goes on behind the scenes of a successful MakerSpace.

- Chapter 1 is an introduction to MakerSpaces.

- Chapter 2 will provide an overview of the history of MakerSpaces and the different types of MakerSpaces.

- Chapter 3 will dive into different maker fields.

- Chapter 4 will cover the tools and equipment needed for MakerSpaces.

- Chapter 5 will describe how to organize a MakerSpace.

- Chapter 6 will show how to operate a MakerSpace.

- Chapter 7 will discuss how to build a community around a MakerSpace.

- Chapter 8 will close with some final thoughts.

CHAPTER 1

Introducing MakerSpaces

In this chapter, we will introduce the idea of the "MakerSpace" which is permeating our world today. We will explore some of the challenges with running them as well as where they can be found. We will then provide an overview of the upcoming chapters.

MakerSpace Primer

Imagine having a room in your house dedicated to woodworking. Woodworking tools abound, and all the supplies you would ever need. As you step into the woodworking room, you're greeted by the sight of a well-organized and inviting space (see Figure 1-1). The walls are lined with sturdy shelves, proudly displaying an impressive collection of hand and power tools. Each tool has its designated place, carefully hung and precisely arranged. You have an assortment of drills and drill bits, different types of saws, clamps of all shapes and sizes, and all kinds of different types of wood for all your projects. Everything has a place, and everything is in its place.

S. G. Mannickarottu et al., *Creating MakerSpaces*, Maker Innovations Series,
https://doi.org/10.1007/979-8-8688-1309-2_1

Figure 1-1. *Wood working space in the "Garage Lab" in Penn Engineering*

Now, picture stepping into a machine shop (see Figure 1-2) that's your ultimate mechanical haven. This dedicated space is filled with an impressive array of industrial tools and equipment, carefully organized to inspire creativity and precision. As you enter, you're greeted by rows of towering steel shelves, displaying an extensive collection of hand tools and power machinery. Each tool boasts its own designated spot, hanging with precision and purpose. There's an assortment of powerful drills and an array of meticulously sorted drill bits. Lathes and milling machines stand ready for your machining projects, while clamps and vices of varying sizes await their roles. Rows of steel and aluminum stock are neatly arranged, offering materials for your mechanical dreams. Every tool, every piece of equipment, finds its home in this well-organized machine shop.

Figure 1-2. *Machine shop of the Precision Machining Laboratory in Penn Engineering*

Or perhaps imagine having a craft room, with a sewing machine, lots of fabrics, various types of needles, threads, bobbins, all kinds of special papers, canvases, paints, brushes, beads, string, metals, stones, and other crafting materials. Like in the imaginary woodworking spaces, the walls are lined with sturdy shelves stacked with yards of fabric, and smaller items are organized in neat grids of perfectly organized and labeled drawers. Perhaps there is a peg board where pliers, hot glue guns and markers are placed within easy reach of the adjustable height workbench. As these examples demonstrate, equipment and supplies can quickly add up for these kinds of hobbies, especially if you are interested in multiple maker fields. For so many of us, having a dedicated space and all the required tools is just not possible. Perhaps it's too expensive, or perhaps our homes simply cannot accommodate it. Without the luxury of having a dedicated space for making in our own home, we either have to make do with the spaces and resources that we have or find somewhere else that we can visit that has the spaces and tools that we want to use.

That's where MakerSpaces come in! MakerSpaces provide the same resources that an experienced maker may have in a dedicated space in their home, but are set up in a space for a community to share. Not everyone can have a large library full of all the books they may ever want to read, their own pool, a home gym, or large backyard, and consequently many people use a community library, a community pool, join a YMCA or gym, or visit their local park. Just as libraries, pools, and parks enrich the lives of the members of the community, so too do MakerSpaces, as they give individuals the freedom to express their creativity through a constructive outlet and learn new skills at the same time.

A fundamental principle of MakerSpaces is that anyone can be a maker. All they need is an idea and a space to facilitate it. MakerSpaces strive to reduce the activation energy required to build any individual's dream. They are places where people teach, tinker, test, and try—together. These spaces encourage experimentation and iteration, where it's okay to fail, pivot, and build again.

At their core, MakerSpaces are about more than tools—they're about a mindset. They represent the idea that creativity and innovation shouldn't be limited by space, equipment, or experience. By offering shared access to tools, knowledge, and a supportive community, MakerSpaces help democratize the process of making.

Often, MakerSpaces are associated with engineering, and are defined by the presence of a 3D printer. These more "classical" MakerSpaces often include equipment and supplies for sophisticated electronics and programmable microcontrollers along with advanced Computer Aided Design (CAD) software for designing enclosures and mechanisms that can be 3D printed or machined in the MakerSpaces (see Figure 1-3). A user would, for example, have the resources and space to create from scratch their own pet robot dog that they can control with a smartphone. This type of MakerSpace has been popularized by universities, and are often housed within their engineering programs.

Figure 1-3. *The rapid prototyping laboratory at Penn Engineering's Department of Mechanical Engineering. It is a traditional MakerSpace with 3-D printers and laser cutters*

Some famous examples include the George H. Stephenson Foundation Educational Laboratory & Bio-MakerSpace which is part of the Department of Bioengineering in the School of Engineering and Applied Sciences at the University of Pennsylvania as well as Yale University's Center for Engineering Innovation & Design (CEID). As these technologies have become more accessible, we are now seeing these types of MakerSpaces entering regular communities outside of engineering schools.

Although these engineering-focused MakerSpaces are becoming more commonplace, you can have MakerSpaces for anything, from the more typical electronics and mechanical design to more niche fields such as metal working or cooking (see Figure 1-4). Recently, MakerSpaces are coming up with a focus on molecular biology and chemistry. What was once reserved for cutting-edge academic labs is now entering the broader community. Advanced technologies like genetic engineering are now accessible to the public in Bio-MakerSpaces, such as the previously mentioned Stephenson Foundation Bio-MakerSpace at Penn or MIT's Huang-Hobbs BioMaker Space.

Figure 1-4. *Test Kitchen in Tangen Hall of Penn's Venture Lab*

Across all these formats, MakerSpaces bring together a community of learners, inventors, and collaborators. These communities often span generations and backgrounds—students working beside retirees, artists learning electronics from engineers, and neighbors teaching neighbors how to sew or solder. MakerSpaces thrive on peer-to-peer learning and shared enthusiasm. Workshops and training sessions help beginners get started, while more experienced makers can mentor others and take on ambitious projects.

In this way, MakerSpaces don't just build objects—they build people. They help individuals gain confidence with tools, deepen their understanding of science and technology, and gain tangible skills in design, construction, and creative problem-solving. In doing so, MakerSpaces enrich not only the lives of individual makers but also the communities that surround them.

Challenges with Having a MakerSpace

Creating and sustaining a MakerSpace can be incredibly rewarding, but it also presents a unique set of challenges. These spaces must support a wide variety of users, accommodate many types of tools, remain safe and flexible, adapt to technological change, and often do all of this with limited resources. Successfully addressing these challenges requires thoughtful planning, a deep understanding of users' needs, and a commitment to continuous improvement. Table 1-1 provides a summary of these.

Table 1-1. *Common Challenges with Running a MakerSpace*

Challenge Area	Description
Space and storage	Balancing equipment storage with open, functional workspace; requires flexible layouts, clear labeling, and thoughtful traffic flow.
Operational complexity	Managing tool maintenance, consumable inventory, user access, and staff support; requires strong systems and oversight.
Safety and liability	Ensuring safe tool use through training, policies, and supervision; addressing legal risk and user accountability.
Accessibility and inclusivity	Reducing barriers for beginners, non-technical users, and those with physical or cultural limitations; fostering a welcoming culture.
Financial sustainability	Funding ongoing costs such as equipment, supplies, staffing, and facilities; requires creative and diversified funding strategies.
Keeping up with technology	Adapting to rapidly evolving tools and maker technologies; balancing innovation with practical, sustainable investment.
Community engagement and culture	Building a strong, inclusive maker community through events, mentorship, shared projects, and celebration of user contributions.

Space and Storage Constraints

One of the most fundamental challenges that MakerSpaces face is the tension between storing equipment and maintaining a functional, inspiring workspace. Every MakerSpace must find ways to efficiently use its available area. Tools, supplies, and raw materials need to be stored in a manner that keeps them accessible without overwhelming the open space needed for working on projects. This balance is rarely perfect and often changes as the needs of the space evolve. It requires careful spatial planning, regular reorganization, and ongoing attention to how the space is actually used.

Storage solutions such as shelving, cabinetry, and tool racks must be strategically placed to maximize capacity while minimizing interference with workflow. Accessibility is key—users should be able to find and retrieve tools easily, without having to search through cluttered drawers or disorganized bins. Clear labeling, logical grouping, and prominent placement of frequently used tools all contribute to a better user experience. In addition to the tools themselves, MakerSpace managers must also think about how people move through the space. It's important to keep walkways clear and maintain smooth traffic flow, especially when users are transporting large materials or navigating around workstations. Flexibility is also essential. Because MakerSpaces serve a constantly shifting landscape of projects and technologies, their layouts need to be adaptable. Moveable furniture, collapsible workstations, and reconfigurable storage systems can help the space evolve as new needs arise. Ultimately, the goal is to create a space that is both organized and dynamic, capable of supporting creativity without becoming crowded or chaotic.

Operational Complexity

Operating a MakerSpace involves far more than just opening the doors and turning on the lights. Tools need to be maintained, consumables must be tracked and restocked, and usage must be monitored in order to ensure fair access. Without a robust operational infrastructure, even the most well-equipped MakerSpace can become dysfunctional. This includes implementing inventory systems, tool checkout procedures, and maintenance schedules to prevent equipment failures and supply shortages.

Staffing is another crucial component. Whether a MakerSpace relies on full-time staff, student workers, or volunteers, there must be someone available to train users, manage equipment, and oversee safety. The need for knowledgeable personnel becomes especially important as the complexity of tools increases. Users may need guidance not just on how to operate a piece of equipment, but also on how to troubleshoot issues, interpret data, or refine their designs. Without proper oversight and support, even enthusiastic users can become frustrated or discouraged.

Safety and Liability

MakerSpaces often house tools that range from relatively safe items like scissors and hot glue guns to high-powered machinery such as laser cutters and CNC mills. The diversity and potential hazards of this equipment bring safety to the forefront of MakerSpace management. Ensuring user safety involves establishing clear rules, offering mandatory training sessions, and posting visible signage to remind users of best practices. Some tools may require certification before use, while others can be more freely accessed.

In addition to safety training, MakerSpaces must also consider institutional liability. This becomes especially relevant when spaces are open to the public or serve minors. Some MakerSpaces implement user agreements or liability waivers, while others limit access to certain tools unless users are supervised. Balancing open access with responsible tool usage is a persistent challenge, and finding the right mix of trust, supervision, and policy enforcement is an ongoing process.

Accessibility and Inclusivity

While MakerSpaces aim to provide broad access to tools and knowledge, they can unintentionally exclude people due to cultural, physical, or educational barriers. New users may feel intimidated by unfamiliar tools, technical jargon, or even the social atmosphere of the space. Assumptions about prior experience, especially in technical areas like electronics or coding, can create friction for those who come from non-engineering backgrounds.

To be truly inclusive, MakerSpaces must actively design for accessibility. This includes making sure that the physical layout is navigable by people with disabilities, that tools and workbenches are adjustable or ergonomically friendly, and that signage is easy to understand. It also means building a culture of welcome—offering beginner workshops, encouraging mentorship, and celebrating all types of making, not just those rooted in engineering or technology. The presence of diverse role models and leaders within the space can help reinforce that everyone belongs, regardless of background or skill level.

Financial Sustainability

The financial realities of running a MakerSpace can be daunting. Equipment is expensive, and keeping it in working order requires a steady supply of parts, tools, and consumables. Ongoing expenses also include software licenses, safety equipment, staff salaries, and facility upkeep. Spaces in public schools, libraries, or underfunded institutions may struggle to maintain even the most basic resources.

Different MakerSpaces approach financial sustainability in different ways. Some charge membership or usage fees to help cover costs, while others are funded through university departments, grants, or corporate sponsorships. Crowdfunding campaigns and community fundraising efforts have also played a role in keeping some MakerSpaces alive. Still, long-term sustainability often remains uncertain. Balancing affordability and access with the need to maintain equipment and staffing is a constant negotiation, and one that demands creative solutions.

Keeping Up with Technology

Technology evolves rapidly, and MakerSpaces must keep pace or risk falling behind. A tool that once seemed cutting-edge—a filament-based 3D printer or basic microcontroller—can quickly become outdated. Meanwhile, newer tools such as resin printers, robotic arms, or biofabrication kits may require significant investment or expertise that the MakerSpace doesn't yet have.

Staying current requires both foresight and flexibility. MakerSpaces must evaluate new technologies not just for their novelty but for their relevance to the community they serve. One strategy is to stay modular, favoring tools and systems that can be expanded or upgraded over time rather than investing in all-in-one machines that may become obsolete. Sometimes, forming partnerships with local universities, companies, or research groups can help bring new technologies into the space without shouldering the full financial burden.

Community Engagement and Culture

At the heart of every successful MakerSpace is a strong, engaged community. Tools alone do not make a space vibrant—people do. Yet building and sustaining that community is one of the most complex and subtle challenges a MakerSpace can face. A space that lacks engagement risks becoming underutilized or fragmented, with little sense of ownership or connection among its users.

Fostering community requires intention. MakerSpaces benefit from regular events that bring people together, whether through workshops, build nights, project showcases, or informal gatherings. Celebrating the work of makers—through exhibitions, social media, or even hallway conversations—can help individuals feel seen and appreciated. Encouraging cross-disciplinary collaboration and mentorship allows people to learn from one another and build lasting relationships.

Over time, these shared experiences create a sense of belonging and collective identity that makes the MakerSpace feel more like a creative home than just a room full of tools.

What Else Can MakerSpaces Offer?

Opportunities for designing and creating something new can lead naturally to entrepreneurship. After all, isn't being able to share your new idea with the world part of the fun of making something in the first place? It's not uncommon for a budding entrepreneur to use the resources of a MakerSpace to develop a new item, prototype a technology, or test an idea—and then use that work as the foundation for launching a business. MakerSpaces provide not only a space and tools to build a prototype, but also a network of other makers who can help guide and support new entrepreneurs. Within this shared environment, individuals can trade advice, offer feedback, and collaborate on the technical and creative challenges that arise when developing something new.

These early-stage efforts often lead to exposure—through project showcases, maker fairs, or word of mouth—which can bring in potential customers, collaborators, or even investors. Once a startup gains traction through sales, grants, or venture capital, it may outgrow the MakerSpace where it began and move into its own dedicated space equipped with more specialized tools, personnel, and infrastructure. In this way, MakerSpaces can serve as powerful incubators—offering low-barrier access to essential tools and knowledge while also forming the social and professional foundation for new ventures.

A great example of this is Stella Biotechnology (`https://www.strellabiotech.com/`), a company that developed sensors to track when fruit begins to ripen, helping farmers prioritize which stock to sell. The company was started by Katherine Sizov, a 19-year-old biology student at the University of Pennsylvania. Katherine had an idea for a new kind of sensor but needed a space to test her concept and build a prototype.

As a student, she was able to access Penn's Stephenson Foundation Bio-MakerSpace, where she learned about electronics and microcontrollers and used those skills to build the first version of her product. With a working prototype in hand, she went on to win competitions, raise funding, and build a company. Importantly, because the Bio-MakerSpace is considered "IP neutral" by the University, Penn did not claim ownership over her invention, allowing her to retain full rights to her innovation while still taking advantage of university resources.

This example also highlights something even more essential to MakerSpaces than tools: community. While someone might be able to set up a personal workspace in a basement or garage, what separates a MakerSpace from a solitary workshop is the social environment it fosters. MakerSpaces bring together people who share an interest in making things—whether that means building robots, sewing clothing, designing jewelry, developing medical devices, or experimenting with new forms of art or science. These shared interests create fertile ground for collaboration, mutual support, and collective learning. Users pass ideas back and forth, help troubleshoot each other's projects, and often spark inspiration through casual conversation or chance encounters.

The community dimension of a MakerSpace also makes the experience of making more enjoyable. For many people, working in isolation can be lonely or demotivating. But in a MakerSpace, the presence of others who are building and exploring creates an atmosphere of energy and shared purpose. It can be likened to joining a gym—many people struggle to maintain a workout routine on their own, but once they join a group, find a partner, or attend regular classes, they suddenly gain motivation and consistency. In the same way, being part of a MakerSpace can turn what feels like a solitary hobby into a shared creative experience.

This community also plays an important role in learning. MakerSpaces provide opportunities for both formal and informal learning. Formal learning includes scheduled classes, safety trainings, or skill-building workshops. For example, a new user who wants to learn how to use a

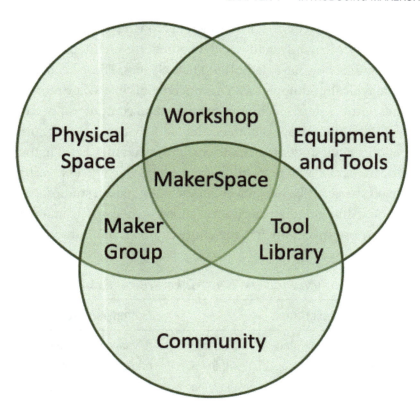

Figure 1-5. *Diagram showing how MakerSpaces sit at the intersection of community, space, and tools*

Where Can You Find MakerSpaces?

While MakerSpaces are often associated with universities and colleges, their roots lie in community-based initiatives. The first spaces to call themselves MakerSpaces—or similar names like hacker labs or fabrication workshops—were created not in academic institutions but by collectives of hobbyists, engineers, artists, and tinkerers who pooled their tools and knowledge to create collaborative environments. These grassroots spaces reflected the DIY ethos of the early Maker Movement: accessible, inclusive, and centered around curiosity and community.

Today, MakerSpaces exist in a wide and growing range of settings (see Table 1-2). Most universities with engineering, architecture, or design programs now have dedicated MakerSpaces. These academic spaces are typically equipped with advanced tools like 3D printers, CNC machines, laser cutters, electronics benches, and computer-aided design software. They often support both curricular activities and extracurricular exploration, giving students a chance to apply what they learn in the classroom to personal or team-driven projects. Some universities have specialized spaces—like bio-maker labs, textile-focused studios, or entrepreneurship-centered fabrication zones—while others maintain general-purpose spaces open to the entire campus community.

Table 1-2. *Common Places Where MakerSpaces Exist*

Location type	Description	Examples/notes
Universities and colleges	MakerSpaces in higher ed institutions, often within engineering or design schools	Advanced tools (e.g., 3D printers, CNC), often open to students and faculty
Community colleges	Spaces that serve students and local residents alike.	Emphasis on workforce training, certification programs, community access
Public libraries	Accessible MakerSpaces promoting lifelong learning and creativity	Often free and open to all; offer tools like 3D printers, sewing machines
K–12 schools	Integrated into classrooms or media centers to support hands-on learning	Age-appropriate tools; fosters creativity, collaboration, STEM skills.

(*continued*)

Table 1-2. (*continued*)

Location type	Description	Examples/notes
Museums and science centers	Maker areas linked to exhibits or programs, often with rotating activities	Interactive exhibits, short-term projects for visitors of all ages
Community centers/ nonprofits	Spaces hosted by local orgs to support youth, education, or civic innovation.	May serve specific groups (e.g., afterschool programs, underserved areas).
Hackerspaces/ fab labs	Independent or network-affiliated spaces focused on open-source innovation	Often membership-based; connected via Fab Foundation or maker networks
Online maker communities	Digital platforms where makers collaborate, share designs, and ask questions.	Found on Reddit, Discord, GitHub, Thingiverse, Instructables, and more.
Mobile MakerSpaces	Traveling labs that bring tools and training to different locations.	Ideal for outreach in rural or underserved communities

Community colleges are increasingly joining the MakerSpace movement as well. These spaces not only support student learning but also serve the broader public by providing access to tools and training for local residents, small business owners, and aspiring entrepreneurs. In many cases, community colleges act as regional innovation hubs, offering workforce development programs, maker certifications, and even hosting local start-up incubators that grow out of the MakerSpace community.

Beyond higher education, MakerSpaces have taken root in public libraries, K-12 schools, museums, and nonprofit organizations. Public libraries in particular have embraced the Maker movement as part of their evolving mission to support lifelong learning. Many now feature dedicated "maker corners" or full-fledged labs with 3D printers, craft supplies, soldering stations, and more. These spaces are typically free to use, making them one of the most accessible entry points into the world of making.

K-12 schools are also embracing hands-on, project-based learning by integrating MakerSpaces into their classrooms and media centers. These spaces may be stocked with LEGOs, cardboard, sewing kits, and basic electronics, or may grow to include higher-end fabrication tools as students advance. They provide a tangible way for students to engage in STEM, develop creativity, and practice collaborative problem-solving—skills that will serve them well no matter what career path they choose.

Museums and science centers sometimes maintain temporary or permanent MakerSpaces, offering visitors the chance to experiment, build, and create as part of their exhibits. Nonprofit and youth organizations, such as the Boys & Girls Clubs or afterschool STEM programs, have also launched mobile MakerSpaces or pop-up labs that bring making directly into underserved communities.

To find a MakerSpace near you, one of the easiest places to start is online. A quick Internet search for "MakerSpace" along with your city or town's name can often lead you in the right direction. You can also search using related terms like "Hackerspace," "Fab Lab," "Idea Lab," "Makers Hub," or simply "makers + [your city]." If nothing comes up in a general search, consider reaching out to local public libraries, community centers, high schools, or school boards—they may have a MakerSpace on-site or know of one nearby.

If you live in a rural area or a place without a local MakerSpace, don't be discouraged. The global maker community is alive and thriving online. Many virtual MakerSpaces and maker communities are organized around common interests—electronics, 3D printing, robotics, cosplay, sustainable design, woodworking, and much more. These groups gather on platforms like Reddit (e.g., r/makers, r/DIY), Discord, GitHub, Stack Overflow, Thingiverse, and Instructables. These digital communities often offer project documentation, open-source files, tool reviews, and forums where you can ask questions, get advice, and connect with others who share your interests.

In addition, networks like the Fab Lab Network and Makerspace. com offer searchable directories of affiliated spaces around the world. MIT's Fab Lab model, in particular, has spread globally and helped seed the growth of MakerSpaces in over 100 countries, often in schools and underserved regions.

Some organizations even offer "mobile MakerSpaces" that bring equipment and training to communities without permanent facilities. These mobile units may appear at schools, fairs, or community events, and they can provide inspiration for how a MakerSpace might start small and grow over time.

In the open-source spirit of the Maker Movement, MakerSpaces— both physical and virtual—tend to be welcoming, inclusive, and driven by the values of accessibility and collaboration. The best way to learn more about MakerSpaces is to visit one, talk to the people there, and try a project yourself. Whether you're prototyping an invention, learning to sew, coding an LED display, or just exploring what's possible, you'll likely find that MakerSpaces are not just about tools—they're about people, and the communities they build through making.

Key Takeaways

- MakerSpaces provide the resources needed to make things, such as art, woodworking, 3D printing, electronics, or food, without the expense of buying all of the material yourself.

- MakerSpaces encourage community and provide opportunities for entrepreneurship.

- MakerSpaces can be found anywhere, from community centers and libraries, to schools and universities.

CHAPTER 2

Introducing Space Types

In this chapter, we will begin by exploring the origins and history of MakerSpaces and describe early historical examples of physical spaces that served similar roles to the MakerSpaces of today. We will then follow up by exploring the common characteristics of several different types of MakerSpaces in greater detail. There are too many different MakerSpace types to attempt to describe in just this book so we have narrowed down the list to a selection based on our impression of the most common types of MakerSpaces that we are familiar with, classified by the setting of the space. The four key types of MakerSpaces that we have chosen to describe in depth in this chapter include Library MakerSpaces, School MakerSpaces (K-12 or primary and secondary schools), University and College MakerSpaces (or other higher education institutions), and Community MakerSpaces (inclusive of all other MakerSpace settings not described by the first three on the list). These categories of MakerSpace types represent the authors' best attempt at segmenting the different types of MakerSpace physical settings that are most commonly seen.

© Sevile G. Mannickarottu, Michael G. Patterson, and Carolyne Godon 2025
S. G. Mannickarottu et al., *Creating MakerSpaces*, Maker Innovations Series,
https://doi.org/10.1007/979-8-8688-1309-2_2

Laying the Groundwork

We recognize that in reality, these four categories describe just a small sample of the myriad of different MakerSpaces that you may find in the wide world around you and we are of course well aware that there are many existing MakerSpaces that may not fall perfectly neatly into one of our specific buckets of MakerSpace types. That uniqueness of MakerSpace settings, and inability of some MakerSpaces to slot into clean-cut defined categories, is definitely not a negative trait at all and can actually be described as one of the most amazing and beautiful things about MakerSpaces, for each space is truly unique in its own way and represents a descriptive picture of the broader community situated around it!

For each of the four key MakerSpaces type segments that we have chosen to include in this chapter, we will describe what they are, what makes them different from some other types of MakerSpaces, what users can typically expect to be able to do in most examples in that type of MakerSpace setting, how users can usually expect to access them, and conclude the description of each type of MakerSpace setting by evaluating some of their pros and cons compared to the other types of MakerSpaces that we are describing in this chapter. At the end of this chapter, after the description of each type of MakerSpace setting, we will also outline some of the reasons that one might decide to choose one particular type of MakerSpace over another, both from the perspective of a MakerSpace user choosing which setting of MakerSpace where they would like to visit in order to make things and also from the perspective of someone who is operating a MakerSpace choosing the type of MakerSpace setting they may want to set up or the changes they may want to explore making to their current MakerSpace.

Please note that this chapter, as well as the entirety of this book, will primarily focus on the United States context of MakerSpaces due to the authors' location and unfortunately severely limited knowledge of and exposure to international MakerSpaces setting types. We recognize this is a serious limitation and will consider remedying this in upcoming future editions of this publication. Finally, we will conclude this chapter by providing a succinct summary of the key takeaways regarding different MakerSpace setting types and we will outline what we believe to be the key considerations relevant to each type of MakerSpace stakeholder.

Throughout the entirety of this chapter, we will regularly refer back to the following matrix illustrated in Figure 2-1. This matrix defines MakerSpace setting types by MakerSpace cost and MakerSpace specialization to compare and contrast different types of MakerSpace settings described in this chapter. In this 2x2 matrix, the X axis (horizontal) describes the user cost. The cost in this case refers to the monetary cost to the user to utilize the MakerSpace. More affordable MakerSpaces would be located on the left side of the figure while more expensive MakerSpaces would be located on the right side. The Y axis (vertical) describes the specialization of the equipment that can typically be expected to be found in that type of MakerSpace. For example, MakerSpaces with relatively common, everyday equipment that would not be surprising to see in someone's garage or craft room at home would be considered lower specialization and would therefore be located on the bottom of the figure while conversely, MakerSpaces setting types that can typically be expected offer very specialized, unique, high-tech, professional, or industrial types of equipment would generally be considered to be high specialization and would be located on the top of the figure.

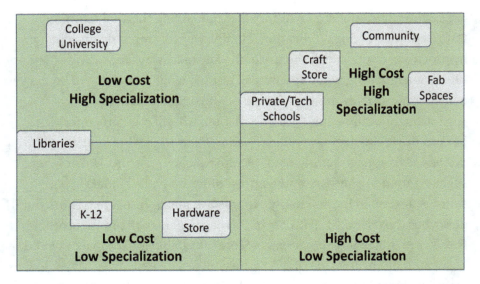

Figure 2-1. *Matrix of MakerSpace types by user cost and equipment specialization. User cost is represented on the X axis (lower cost to the left and higher cost to the right). Equipment specialization is represented on the Y axis (lower specialization at the bottom)*

In Figure 2-1 above, you can clearly observe that the various different types of MakerSpaces each have their own unique niche and occupy different quadrants and areas of the cost-specialization matrix. At one end, K-12 (also known as primary and secondary) school MakerSpaces are typically expected to be located in the lower cost and lower specialization quadrant of the MakerSpace cost-specialization matrix (except perhaps for MakerSpaces found in a minority of generously funded private schools or technology-focused high school programs). Meanwhile, community MakerSpaces can usually be expected to occupy the opposite corner of the same matrix, where there are often high user fees charged for those seeking to use the space but there is also highly specialized equipment available for use in that type of MakerSpace setting. MakerSpaces located in public libraries are typically available to anyone in the community and can usually be accessed at very low (or no) cost to the user and their level of equipment specialization can vary broadly depending on the library. College and university MakerSpaces are typically available at low (or no) cost to the user as well (besides the cost of tuition to attend the college or university, as MakerSpaces in higher education settings are often designed for and restricted to students attending the institution). These types of MakerSpaces typically offer highly specialized professional-grade equipment and universities commonly have multiple MakerSpaces on campus that each have their own unique focus (see Chapter 3 for more in-depth description of different Maker fields).

History of MakerSpaces

While the name MakerSpace may be considered a relatively new term, apparently dating back to sometime in the early 2000s, the concept of having a shared community space to be used for activities focused on making can be considered to be as old as humanity itself (see Table 2-1 for an overview). As early as the Stone Age, prehistoric humans seemingly engaged in community-making activities in specific locations that could be the ancestors of the modern MakerSpaces as we know them. There is vast archeological evidence that early humans gathered as a community in specific locations and shared knowledge with each other about many different things like crafting tools, cooking food, making clothing, building shelter, and making all kinds of other items. Or, it could be summarized as gathering as a community, sharing knowledge and making. That description kind of sounds like the definition of a MakerSpace, doesn't it? This type of community making collaboration is considered by historians to have helped early human communities pool their skills together and jointly develop better tools and improved the sharing of technology that were essential for human social and economic survival without which the current modern world would not even exist.

Table 2-1. *Overview of the History of MakerSpaces*

Era/period	Example(s)	Maker-like features	Shared space type	Continuity to modern MakerSpaces
Stone age	Prehistoric cave sites	Tool crafting, communal knowledge-sharing, collaborative learning	Open cave spaces	Earliest DIY culture, community learning
Ancient civilizations	Deir el-Medina (Egypt), Greek agoras, Roman forums	Artisans living and working together, mentoring, collaborative production	Workshops in cities, temples, civic centers	Foundation of vocational making and apprenticeship models
Roman empire	*Fabricae*, Hagia Sophia construction teams	State-sponsored collaborative production, apprenticeships	State and church-run workshops	Scaled making, specialization, and knowledge transfer
Islamic golden age	House of Wisdom (Baghdad)	Interdisciplinary knowledge sharing, scientific prototyping	Scholarly and artisan institutions	Integrated making and learning, cross-disciplinary culture

(continued)

Table 2-1. (*continued*)

Era/period	Example(s)	Maker-like features	Shared space type	Continuity to modern MakerSpaces
European monasteries	Scriptoriums, blacksmith sheds	Communal crafting, tool production, manuscript making	Religious workshop spaces	Preservation of knowledge through hands-on making
High Middle Ages	Cathedral construction lodges	Multi-disciplinary teamwork, apprenticeship, shared infrastructure	Construction site lodges	Project-based, multi-skill collaboration
Renaissance	Florence artisan guilds	Trade-based collaboration, innovation, technical mastery	Guild halls, workshops, trade streets	Structured communities of practice and skill development
Early modern art studios	Atelier system	Tiered skill-learning, master–apprentice reproduction	Shared studio spaces	Model for mentorship-based creative spaces
Late 20th century	TechShop (2006–2017)	Open access to tools, prototyping, entrepreneurship	Membership-based shared labs	Birth of modern MakerSpaces
21st century	Forums, online communities, local MakerSpaces	DIY culture, peer learning, open-source knowledge	Physical and virtual spaces	Convergence of tech, access, and community building

Archeological evidence obtained from caves occupied by humans in the Lower Paleolithic (Old Stone Age) located in a part of the world that is now known as Israel shows evidence of physical spaces that were commonly used by communities of early humans for "learning through sharing," making, collaborating, and exchanging knowledge and ideas. At the same sites, archeologists also uncovered evidence of tools that these communities of early humans used to teach others how to make tools, the oldest evidence of DIY tutorials found to date. Though these spaces were seemingly unimaginably far from looking anything like the modern MakerSpaces that we have come to expect today, these types of spaces served essentially the same purpose as today's MakerSpaces, which is for a community to gather together, share knowledge, and make things.

Evidently, the development of human community knowledge-sharing about making did not end with early humans making simple tools in caves hundreds of thousands of years ago during the Old Stone Age. Across the ancient world, there is significant evidence of shared spaces dedicated to crafting, building, and knowledge transfer. Ancient civilizations like Mesopotamia, Egypt, Greece, and Rome developed structured environments for collaborative making, often tied to temples, palaces, or civic centers. For example, in Ancient Egypt, entire artisan villages such as Deir el-Medina were organized to support the construction of royal tombs. These communities lived, worked, and learned together, passing down skills in stone carving, metalworking, and painting from generation to generation in a shared workshop model that echoes modern MakerSpace principles.

Similarly, across the ancient Mediterranean, tradespeople gathered in agora workshops in Greece or in the bustling forums of Roman cities, where communal crafting and the informal sharing of tools and techniques were part of everyday life. In Asia, imperial China's dynasties maintained state-sponsored artisan workshops—highly organized spaces where skills were shared across generations. In Japan, temple carpenters (known as miya-daiku) worked in deeply collaborative guilds, often building intricate wooden structures that required decades of mentorship and knowledge transfer.

In both the late Roman Empire, and its continuation in the east, collaborative making continued through state-sponsored and ecclesiastical workshops known as fabricae. Originally established to support the Roman military with arms and armor, these fabricae evolved into large-scale manufacturing centers producing everything from textiles and metal goods to mosaics and religious artifacts. They were staffed by teams of skilled artisans, apprentices, and administrators who worked under imperial oversight.

In eastern Roman cities (sometimes referred to as "Byzantine") like Constantinople, craftsmanship became increasingly tied to religious and courtly patronage. The construction of monumental structures—such as the Hagia Sophia (Figure 2-2)—involved extensive teams of masons, glassworkers, mosaicists, and engineers, who collaborated in shared spaces much like modern interdisciplinary maker teams. These large-scale projects required not only technical skill but also coordination, knowledge sharing, and iterative problem-solving within the making community. While not "public" in the way modern MakerSpaces are, these imperial and religious workshops preserved the collaborative essence of community-based making and served as centers of innovation for centuries.

Figure 2-2. *The Hagia Sophia in modern day Istanbul (formerly Constantinople). Originally constructed as a church building, it was converted into a mosque in the 15th century, and then a museum in the 20th century (Designed by Freepik)*

During the Islamic Golden Age, the House of Wisdom in Baghdad blended scholarship and invention in one location, with scholars and artisans developing scientific instruments, automata, and other early prototypes in shared spaces that fused learning and making. At the same time, European monasteries quietly preserved traditions of collaborative craftsmanship through their scriptoriums, blacksmithing sheds, and woodworking rooms—producing not only manuscripts but tools, textiles, and other physical goods.

In medieval Europe, particularly during the High Middle Ages (roughly 1000–1300 CE), cathedral construction sites became hubs of collaborative making and technical innovation. These massive projects often took generations to complete and brought together a wide range of skilled tradespeople—stone masons, carpenters, glaziers, blacksmiths, and sculptors—who worked side by side in what could be considered one of the most advanced "maker communities" of their time. The construction site itself functioned like a temporary village, with workshops, shared tools, and apprenticeships all organized around a common project. Knowledge was passed down orally and through direct mentorship, and many techniques were refined in real time as workers solved practical challenges together on-site.

This trend continued to flourish in the city of Florence during the Renaissance period, which saw a truly remarkable convergence of art, science, and craftsmanship. During this time, the city of Florence had entire streets and specific neighborhoods dedicated to a particular trade that were concentrated in a defined area of the city, allowing for close-knit collaboration and free-flowing exchange of technical knowledge and innovative ideas between various members of that specific trade's community. Artists, scientists, and artisans were not isolated by themselves in their pursuits of excellence in their discipline during the Renaissance period in Florence; they were brought together to create a vibrant intellectual and creative ecosystem, inspiring all kinds of inventions and progress.

Around the same historical period, guilds were formed so merchants and craft workers could band together to help each other out, both with the purpose de-risking and benefiting their business ventures as well as to encourage and nurture technical competency development and skill-sharing among the various guild members. Skilled artisans formed guilds where workers in craft industries joined together to enjoy the mutual benefits of collaboration. For example, there were guilds for leather workers, weavers, blacksmiths, or jewelers, who were each concentrated in certain neighborhoods and streets of Florence. To this day, many streets still carry the name of craftspeople who occupied them hundreds of years ago.

Many cities and communities all around Europe had similarly structured communities of artisans. These guilds were usually organized and specialized in different ways depending on the cities and regions where they were located, so not every city or town was set up exactly like

Florence during the Renaissance. However, in essence, they consisted of highly organized groups of individuals skilled in making similar things, sharing a profession. Now, just like with the Stone Age communities described earlier, you might begin to think (understandably so) that the history of Renaissance guilds in Florence seems a little out of place in a 21st century book about MakerSpaces, which are typically modern high-technology spaces that would not exist without contemporary inventions like electricity and microprocessors. However, just like modern MakerSpaces, these craft guilds, such as the ones established in Florence during the Renaissance, fostered community collaboration and the sharing of techniques, knowledge, and artistic inspiration between members of the community. Though guilds also had important financial, business, and trade components that are typically seen as their defining features, at their core they were also organizations of makers and so can be considered early instances of MakerSpaces or at least organized maker community groups. Florence, during the Renaissance, perfectly exemplified the timeless human endeavor of collaborative knowledge-sharing and pursuit of innovation, which continues to resonate with the principles of modern-day MakerSpaces and current maker communities.

Furthermore, across history, there have been very clear signs of regional specialization in certain skills and techniques that can be traced back to the path of organized communities fostering knowledge-sharing between members. For example, in the arts, the atelier (or studio) system has been around for thousands of years and is a prime example of a controlled flow of information leading to hyper-specialization of artistic techniques at the local level. The atelier system is designed to operate in such a way that students of all skill levels work together in the same shared community physical space and spend the majority of their time learning specialized techniques from the experienced and well-renowned studio masters who lead the instructional sessions. Students learn the unique techniques of the master artists of the atelier at which they belong by spending their days copying the work of the masters and ultimately set out on the path to progress to making their own unique personal artwork one day once they are deemed to have acquired sufficient skills through reproduction of other works.

The similarities in techniques are so clear between studio masters and their atelier trainees that even with modern technology, art historians sometimes don't know for certain if a work was done by a master or by their apprentice. One recent example of the very strong similarity in techniques is the discovery in 2022 by the American National Gallery of Art in Washington, DC (United States) that "Girl with a Flute," a famous painting long attributed to 17th-century Dutch painter Johannes Vermeer, was actually completed by an assistant, not by the famous artist himself, who, incidentally, was a member of the Delft Painter's Guild but there are no records indicating he had any registered apprentices.

Jumping forward a few centuries, one of the first examples of contemporary MakerSpaces as we currently know them was called TechShop. Founded in 2006 by a group of artists and engineers, this innovative community space provided its members with access to high-quality tools, 3D printers, laser cutters, and other cutting-edge machinery that would typically be well out of reach for individual hobbyists or budding entrepreneurs. TechShop not only promoted a collaborative and supportive environment for creative enthusiasts but also facilitated the transformation of ideas into tangible prototypes or products. Unfortunately, TechShop filed for bankruptcy and went out of business in 2017 but is still considered the blueprint for community MakerSpaces around the world.

Innovative new advances in computing power rapidly unlocked what could be made with regular personal-scale computers and inexpensive components. Technology enthusiasts were inspired by the progress and excited to dive in and explore the boundless new possibilities of making! Things that were only possible on enormous academic or industrial laboratory computers just a few years prior were now possible to accomplish at home or with a regular school or library computer.

Components for electronic projects have also rapidly become more accessible. Widescale adoption of the Internet also facilitated accessibility and ordering of tools and equipment. Previously, one had to find a company's phone number or address to request a hard copy catalog and mail or phone in orders of what they needed. Detailed spec sheets were available on request but also often required long wait times. With the advent of the World Wide Web and digitization of catalogs and product information, all of this became infinitely easier to accomplish. Search engines like Google allowed interested makers to search for a product across all the websites on the Internet. This was a quick and efficient way to not only learn more about the product but also get the best price and/or fastest delivery option.

Forums on making also emerged and rapidly grew in popularity, acting essentially as virtual MakerSpaces hosted on the Internet. Users could ask questions and share knowledge, just like they might do in person at a physical MakerSpace.

Around the same time as TechShop was operating in the mid-2000s to mid-2010s, there were also other MakerSpaces and hackerspaces that began to emerge independently in different parts of the world. Fueled and inspired by the open-source software movement widely documented on the Internet and the sharing of knowledge, these spaces aimed to create physical locations where community members could gather to work on projects, share expertise, and learn from each other. Often, these started as an online community that realized that several users were located near enough to each other that it made sense to get together to collaborate in the same physical space. Or, they evolved from existing groups of individuals who had adjacent interests to making, either in engineering, arts, or other disciplines. These early MakerSpaces were driven by the principles of community, collaboration, and open access, where like-minded individuals from diverse backgrounds could learn new skills, design new things, and invent together.

MakerSpaces and the Open-Source Movement

The open-source movement first started in the software industry with the hope of creating a global unrestricted collaborative community of developers, testers, and users who could all work toward a common goal of creating a new product without cost or license barriers. At its core, the movement was dependent on the symbiotic relationship between all of these stakeholders in the field. If just one of these important pillars were not strong enough to support the platform then the reach of the product could be severely limited (see Table 2-2 for an overview).

Table 2-2. *The MakerSpaces and the Open-Source Movement*

Theme	Description	Example
Open-source principles	Free access, collaborative improvement, community ownership	Wikipedia, GitHub projects like OSP
MakerSpace role	Physical hub providing tools, training, and community	University MakerSpaces, library fab labs
Knowledge-sharing	Workshops, peer-to-peer learning, interdisciplinary exchange	Bioengineering students teaching coding to designers
Resource accessibility	Removing barriers through shared access to tools and equipment	3D printers, laser cutters, electronics benches
Rapid prototyping	Allows real-time iteration and troubleshooting for projects	OSP's multiple design revisions done on-site
Global collaboration	Shared repositories and communication across borders	OSP team collaboration between the USA and the UK
DIY movement connection	Values of independence, creativity, and self-reliance	YouTube DIY creators, Make: Magazine, Maker Faires
Impact on innovation	Supports grassroots inventors and entrepreneurs	Startups launching hardware products from MakerSpaces
Cultural evolution	Transition from DIY → Maker → Open Innovation ecosystems	Online communities + physical spaces driving tech access

Over time, the open-source movement has also slowly seeped into other fields besides its origins in the software space. The main principle driving a successful open-source project is that any user of the platform can spark new ideas or determine future growth for the project. As such, the overall impact and success of an open-source project is entirely dependent on the participation and commitment of the community in which it is deployed. This is in direct contrast with a traditional private venture type of software projects where the overall success of the product and future growth directions are entirely dependent on the initial inventors and governing company.

Perhaps one of the most well-known and most-used examples of the open-source movement is Wikipedia. Wikipedia is an open-source encyclopedia website with which you are probably very familiar. Anyone and everyone can contribute to Wikipedia articles and has the freedom to make any changes they desire to any page, adding any information that they wish to add whether it's truthful or entirely incorrect. You can try it right now by visiting any Wikipedia page on the Internet browser of your choice and editing anything on the page. However, don't be surprised if your change does not end up appearing in the published version of the page that you choose to edit. Teams of volunteer moderators and editors review all of the proposed edits made by users and aim to prevent the spread of misinformation by correcting inaccurate information and flagging any content that may be missing references. However, as you probably know and as teachers like to frequently remind their students, the information that you find on Wikipedia can ultimately not be considered reliable because it is open-source and anyone can make changes. It does, however, serve great utility as a quick and easy general introduction to all kinds of different topics, which is why the site remains one of the most visited websites on the Internet.

It is not difficult at all to see how MakerSpaces and the open-source community could have a highly successful pairing (see Figure 2-3). The open-source community is consistently looking for a place to collaborate, share ideas, and foster creativity to improve upon a project. MakerSpaces are ideal locations for this intersection of needs. Unsurprisingly, open-source projects often thrive in MakerSpace environments as they rely on the same kind of collective efforts of a community. In addition, MakerSpaces often attract a wide range of different people, including engineers, artists, designers, and hobbyists. This diversity of user backgrounds and interests can be a great strength for open-source projects as it brings together a variety of individuals with different skill sets who can all contribute in their own way to various aspects of a project. Open-source projects by design rely on knowledge-sharing and the free exchange of ideas between users of the platform to maintain and improve it. MakerSpaces also promote this same sharing culture by offering workshops, classes, and other events where members can share knowledge and learn new skills, which they can then choose to apply to open-source projects.

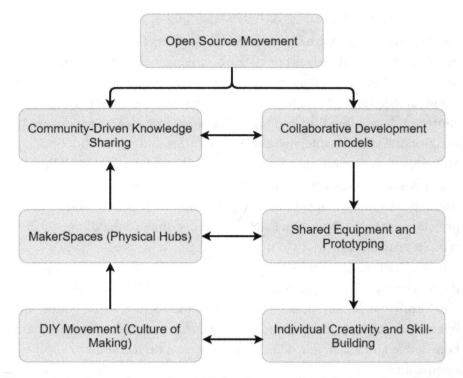

Figure 2-3. *Overview of how MakerSpaces are closely tied to the Open-Source Movement*

Another reason MakerSpaces and open-source projects make a great pairing is that not all open-source contributors have full access to the tools and equipment required for their projects, as these can often be quite cumbersome and expensive. This is where MakerSpaces come in very handy to help remove barriers to getting more people involved in open-source projects. MakerSpaces can offer a wide range of tools and equipment, from 3D printers to laser cutters, which can be used to create or enhance open-source hardware projects.

In addition to providing a location where open-source projects can be maintained and enhanced, MakerSpaces have also been the birthplace of many new open-source projects. As a physical space that brings together people from various backgrounds sharing the spirit of making, they are an excellent catalyst for creative interdisciplinary pursuits and often have lots of tools and equipment available to enable rapid prototyping and troubleshooting, removing common stalls in project development often caused by needing to order new parts to test something slightly different than what was originally expected to be required.

An example of such an open-source project that was fully developed in a MakerSpace is OSP: An Open-source Plate Reader (`https://github.com/brianchowlab/OSP`). The OSP project started as a student project for a submission for the International Genetically Engineered Machine (or better known as iGEM) Competition. However, following the end of the competition, the creators of OSP were inspired by the open-source movement and decided on continuing to develop the project at their university MakerSpace. They benefited from the open resources at the makerspace where they were able to rapidly iterate over new and improved designs of their original plate reader. Without open access to the MakerSpace, these improvements would have been incredibly challenging and even more time-demanding to complete. They were able to leverage the maker community at their university MakerSpace to ask questions to other users with different backgrounds and expertise and learn more about different aspects of their project with which they were struggling.

Outside of being an example of the benefits of the synergies between MakerSpaces and the open-source movement, OSP is also a prime example of just how far-reaching the global open-source movement community can truly be. The OSP project, which was based in Philadelphia, ultimately had supporters around the world, including in the UK where a completely different team went on to feature it in a local hackathon competition. Thanks to the collaborative openness of the open-source movement, the UK team members were able to reach out to the original American OSP team to ask them questions and discuss how best to approach building their own plate reader in their home country.

Modern, post-2000s MakerSpaces can also be considered to have evolved from DIY (do-it-yourself) culture, a movement that had its origins around the 1950s. Before that time, most things were made by hand or industrially manufactured on a relatively small scale. By the mid-20th century, with the economic expansion and increased globalization following World War II, more and more consumer goods were being manufactured industrially at a large scale and often in faraway places. Consumerism culture also grew, and the expansion of a strong middle class, particularly in North America, led to increased spending and perceived need for new luxuries and trendy goods. Participants in the DIY movement, known as DIYers, rejected the consumerist attitude of buying new fewer durable items. They made the very deliberate decision to make things themselves and repair things themselves, often at a higher cost and at the expense of more time than the alternative. Publications such as Family Handyman Magazine exemplified the height of the DIY movement; older existing publications, such as Popular Mechanics, also began to feature more do-it-yourself articles as interest in this movement grew and became more mainstream. In 2005, Make: magazine was published formalizing the "MakerSpace" movement and supporting Maker Faires and other community do-it-yourself activities.

More recently, there have also been many YouTube channels dedicated to DIYing, including "I Like to Make Stuff," "Totally Handy," "DIY Perks," and "This Old House" (which originally started as a TV show in the 1970s) among others. These channels will have a mix of videos ranging from all different skill levels. You can learn everything from how to build a simple shelf to how to integrate electronics into homemade furniture. With an abundance of DIY tutorials available for free on YouTube and broad access to MakerSpaces with all the tools and equipment one would ever dream of needing, the only limit to making is a user's creativity.

Today, MakerSpaces have evolved to cater to a wide range of user interests and types of maker fields, covering everything from electronics and robotics to woodworking, textiles, and culinary arts. MakerSpaces have also found their way into schools, libraries, universities, and other community spaces, fostering education, learning, and creativity in various fields. Additionally, MakerSpaces continue to play a vital role in promoting entrepreneurship and innovation, providing a launchpad for many startups and small businesses.

MakerSpace Types

There are four broad categories of MakerSpaces that you can usually find: those associated with public libraries, MakerSpaces tied to K-12 schools (primary and secondary schools), college and university MakerSpaces, and community MakerSpaces which require a paid membership (see Table 2-3 for an overview).

Table 2-3. Overview of MakerSpace Types

Type	Typical users	Access model	Common tools and activities	Challenges	Distinct features
Library MakerSpaces	General public— all ages	Free or very low-cost, open to all	3D printing, sewing, crafting, basic electronics, quilting, tool lending	Limited capital budgets, staffing for events, equipment maintenance	Strong outreach (mobile units, workshops), digital integration, equity-focused
School MakerSpaces (K–12)	K–12 students, teachers	Tied to classes; also used by after-school clubs	Cardboard prototyping, 3D printing, Makey kits, crafting, LEDs	Underfunding, lack of support staff, bureaucratic barriers	Project-based learning (Constructivist model), mobile kits, STEM skill building

College / university MakerSpaces	University students, faculty, staff	Usually free for students; some require training	3D printing, laser cutting, wet labs, electronics, machining	Varies by department; access restrictions, staffing for broader use	Multidisciplinary, tied to research and entrepreneurship, IP-neutral environments
Community MakerSpaces	Hobbyists, artists, entrepreneurs, learners	Paid membership, class registration, or usage fees	Woodworking, ceramics, laser cutting, sewing, CNC, jewelry making	Cost barriers, tool access, variable skill support	Reflect local culture and needs, range from hobbyist spaces to fab labs

Library MakerSpaces

Libraries have always been much more than just a space full of books to borrow. Since their inception, libraries have also served as places for members of the community to gather together and exchange their thoughts, ideas, knowledge, and information. Libraries commonly host all kinds of community events, such as book clubs, educational workshops, and children's storytime. Many have specific spaces designed for community events, such as classrooms and computer labs. It's no surprise that libraries were early adopters of MakerSpaces, since the guiding principles of the maker movement overlap significantly with the mission of most public libraries. Naturally, public libraries are also an important type of MakerSpace setting, and since they are usually open to the public and free of charge to use, they are often the most widely accessible MakerSpaces available to anyone in any community.

Since the beginning of the modern Maker movement, public libraries have been quick to embrace the growing trend and carve out physical space within their facilities to add one or more MakerSpaces, and allocate budget to set up a MakerSpace and run events. Many public libraries now include a space dedicated to making, crafting, or creating. They are often called MakerSpaces, but sometimes have other names unique to their library like idea space, hackerspace, or workshop. As mentioned in Figure 2-1, Library MakerSpaces generally operate in the lower-cost region of the cost-specialization 2x2 matrix, as they require no or very low user fees to enjoy. However, the same thing that makes them so broadly accessible does add a unique challenge to their operation. Since libraries are publicly funded and typically don't charge user fees, they can struggle to obtain the capital funds needed to create a space that can truly compete with other higher-cost MakerSpaces, such as community MakerSpaces targeting entrepreneurs that operate on a membership model.

However, even though library MakerSpaces typically have relatively limited budgets, they can vary in their level of specialization. Some libraries have the funds available and are still able to offer a large swatch of MakerSpace services to the public, while others are only able to provide one or two services.

Libraries are also often earlier adopters of new technology and serve as a place for community members to use and learn new technology. When personal computers became mainstream in the 1990s, libraries quickly adopted them. In fact, libraries made Internet access accessible to people without phone-line modems. In the 2000s, when "Internet Cafes" became popular, libraries still welcomed users because their services were free. Many individuals had their first experience with computers at a library, and public libraries continue to offer computer and technology workshops in 2023, such as tablet or video-calling classes for seniors, or online job searching workshops.

In the same manner, libraries have begun setting up their own MakerSpaces, giving free access to members of the community who want to use the space. This is in contrast to community MakerSpaces, which normally require a paid subscription or drop-in fee, or university and school MakerSpaces, which generally require that you be a member of those educational institutions in order to get access to the space.

Similarly, libraries have expanded to allow community members to check out all kinds of other things. This has included museum passes, puzzles, and games, or even hiking gear. Now, libraries have further expanded their collections to allow people to check out home improvement tools, cooking gear, or electronics, encouraging making in people's homes.

In addition, libraries have become champions in providing opportunities for non-readers and breaking down barriers to education and cultural enrichment. For individuals who may not be avid readers, libraries offer alternative avenues for engagement, such as hands-on workshops, interactive exhibits, and multimedia presentations. These initiatives not only appeal to non-readers but also enhance the overall accessibility of library services.

For example, the Upper Dublin Public Library in Fort Washington, Pennsylvania (Figure 2-4), holds regular workshops on quilting in their MakerSpace, where quilters of all levels can participate and work on making a unique tapestry by hand, under the guidance of the expert quilters leading the workshops. To help tackle the operational challenges of hosting events in their space, numerous software companies provide support for libraries in helping to manage all of their activities, from space reservation, event support, and inventory management, to even scheduling appointments with staff for support.

Figure 2-4. *MakerSpace in the Upper Dublin Public Library in Pennsylvania*

Moreover, libraries have regularly embraced extensive outreach activities. They understand that not everyone can easily access library facilities, so they take their services directly to the people, transcending physical boundaries. These outreach initiatives often involve mobile libraries, where library resources are brought to schools, community centers, retirement homes, and other local venues. They offer a plethora of books, educational materials, and digital resources, making knowledge more accessible to a broader audience.

Libraries also partner with local schools, organizations, and social service agencies to provide tailored programs and resources, bridging educational gaps and supporting lifelong learning. Furthermore, public libraries conduct events and programs that cater to the specific needs and interests of different demographic groups, fostering community engagement and personal development.

In a similar vein, MakerSpaces in libraries have become instrumental in expanding STEM outreach efforts to engage with diverse communities, who may otherwise face barriers accessing STEM equipment through traditional means such as schools and commercial laboratories. These spaces extend the reach of libraries beyond their physical locations and into various community settings. Libraries recognize that not everyone can easily access a dedicated MakerSpace, so they have taken proactive steps to make maker resources more accessible to all members of their community. One approach involves creating mobile MakerSpaces, much like their mobile library counterparts. These mobile MakerSpaces are an all-in-one solution that can visit local schools, community centers, and even retirement homes, providing hands-on creative opportunities to people who might not otherwise have the chance to explore their innovative potential.

These outreach initiatives offer a wealth of maker tools, equipment, and expertise, encouraging community members to experiment, invent, and collaborate to make an array of exciting projects. Whether it's a school seeking to integrate hands-on STEM education into their curriculum, a retirement home aiming to inspire lifelong active learning among its residents, or a community center looking to spark creativity among its members, library MakerSpaces play a pivotal role in meeting the unique needs of various groups.

Furthermore, public libraries, through their MakerSpaces, often partner with local schools, community organizations, and social service agencies. Together with these organizations, they can create tailored programs and develop resources that help bridge educational gaps and support lifelong learning opportunities for all members of the community. These partnerships are essential in fostering a sense of community engagement and personal growth and development, making technology and hands-on creative experiences available to all, irrespective of age, background, or location. The ever-expanding reach of MakerSpaces beyond the library walls is a testament to their commitment to democratizing innovation and learning and enhancing the lives of community members in a myriad of ways.

In addition to physical outreach conducted live and in-person, libraries often maintain a strong online presence. Many libraries host virtual events, provide e-resources, and engage with the community through various social media and digital platforms. This online presence ensures that individuals who may not have the means to visit the library physically (for any variety of reasons) can still access its resources and connect with the library community. For library MakerSpaces, this means extending their reach beyond the physical confines of the library walls. Libraries have recognized the importance of inclusivity and accessibility in the digital age, and they are actively leveraging technology to serve their communities more effectively.

Libraries have embraced the digital realm, offering a wide range of online resources and services that complement their physical MakerSpaces. This not only caters to the needs of those who may find it challenging to visit the library in person but it also brings the Maker movement to a broader audience. Through online platforms, libraries conduct virtual workshops and provide instructional videos, allowing community members to learn and create from the comfort of their own homes. These resources cover a variety of interests, from 3D printing and electronics to woodworking and sewing, making DIY projects more accessible than ever before.

In addition to workshops, libraries maintain active social media profiles and websites dedicated to MakerSpaces. They share project ideas, success stories, and user-generated content, fostering a sense of community among makers. Online forums and discussion groups provide a space for members to exchange ideas and troubleshoot projects, creating a virtual hub for collaborative creativity. Public libraries understand that fostering a vibrant online maker community is just as important as providing physical spaces, and they invest in maintaining and expanding their digital presence.

Moreover, libraries are adapting to the changing landscape of technology by investing in emerging trends. As new tools and equipment emerge in the Maker movement, libraries are quick to make them available to the public. For instance, libraries now offer access to cutting-edge 3D printers, laser cutters, and virtual reality equipment. These advancements not only keep libraries relevant in a rapidly evolving tech landscape but also empower community members to stay at the forefront of technological innovation.

The expansion of MakerSpaces in libraries, both physically and virtually, underscores their commitment to fostering a culture of learning, creativity, and collaboration within communities (see Table 2-4 for a summary). These spaces continue to be at the forefront of democratizing access to tools and knowledge, making creativity and innovation accessible to everyone, regardless of age, background, or economic status. In an ever-changing world, libraries stand as beacons of innovation and community engagement, serving as dynamic resources that evolve to meet the diverse needs of their users.

Table 2-4. *Library MakerSpace Summary*

Feature	Description
Typical users	General public—all ages and backgrounds
Access model	Free or very low-cost; open to all community members
Specialization level	Low to Moderate (varies by library size and funding)
Cost to user	None or nominal
Common tools and activities	3D printing, sewing, crafting, basic electronics, quilting, tool lending
Programming examples	Workshops, storytime crafts, senior tech classes, mobile MakerSpace events
Outreach and accessibility	Mobile MakerSpaces, school visits, retirement homes, virtual workshops, online resources
Staffing model	Operated by library staff; may use scheduling software for events and training
Digital integration	Online classes, instructional videos, virtual events, active social media presence
Community role	Democratizes access to tools and knowledge; fosters lifelong learning and creative equity
Challenges	Limited capital budgets, equipment maintenance, staffing for specialized programs
Partnerships	Schools, community centers, social service agencies, local organizations
Innovation and adaptation	Quick adopters of new tech (e.g., 3D printing, VR); maintain relevance through continuous evolution

School MakerSpaces

Another location where MakerSpaces are commonly found are primary and secondary schools (see Table 2-5 for a summary). MakerSpaces fit in a teaching model known to education theorists as "Constructivism." In constructivism, rather than students passively listening to a teacher, the students learn by "constructing" knowledge. While this model can be applied to any type of learning domain, MakerSpaces are an obvious fit for this method. Indeed, a tenet of this theory is that learning is inherently social, and thus works best in a community environment, something for which MakerSpaces are apt. As outlined in Figure 2-1, Secondary School MakerSpaces in the United States generally fall in the low-cost and low-specialization region of the chart. While there may be a few outliers, such as generously funded private/charter schools or technology-focused programs, the bulk of these schools operate under very strict budgets. However, they do recognize the importance a MakerSpace can provide to their students.

Here, students are presented with a problem and, working in groups, are freely able to use the resources available to them, in order to find a solution. This requires brainstorming, learning new tools, and sharing what one learns. In this type of learning, the instructor acts more as a guide, engaging the students in dialog, rather than just merely lecturing. Students normally work in teams of three to four, giving the students an opportunity to learn from each other. One example involves students designing a holiday light show. They apply what they learned related to electronics and microcontrollers to put something together in whatever manner they like.

Another example is in middle school, where students are given kits by Makey Makey or SAM Labs. Students are first taught about human systems in their science class. They then use the MakerSpace to learn basic electronics, after which they are to design a rudimentary medical device.

Table 2-5. *Overview of School MakerSpaces*

Feature	Description
Typical users	K–12 students; teachers and club advisors
Educational model	Constructivist, project-based learning; emphasizes teamwork and exploration
Access model	Usually tied to specific classes; may also be used by after-school clubs
Specialization level	Low to Moderate (varies widely with funding)
Cost to user	Free to students, though often funded by teacher, PTA, or school budget
Common tools and materials	Cardboard, 3D printers, Makey Makey kits, LEDs, crafting materials
Technical support	Often limited; maintenance falls to teachers or student volunteers
Space constraints	May be single-use rooms or mobile kits stored in libraries or classrooms
Staffing model	Operated by teachers, librarians, or parent volunteers
Challenges	Limited funding, lack of technical support, bureaucratic purchasing hurdles
Innovative solutions	Mobile kits, cardboard for prototyping, free platforms like TinkerCad
Extended access options	Robotics/tech clubs, partnerships with local universities, public libraries

Just as in the previous examples, school MakerSpaces tend to fall into STEM fields, specifically in engineering. These might include woodworking, metal fabrication, and electronics. 3-D printers are becoming more common, and some schools go so far as to have laser cutters. However, this is generally defined by budgetary and space constraints. For example, in the United States, it is not uncommon for teachers to purchase classroom supplies out of pocket, pulling from their own salaries or relying on contributions from students' parents to obtain anything beyond the bare minimum of supplies for their classroom. Teachers have been known to solicit parents to contribute money to help support their spaces.

Another challenge schools have is that they lack technical staff to support the teachers. Equipment maintenance is left to the teacher who might not have the time amid teaching responsibilities. In some cases, maintenance is left to student volunteers. In addition, it is also difficult to track equipment and supplies, and it's difficult to obtain the funds to replace them. In contrast, a well-funded school would have the staff, equipment, and space to provide exceptional opportunities for students.

Depending on the school district, the bureaucracy required to set up, purchase, or maintain a MakerSpace can become very complicated and the bureaucratic challenges of securing a MakerSpace for the school can often lead to delays and suboptimal equipment selection due to budgetary or supplier constraints. This is especially true when safety becomes a concern. Unfortunately, teachers are often not incentivized or rewarded for their efforts in navigating through the bureaucracy so even the most motivated and well-meaning engineering-minded teacher will face major headwinds against their efforts to set up a school MakerSpace. In addition, schools often only have one such facility, so a new teacher in the space cannot rely on support from others.

Fortunately, there are many free online learning resources available to students. TinkerCad provides free resources for students to make mechanical and electrical designs. Students can even model and code using the Arduino package. Similarly, for more advanced students, **Onshape** provides professional-level drafting, accessible on any computer, and free to students. From the standpoint of creating educational modules, organizations such as e4USA supports collaborations between schools and colleges. For materials, cardboard can be an excellent low-cost alternative to acrylic or wood.

To combat physical space and storage space limitations, school libraries may consider developing shared MakerSpace kits that can be stored in a central location like the school library and brought to the appropriate classrooms for specific projects as needed. These may be adapted to different grade levels. For example, a MakerSpace kit for first graders could include simple low-tech components such as batteries, aluminum foil, and LEDs. On the other hand, a MakerSpace kit for 5th graders would include more sophisticated components.

Figure 2-5. *MakerSpace for grade school students (Designed by Freepik)*

One drawback of school MakerSpaces is that they are not freely accessible and are traditionally tied to a class. Consequently, a student would need to be enrolled in a class which uses the MakerSpace in order to access it. However, many schools also have technology or robotics clubs that students may join, typically meeting during the school's lunch break or after classes have ended for the day, and run by teachers. These groups may also utilize the school MakerSpace, and may in fact be the main users of the MakerSpace. Some groups have collaborations with local colleges and universities that allow students to get exposed to more advanced tools and equipment and the interactions these young students have with college and university student mentors help inspire them to continue their education in STEM fields.

While not every school will be able to have a full-scale MakerSpace, teachers, and school librarians can also be aware of MakerSpaces and resources elsewhere in the community, especially low/no cost options like public libraries and free community spaces with programming for kids and teens. They can steer interested students toward those options and help foster curiosity for learning and STEM skills. If those other spaces have marketing materials (see more about marketing your MakerSpace in Chapters 7 and 8), they can encourage students to visit these other spaces.

College and University MakerSpaces

Next, MakerSpaces are also found in colleges, universities, and other post-secondary education institutions (see Table 2-6 for a summary). One exclusive to engineering departments, multidisciplinary MakerSpaces are now popping up in many different schools and departments all across campuses, as well as in some dining halls and other non-instructional spaces. College and university MakerSpaces stand as dynamic hubs of innovation, creativity, and hands-on learning within the higher education landscape. These spaces serve as catalysts for fostering a culture of making, offering students, faculty, staff, and often the broader community a unique opportunity to turn their ideas into tangible creations. As outlined in Figure 2-1, College and University MakerSpace, typically operate at a low cost to the user (no to low additional fees after tuition), but offer a very high level of Specialization. Typically, colleges and universities will provide multiple different MakerSpaces to their students, each with a specific genre in mind. For example, they may have dedicated 3D Printing zones where students can gain access to high quality printers, or they may have a Precision Machining Area where students can gain access to more specialized equipment for manufacturing.

Table 2-6. *Summary of College and University MakerSpace Types*

Type of university MakerSpace	Access model	Specialization level	Example activities/ tools	Notes
Department-based educational labs	Restricted to students in specific courses	High	Course-specific labs: electronics, bioengineering, machining	Often evolve into open-access MakerSpaces if curriculum changes
Open-access departmental MakerSpaces	Open to all university students (after training)	High	3D printing, laser cutting, wet lab work, electronics	Example: Penn's Stephenson Foundation Bio-MakerSpace
Library-managed MakerSpaces	Open to all students, staff, faculty	Medium to High	3D printing, crafting, poster printing, electronics	Inclusive; often host workshops; modeled after public libraries
Entrepreneurship-focused MakerSpaces	Open to students working on ventures	High	Prototyping, product design, business development	IP-neutral; integrated with campus entrepreneurship programs

College and university MakerSpaces come in a variety of sizes and layouts, but they all share a common goal: to provide a dedicated environment for hands-on making. These spaces are often housed in purpose-built stand-alone facilities or are integrated into existing academic buildings. They feature an array of workstations, project areas, and storage facilities, all designed to support a wide range of making activities.

Most college and university MakerSpaces are specialized in certain fields or combinations of fields, such as chemical/biological MakerSpaces or mechanical/electrical MakerSpaces. Often, colleges and universities will have a variety of different MakerSpaces that suit different users' needs. By design, college and university MakerSpaces prioritize safety and accessibility as the most important factors for their space, ensuring that users have the space they need to work on diverse projects, from electronics and robotics to woodworking, laser cutting, and 3D printing.

MakerSpaces are especially popular in engineering programs within universities and colleges. Oftentimes, these MakerSpaces would have started as the educational laboratory for the department and evolved over time from a traditional instructional space where lab classes are held to a more flexible MakerSpace where students and other community members have more freedom to work on personal projects. For example, an educational lab designed to teach undergraduate electrical engineering courses would already house all the relevant testing and prototyping equipment for making electronic projects. In the traditional educational lab mode, the space would only be open and available when classes are being taught. By contrast, as a MakerSpace, the lab would remain staffed and open for extended hours outside of scheduled class time and be available for students to access outside of class hours, often until late in the evening. In the same manner, mechanical engineering departments opened up outside of regular hours to support their students.

Figure 2-6. *The George H. Stephenson Foundation Educational Laboratory & Bio-MakerSpace at Penn Engineering*

Located within the University of Pennsylvania's Bioengineering department, the Stephenson Foundation Educational Laboratory originally served students for specific classes in Bioengineering (Figure 2-6). The entire lab space essentially served only as a classroom and the door was locked outside of scheduled class time, so students could only use the space and equipment while attending classes in which they were enrolled. However, the undergraduate bioengineering curriculum changed to be more project-focused, requiring students to spend time outside of regular scheduled class time to work on their projects and requiring them to gain access to specialized equipment to perform this work and advance their projects. This in turn required a new outlook on the operations of the lab facility, since students now needed access to a space where they could work in project teams, collaborate and use equipment and tools that they needed to complete their projects. In addition, since Bioengineering is fundamentally interdisciplinary, the single laboratory housed and maintained equipment to support a broad range of fields, including electronics, chemistry, biology, and mechanical fabrication through laser cutters and 3-D printers.

This "one stop shop" model to house all the different tools and equipment that students might need all in the same space spread throughout the university and attracted interest from students in other departments who were also interested in interdisciplinary projects, encouraging the lab to open up to all students, and not just those enrolled in the Bioengineering program. This posed additional operational challenges, as the number of users in the space at any one time quickly increased and students from various programs all needed to be trained to safely use all the equipment found in the lab such as the laser cutters. Laser cutter training was already included as part of the bioengineering curriculum, but students from other disciplines didn't usually get trained for the same equipment, so a comprehensive training module and validation test needed to be developed to ensure all users of the laser cutters were adequately trained in their safety and operation. Also, given that the facility hosts many life sciences projects beyond those of traditional mechanical and electronic-focused MakerSpaces, the laboratory has defined itself as a Bio-MakerSpace. The Stephenson Foundation Bio-MakerSpace has since expanded its support of the broader university community by creating and making available online guides and other resources, as well as constant staff support, in order to encourage people from anywhere throughout the university to feel welcome and use the space.

Figure 2-7. *Example of a sign restricting access*

Unfortunately, not all department MakerSpaces are as open and supportive to the broader maker community as the University of Pennsylvania's George H. Stephenson Foundation Bioengineering Laboratory and Bio-MakerSpace described above. Many engineering departments and programs limit access to their facilities to students enrolled in their department only (Figure 2-7).

However, the university libraries are usually much more inclusive and often provide this service for the broader university community with no restrictions on department affiliation. Libraries often manage 3-D and poster printing facilities for the entire campus. They may also support other activities such as crafting and electronics and library staff may host workshops to learn more about various maker disciplines independently from any university department. In a way, just as public libraries support their community with their MakerSpaces, university library MakerSpaces do the same.

At universities, MakerSpaces are sometimes tied with entrepreneurship. MakerSpaces give students access to the materials and tools to develop their ideas without having to buy these resources themselves. Oftentimes these spaces are considered to be "IP neutral," meaning that any intellectual property developed in the space would not be owned by the university but rather wholly owned by the student.

Community MakerSpaces

Finally, for the fourth and final classification of MakerSpaces, the authors have considered community MakerSpaces to encompass all other types of MakerSpaces that are not within public libraries, K-12 schools, or higher education institutions. Community in this sense is a catch-all term to refer to any spaces not included among the other three types described in earlier sections, Even more than the other types of MakerSpaces, these spaces may vary widely in terms of scale, purpose, and available resources, reflecting the rich tapestry of interests and skills within the community in which they are located. Examples of Community MakerSpaces may include anything from stand-alone community fabrication and prototyping spaces (e.g., fab spaces, community art studios, tech shops, etc.) with a full suite of high tech mechanical and electronic capabilities, to smaller scale specialized spaces found in craft stores, hardware stores, or other community spaces (see Figure 2-8).

Figure 2-8. *Community MakerSpace (Designed by Freepik)*

What makes community MakerSpaces truly remarkable is their ability to adapt and cater to the unique interests and needs of the people they serve. Community MakerSpaces are, by nature, embedded within the community in which they are located and are true reflections of that community's creativity, ingenuity, and cultural diversity. Whether it's through building an innovative high-tech prototype for their startup, crafting a beautiful piece of fine art, or committing the time and effort to perfecting a traditional handiwork skill, these MakerSpaces empower individuals to explore, experiment, and innovate in their own way.

In the grand tapestry that is the Maker Movement, community MakerSpaces (see Table 2-7 for a summary) can be considered the vibrant threads that weave together the diverse skills and passions of a community, helping to foster an empowering culture of collaboration, discovery, and continuous learning for all individuals who use the MakerSpace. Whether you're a seasoned inventor or a novice artist, there is likely a community MakerSpace waiting to welcome you and help turn your dreams into tangible creations.

Table 2-7. Overview of Types of Community MakerSpaces

Subtype of community MakerSpace	Typical users	Specialization level	Cost to maker	Example activities/ tools	Operational model
Community education center MakerSpaces	Adult learners, hobbyists, artists	Moderate	Moderate	Painting, woodworking, ceramics, open studio hours	Non-profit, fee-based
Fab spaces	Entrepreneurs, experienced makers	High	High	3D printing, CNC, laser cutting, electronics	For-profit, membership or course-based
Craft store MakerSpaces	Hobbyists, casual creatives, social learners	High	Moderate to High	Jewelry making, scrapbooking, sewing, painting	Retail-based, class/ event model
Hardware store MakerSpaces	DIYers, home improvement enthusiasts	Low	Low	Basic woodworking, tool use workshops	Retail-based, promotional classes

Community Education Center MakerSpaces

Community education centers may also host their own MakerSpaces. Community education centers are organizations that offer non-degree educational programs to members of their community, generally targeted at adult learners but may also offer programs for children of all ages. For example, community education centers often offer language classes, technology or financial literacy classes, visual arts classes such as painting or drawing, and may also offer lecture series on liberal arts on various topics such as history or philosophy. Often these centers have woodworking or art studio space that can be used at different times to provide a variety of instructional courses for all levels or offer open studio space for experienced participants. Artists of all backgrounds and levels of expertise congregate here to paint, sculpt, sketch, and experiment with various mediums. These studios may provide easels, pottery wheels, kilns, or even darkrooms for photographers. Collaboration, critique, and inspiration flow freely in these creative sanctuaries. Sometimes, open studio time is restricted to participants who have completed a previous course at the center and are sufficiently skilled to use the equipment safely and correctly with minimal supervision. Upon successful completion of a course and any required training, they may enroll in open studio hours, usually for a small fee and either bring their own materials or pay for what they used.

Cost for using these types of space varies greatly by community, though many community education centers are not-for-profit organizations and try to make their programming affordable for community members. Community MakerSpaces in educational centers are usually more expensive for the user than the (usually free) public library MakerSpaces, but they often offer a lot more specialized tools and equipment and can cost less for a casual maker than more professional fabrication spaces that are capable of manufacturing products at tighter specifications and on a larger scale. In essence, they generally offer a middle-of-the-road level of specialization, for a mid-range cost, as shown in Figure 2-1.

Community education center MakerSpaces are generally geared toward beginner to intermediate makers and are more hobby-oriented, though this can also vary a lot by each individual center. Some users eager to improve their skills may find that they outgrow these spaces and decide to create their own spaces if they have the room and resources to do so, or they may move to a more professional MakerSpace geared toward supporting more skilled makers and entrepreneurs.

Fab Spaces

At the broad end of the spectrum, you'll find stand-alone community fabrication and prototyping spaces often referred to as "fab spaces." These are fully equipped facilities that offer a wide range of high-tech mechanical and electronic capabilities. Inside these makerspaces, you might find 3D printers, laser cutters, CNC machines, and a plethora of hand and power tools. They serve as hubs for innovation, attracting inventors, tinkerers, and entrepreneurs. These spaces foster a DIY ethos and serve as breeding grounds for turning innovative ideas into reality.

Fabrication spaces, often shortened to Fab spaces, are more specialized MakerSpaces designed for more experienced users. They operate almost as a shared commercial manufacturing space and are generally run as for-profit specialized spaces. These facilities usually charge high fees for makers to utilize the space and offer one-off classes and/or longer courses typically with weekly classes for blocks of 6–12 weeks. They are typically at their busiest on evenings and weekends, but many fab spaces also offer weekday classes aimed at retirees or individuals with flexible work schedules. They may also sometimes offer summer camps or on-site hands-on educational programming for school groups during the day. As shown in Figure 2-1, Fab space MakerSpaces provide higher specialization at a higher cost.

Craft Store MakerSpaces

At the smaller scale, community MakerSpaces can be found within craft stores, framing shops, or other community spaces. These may not have the extensive array of high-tech equipment that larger MakerSpaces boast, but they excel in specialization. Craft stores offer the materials and guidance for those interested in knitting, beadwork, scrapbooking, and other handcrafts. Framing shops provide the expertise and tools necessary for custom framing, adding an artistic touch to cherished memories. These spaces play a vital role in fostering localized skills and crafts.

Some stores selling supplies for making crafts or other stuff will have a space for making on-site. The room can be in the store itself (sometimes workshops are held after retail hours) or in a separate room. Knitting stores, woodworking stores, figurine stores, bead/jewelry supply stores, pottery stores, board game stores, etc. Offering MakerSpaces can be a way to diversify the store's revenue by collecting registration fees, may also allow potential customers to demo higher margin equipment such as sewing machines, and can help attract people to shop for supplies while they are in the store before and after attending a scheduled class. Offering programming also creates a sense of community at the store and encourages return customers.

Oftentimes the owners who run the craft store are very passionate hobbyists as well and enjoy the opportunities to interact with the Maker community that hosting these classes offer them. Classes at craft store MakerSpaces can be one-off themed events targeting a broader crowd not usually involved in the Maker community, like a paint and wine night event hosted in their space, or they may be multiple recurring classes centered around making a defined thing or learning a specific specialized more advanced technique. Classes at craft store MakerSpaces will have one or more facilitators, usually part-time workers who are passionate about making and experienced in our or more maker fields. Sometimes the facilitators may be art students from a local college or university. People choose to attend these spaces for various reasons. It could be as simple as an excuse to get out of the house and socialize. Sometimes, they choose to attend these classes just to try something new before committing to a new hobby and getting all the equipment to do it at home. Or, it may be to broaden their skills within a specific discipline they already know (e.g., an accomplished watercolor painter may choose to take a community class to learn acrylic or oil painting), or learn a completely new skill in a totally different discipline (e.g., said watercolor painter decides to learn sculpting or crochet). Or, they may sign up to a one-off class just as a fun activity to do with friends or on a date. Some of these specialized spaces also host children's birthday parties where kids make one or more crafts guided by a trained facilitator.

Craft store space MakerSpaces can vary a lot by individual location, but generally provide pretty high specialization at a pretty high cost, though less so on both metrics than Fab Spaces, since they are still home-made crafty spaces rather than near-commercial manufacturing spaces. The key advantage to using a craft store MakerSpace is the high level of specialization in one or more specific craft disciplines and the large inventory of supplies for those craft disciplines. To make something like that at a less-specialized different type of MakerSpace, the user would need to spend a lot of time researching tools and techniques and scouring pages and pages on the Internet, watching countless videos, or reading several different reference books to learn from others about the best supplies to use to achieve the result they aspire to achieve. By contrast, at a craft store MakerSpace, an expert maker in that craft discipline will be available immediately to answer their questions live and will have recommendations on the best equipment and supplies to use (or best value for money supplies!) based on their extensive experience in that discipline and their knowledge of the inventory that is stocked and sold in their store.

Hardware Store Makerspaces

Another unconventional location for MakerSpaces is hardware stores. Several big international chains of hardware stores offer courses and workshops in their retail locations, where trained employees guide customers to complete projects. Classes are often offered during weekends and take place in a special room within the store that doesn't look too different from a community education center woodworking studio or a mechanical engineering department MakerSpace at a college or university.

The space is typically set up with multiple workstations on high top work benches, and all the tools, equipment, and materials needed to complete the project are provided to registered attendees. Classes are generally advertised in stores on posters and a schedule is published on the store website. Employees may also promote upcoming events to customers with whom they interact in store. Compared to other MakerSpace types, hardware store MakerSpaces typically fall in the lower cost, lower specialization end of the spectrum, since the fees to attend workshops hosted in hardware store MakerSpaces are generally pretty affordable (after all, the business purpose of offering these classes is probably to drive sales by having more people visit the store more often, not to make profit from registration fees) and the equipment used is pretty standard stuff that one wouldn't be surprised to see in a hobbyist's garage or home workshop.

Conclusion

For someone trying to choose a MakerSpace, it's important to consider your specific needs, such as cost, tools, and community, depending on whether you are a parent, entrepreneur, hobbyist, artist, or senior. For someone who is creating a MakerSpace, it's essential to define your niche, offer diverse programs, and create a strong community atmosphere to attract and retain users. For someone who manages an existing MakerSpace, understanding why users choose your space and continuously gathering feedback can help you improve and adapt to their evolving needs.

Key Takeaways

- The concept of shared community spaces for making, like modern MakerSpaces, has deep historical roots, dating back to early human history when communities collaborated to craft tools, cook, make clothing, and build shelters.

- Modern MakerSpaces cater to a wide range of interests and maker fields, from electronics and robotics to woodworking, textiles, and culinary arts, and they are found in various educational and community spaces, promoting learning, creativity, entrepreneurship, and innovation.

- Public libraries are often among the most widely accessible MakerSpaces in communities, offering free access to making and crafting resources.

- Libraries play a crucial role in fostering a culture of learning, creativity, and collaboration within communities, democratizing access to tools and knowledge.

- MakerSpaces are commonly found in primary and secondary schools, aligning with the educational theory of constructivism, which emphasizes active learning and knowledge construction in a community environment.

- School MakerSpaces typically focus on STEM fields, especially engineering, and the equipment available may vary based on budget and space constraints. 3-D printers and laser cutters are becoming more common.

- Community MakerSpaces are highly adaptable and cater to the unique needs and interests of the communities they serve. They empower individuals to explore, experiment, and innovate, fostering a culture of collaboration, discovery, and continuous learning.

CHAPTER 3

Introducing Maker Fields

The definition of "making" may appear to be pretty straightforward at first glance, implying the act or process of creating or crafting something. However, there is much more to making than the simple act of producing something new from raw materials. Making is a process that comes from a place of passion, creativity, ingenuity, and resourcefulness. From electronics and robotics to woodworking, metalworking, textile arts, culinary arts, and beyond, making embraces the confluence of technology, artistry, and craftsmanship. It is a manifestation of the human spirit's perpetual quest to explore, tinker, and express itself through creation and innovation. Inside each person is a deep passion to express oneself, making being the optimal outlet for this fire burning inside each one of us. In essence, making is not merely a process; it is a testament to the human capacity for invention and the enduring quest to leave an indelible mark on the world.

Laying the Groundwork

There are many reasons one might choose to make. Some people make things just for fun, while other people make things with a purpose and to solve a problem, be it a very simple everyday inconvenience like an uneven

© Sevile G. Mannickarottu, Michael G. Patterson, and Carolyne Godon 2025
S. G. Mannickarottu et al., *Creating MakerSpaces*, Maker Innovations Series,
https://doi.org/10.1007/979-8-8688-1309-2_3

piece of furniture that can be solved with a perfectly shaped 3D-printed wedge or a more complex big-picture problem that can be solved with breakthrough high-tech innovations that can help save the lives of millions of people. Making empowers individuals to unleash their creativity and make meaningful contributions to improve their surroundings or the world at large.

One of the most classical and fundamental maker fields is arts and crafts. Arts and crafts MakerSpaces go well beyond the basic rainbow colored sheets of construction paper, crayons, and pipe cleaners that may first come to mind when thinking of an arts and crafts space, though the utility of these basic items should not be underestimated even in higher education MakerSpace settings, where crayons have been used for all kinds of purposes, including the creation of high-tech microfluidic devices, which were eventually spun out to a commercial company. Arts and crafts MakerSpaces can include textile arts such as sewing, knitting, crochet, and embroidery. They can also include painting, drawing, sculpting, pottery-making, jewelry-making, glassblowing, etc. Combined with other fields, arts and crafts MakerSpaces can even extend into the ongoing boom in wearable technology.

Like arts and crafts, electronics are another classic maker field. After all, what would a MakerSpace be without some flashing LED lights? Some of the most classic electronics MakerSpace introductory projects include a blinking LED or a display that prints "hello world." In electronics MakerSpaces, users can create all kinds of projects, ranging from these simple circuits on breadboards to more complex AI-driven human–computer interaction devices.

Finally, another important field is mechanical making. Mechanical making encompasses anything that primarily deals with the tangible and functional aspects of creation, focusing on the construction of mechanical objects such as machinery, mechanisms, or assemblies. With recent improvements in performance and reliability of lower priced models, 3D printers have become a ubiquitous defining feature of MakerSpaces, to the point where any space that includes a 3D printer is labeled as a MakerSpace, much to the disdain of many purist multidisciplinary Makers. For them, true making transcends the mere possession of a single tool or technology, emphasizing instead a holistic approach that embraces a diverse array of disciplines and methodologies.

In recent years, biology and chemistry have also become important maker fields. Making with chemistry can range from the classic elementary school lemon-powered clock to the design and synthesis of new molecules. Similarly, making in biology can be anything from growing mold or cultivating bacterial colonies from unwashed hands-on petri dishes to hacking natural chemical sensing processes in fruits to developing complex bio-inspired sensors that detect ripeness of apple crops in storage.

There are also many more fields beyond what we define as the four core maker fields. In fact, by definition, there are absolutely no limitations to what can be made in a MakerSpace. The four fields described in detail in this chapter would in no way be perceived as a mutually exclusive collectively exhaustive list of maker fields. New and existing maker fields are constantly evolving. Some examples of alternative and emerging maker fields include culinary, fashion, gaming, AR/VR, and there are many more.

Of course, few MakerSpaces cater to only one maker field, with most MakerSpace providing the physical space and community to explore and combine two or three different fields within the same project and allow users to be creative, blurring the lines between several different maker fields. For simplicity, this chapter will explore each of the above categories of maker fields in detail separately, then provide some perspective on the opportunities and challenges of combining different maker fields within the same MakerSpace.

This chapter will focus on the disciplines and what can be made and considerations when setting up such spaces. The next chapter will focus more specifically on the equipment and tools that enable each maker field.

Arts and Crafts

Arts and crafts, also known as artisanal handicrafts, are a form of expression of human creativity. They are essentially a form of making that involves creating useful or decorative objects mostly by hand or with simple tools, though increasingly more and more technology is being used to supplement traditional manual techniques. In this book, we consider arts and crafts to include any form of making traditionally done mostly by hand, even if modern technological tools are used. For example, knitting computer-designed patterns using a digital knitting machine would still be considered arts and crafts, just like making a collage with digitally designed vinyl pieces cut using a digitally controlled cutting machine instead of old-fashioned scissors and glue.

Anyone and everyone can make arts and crafts projects! In the distant past, making was considered a necessity and humans made things to help them live their lives, such as cooking tools, clothing, and weapons for hunting. However, even back then, making wasn't always 100% utilitarian. There is early evidence of human art, such as painting, drawing, sculpting, beading, and knitting, that was seemingly made with no other known purpose than the expression of creativity. The desire to express oneself through making is a defining feature of humankind. Since the 19th century, as production of day-to-day goods became more industrialized and economy of scale was realized by mass-producing day-to-day necessities in factories, crafting became more of a hobby than a necessity, and making for art overtook making for utility. This is what we refer to as arts and crafts.

What Can You Make?

Arts and crafts may be the most wide-ranging of all the maker fields when it comes to the types of projects that users create. Some projects are purely expressive, while others have a functional purpose or a social message.

Many blend aesthetics with storytelling or cultural meaning. The only real constant is that these projects typically involve hands-on engagement and emphasize visual, tactile, or textural creativity (see Figure 3-1).

Figure 3-1. *Origami paper folding (Designed by FreePik)*

A user might create a hand-sewn sketchbook, a mixed-media protest poster, or a digitally designed stencil for screen-printing t-shirts. In a school setting, younger makers may experiment with collages or handmade cards, while advanced users may explore textile design, sculpture, or laser-engraved block printing. Arts and crafts projects can also be deeply interdisciplinary—for example, a student might combine illustration with electronics to create a light-up shadow box, or integrate embroidery into a wearable sensor project.

Some projects are made quickly, in under an hour. Others stretch over days or weeks, involving experimentation, iteration, and reflection. Regardless of complexity, these projects allow users to express identity, emotion, and curiosity—often while learning new materials, tools, and techniques along the way.

Importantly, arts and crafts in MakerSpaces are not restricted to "traditional" media. They also include digitally designed and machine-assisted work. A vinyl cutter can transform a digital illustration into a wall decal or wearable patch. A Cricut machine can produce intricate folded paper structures. A digital embroidery machine allows users to upload designs and stitch them onto fabric with precision. These tools expand what's possible while still preserving the handmade character of the final product.

Many users engage with this field not to prototype or solve technical problems, but to create something that is meaningful, beautiful, or fun. That is not only valid—it's essential. Arts and crafts anchor the emotional and expressive side of the MakerSpace, and serve as a gateway to deeper confidence and broader engagement across fields.

Table 3-1 outlines some of the types of projects that can be made in an arts and crafts MakerSpace. These include paper arts, mixed media, textile arts, and sculpture. However, the list provided in the table below is just a starting point should not at all be considered exhaustive. There are many other disciplines and types of projects that could be made in an arts and crafts MakerSpace. The opportunities are endless for a motivated Maker.

Table 3-1. *Table Which Outlines the Types of Projects That Can Be*
Made in an Arts and Crafts MakerSpace

Arts and crafts discipline	Project example
Paper arts	Painting (acrylic, oil paint, watercolors)
	Drawing (pencil, colored pencil, ink, pen, pastels)
Mixed media	Collage
	Assemblage
Textile arts	Upcycling/restoration
	Sewing
	Quilting
	Knitting
	Weaving
	Crochet
	Cross stitch
	Embroidery
Sculpture	Clay modeling
	Casting
	Carving
	Ceramics
	Pottery

The Space

Have you ever been inside a high school or middle school art classroom? That type of space can give you an idea of what an arts and crafts-focused MakerSpace may look like. As you enter the space, the chemical scent of paints and varnishes overwhelms your senses. The room's surfaces are covered with bright, colorful stains and splattered with blotches of various colors from many years of creative projects. In the back of the room by the windows, you can see the semi-organized mess of finished colorful projects in the drying rack area, waiting to be claimed by their respective makers. It's a symphony of hues and textures, a tangible manifestation of boundless imagination and artistic expression.

Arts and crafts MakerSpaces don't spontaneously appear fully formed. There is a lot of thought and deliberate planning that goes into designing and executing the space. It should also be a fluid space that naturally evolves over time based on how the users experience it and their evolving needs. Starting with the basics, if designing a space for your arts and crafts MakerSpace from scratch is an option, the flooring surface should be carefully selected to be a uniform surface and easy to clean in case of inevitable arts and crafts incidents like spilled paint, splatters of clay or plaster, and devastating glitter explosions.

Just like high school art classrooms, arts and crafts MakerSpaces typically consist of several rows of large tables in the center of a room surrounded by stools or tall chairs, and walls lined with shelves containing all the necessary supplies and equipment. There might also be a storage room or closet adjoining the main space, where additional less frequently used equipment and supplies are kept.

Power outlets are typically available throughout the space in convenient locations to the tables to allow users to easily make use of electric-powered arts and crafts equipment like hot glue guns or sewing machines (Figure 3-2). Large sinks are also available for washing paintbrushes and cleaning up any other messy supplies. A sufficiently large area of the space, ideally with natural light and good airflow, should also be designated for letting finished masterpieces dry.

Figure 3-2. *Person using a sewing machine (Designed by FreePik)*

Furniture and accessories for the space are also very important to consider thoughtfully. Tables in arts and crafts MakerSpaces are typically made of surfaces that can easily be wiped and are less prone to permanent staining. It is also important to provide large flat surfaces that don't have many cracks or gaps (i.e., no tiled work surfaces, no merging of multiple small decks together to form a larger table, no wobbly tables, etc.). Chairs should be chosen that can be moved around easily for group projects and for making space for larger format projects like sculptures. They should also be comfortable and adaptable to a wide range of body shapes and sizes. If the target audience for your arts and crafts MakerSpace includes children, especially younger children under age 12, consider investing in child-sized furniture and additional safety features to make sure your MakerSpace is a fun and safe space for all ages to enjoy.

Environmental conditions of the space are also important to think about. While arts and crafts MakerSpaces don't typically require as sophisticated an HVAC system as biological or chemical MakerSpaces, and don't have the structural or electrical requirements of a machine shop or mechanical MakerSpace, there are still some decisions that can make the space more pleasant and more suitable for the users and produce better outcomes in their arts and crafts products by having a more predictable constant environment. For example, in a well-designed environment, paint will dry quickly and evenly year-round and curing times will be predictable and constant.

Ventilation and fresh air is also always important, as well as maintaining a constant comfortable temperature, good lighting, and the ability to change lighting for different needs. Depending on the setting of your arts and crafts MakerSpace, you may also wish to dedicate part of the space to product photography or provide an area where this could easily be done with a portable light box. In these digital times, the original physical prototype may live a relatively short life with minimal travel, but professional-quality images of the final product will last forever on the Internet and have a global reach beyond what the physical product could ever achieve. High quality photography of final products can easily be achieved with modern smartphones and a few simple pieces of equipment and can help tremendously in promoting your MakerSpace, which is the subject of Chapter 8 later in this book.

Beyond these general considerations, there are also specialized disciplines within arts and crafts that may be included in MakerSpaces, which are far less common. For example, an arts and crafts MakerSpace could include a pottery wheel and kiln for making ceramics. It could also include a loom to weave large scale textile arts projects, or even an industrial knitting machine. In recent years, technological innovation has allowed many previously industrial-only machines to enter the consumer realm of MakerSpaces, equipping amateur enthusiasts with capabilities previously reserved for large scale manufacturing operations. One such example is the Kniterate digital knitting machine (`https://www.kniterate.com/product/kniterate-the-digital-knitting-machine/`). Priced at just under $16,000 as of December 2023, this machine is a relatively affordable and relatively compact footprint digital knitting machine that provides hobbyists with the capabilities of an industrial knitting machine. It comes with software for programming knitted projects and is marketed toward individual consumers and shared MakerSpaces. Consider allocating space for this or any other larger pieces of equipment that may be appropriate for your MakerSpace's users, such as sandblasting stations or spray-painting setups.

Case Study

A popular and meaningful project that has emerged in many arts and crafts-focused MakerSpaces—especially those based in public libraries—is the Community Quilt. This initiative typically invites individuals of all ages and backgrounds to participate in a collective art-making effort over the course of several weeks or months. While the specific materials and methods may vary, the core idea is always the same: each participant creates one square of the quilt, which is then stitched together into a single unified work.

Participants often begin with little or no sewing experience. Workshops and open drop-in sessions offer basic instruction on how to design and sew a patch (Figure 3-3), giving community members the chance to learn fundamental textile skills in a low-pressure, collaborative environment. Some MakerSpaces provide templates or themes for the squares—such as "home," "hope," or "my neighborhood"—while others encourage complete creative freedom.

Figure 3-3. *Working with a sewing pattern (Designed by FreePik)*

Because the quilt is composed of so many unique contributions, it becomes a visual representation of the diversity, creativity, and lived experience of the community itself. The final product is more than just a textile object—it's a conversation across generations and backgrounds, stitched together one piece at a time.

In many cases, the completed quilts are donated to local shelters, refugee support centers, or housing nonprofits. Other quilts are displayed in the library or other civic buildings as public art. This dual purpose— both expressive and charitable—adds to the power of the project. Makers aren't just learning how to sew; they're connecting with their neighbors and giving something back.

For many library MakerSpaces, the Community Quilt has become an annual tradition—an opportunity to welcome new users, rekindle relationships with returning ones, and reassert the MakerSpace's role as a creative and civic commons.

Biology and Chemistry

In recent years, the emergence of MakerSpaces in the realms of biology and chemistry has signified a remarkable shift in the landscape of making and innovation. These spaces, equipped with a growing array of specialized tools and facilities, allow people to explore the living and molecular world through hands-on experimentation. Just like the early days of the scientific revolution, when curious minds could conduct meaningful work without an advanced degree or a formal laboratory, these MakerSpaces open up the world of biology and chemistry to a much broader and more diverse population.

In the same way that crayons and scissors in a kindergarten classroom can set the stage for future design thinking, a lemon-powered clock or a DIY microscope in a biology MakerSpace can spark a lifelong interest in science. The essential spirit of making—tinkering, testing, adjusting, and discovering—is just as strong in these MakerSpaces as it is in the traditional fields of woodworking or robotics.

What Can You Make?

The types of projects that can be created in biology and chemistry MakerSpaces are surprisingly broad, ranging from artistic to analytical. Some projects use biology or chemistry as a medium for expression, while others are aimed at solving real-world problems such as food spoilage detection, rapid diagnostics, or new material development.

Table 3-2 below outlines some of the types of projects that can be made in a biology or chemistry MakerSpace. These include scientific equipment development, chemical synthesis, and synthetic biology. As with the arts and crafts table, this list is just a starting point and should not be considered exhaustive. The possibilities are limited only by imagination and available resources.

Table 3-2. *Table Outlining Some of the Types of Projects That Can Be Made in a Biology or Chemistry MakerSpace*

Biology and chemistry discipline	Project example
Scientific equipment development	DIY plate reader
	DIY microscope
Chemical synthesis	Custom fragrances
	New adhesives
	Hydrogels and other materials
Synthetic biology	Bacterial transformation
	PCR work
	DNA sequencing
	Gel electrophoresis
Bio-inspired sensing devices	Apple ripeness sensor
	pH-reactive packaging
Environmental testing	Water quality sensors
	Soil health kits
Edible chemistry	Flavor emulsions
	DIY molecular gastronomy
Artistic biology	Petri dish art
	Living microbial "paintings"

Anyone and everyone can engage in biology and chemistry making! You don't need to have taken AP Biology or college-level Organic Chemistry to start experimenting in a bio/chem MakerSpace. While there are certainly best practices and safety protocols to follow, much of the necessary knowledge can be learned through mentorship, guided workshops, and exploration.

The Space

A typical biology or chemistry MakerSpace has a very different vibe than an arts classroom or a woodshop. Instead of dried paint and scattered fabric scraps, the environment here tends to be more organized and clean, often with a faint chemical scent and the low hum of ventilation equipment. Stainless steel or epoxy countertops, clearly labeled storage cabinets, and areas designated as "wet benches" or "clean zones" are common. Depending on the nature of the work being done, the MakerSpace may be partially enclosed or have distinct boundaries within a larger space.

Some bio/chem MakerSpaces are built to enable professional-grade work, including PCR machines, fume hoods, and -80 °C freezers. Others are more DIY-oriented, using modified kitchen tools, household items, or open-source labware to make experimentation more accessible. Some even include makeshift incubators made from styrofoam coolers or low-cost Raspberry Pi-controlled centrifuges made with 3D-printed parts.

Furniture and layout in a biology or chemistry MakerSpace should be planned with workflow and safety in mind. Tables are typically made from non-porous materials, and there should be large sinks for handwashing and cleaning glassware. Dedicated storage areas for chemicals and biological samples should be secure and clearly labeled, and personal protective equipment (PPE) like gloves, goggles, and lab coats should be readily available. Ideally, there will also be a designated biohazard or sharps container for waste disposal, especially if students or users are working with live cultures or hazardous materials.

For bio/chem MakerSpaces located in educational institutions, zoning the space into "introductory" and "advanced" areas can allow for different levels of risk and complexity. For example, the introductory side might support fruit DNA extraction or pH indicator testing using red cabbage, while the advanced side might include PCR thermocyclers, gel electrophoresis systems, or chemical synthesis workstations (see Figure 3-4).

Figure 3-4. *Working in a typical biology MakerSpace (Designed by FreePik)*

Ventilation and temperature control are even more important here than in most MakerSpaces, as many biological or chemical reactions are sensitive to environmental conditions. Some projects, such as agar-based microbial art or DNA amplification, require incubators or heating blocks to maintain a consistent temperature.

Furthermore, these spaces cater to a wide spectrum of biological work, including experiments involving animals. Proper surfaces for animal work, along with storage and disposal facilities, are integral components of these spaces. However, such facilities are expensive to maintain, particularly due to the necessity of safety features like chemical fume hoods with complex ventilation systems. Ideally, certain areas would be marked off and access controlled based on work being carried out.

Ethics

An aspect of paramount importance that must not be overlooked is the ethical considerations, particularly when working with bacteria and mammalian cells. These ethical dimensions add an essential layer of responsibility and awareness to the scientific curiosity and innovation fostered within these spaces.

Ethical considerations in these MakerSpaces span a range of issues. When working with bacteria, it is crucial to consider both the potential environmental impact and the risk of creating harmful pathogens. Responsible handling of bacteria involves strict adherence to safety protocols to prevent accidental release or contamination. Furthermore, there is an ethical imperative to avoid genetic modifications that could lead to unforeseen and possibly detrimental consequences.

Similarly, when dealing with mammalian cells, ethical concerns are multifaceted. The source of these cells, whether they are derived from human or animal tissues, raises questions of consent and animal welfare. The use of human-derived cells necessitates stringent consent processes and privacy protections. In the case of animal cells, ethical considerations revolve around the humane treatment of animals and the justification of their use for experimental purposes.

Additionally, in MakerSpaces, where resources and oversight might be less rigorous than in professional research institutions, there is a heightened need for self-regulation and ethical awareness among users. It becomes crucial for these spaces to foster an environment of ethical consciousness, where users are not only informed about the potential risks and ethical implications of their work but also encouraged to critically evaluate the moral dimensions of their experiments.

While these MakerSpaces serve as fertile grounds for exploration and innovation in biology and chemistry, they also bear the responsibility of instilling a strong ethical framework in their community. This includes providing education on bioethics, ensuring compliance with legal and safety standards, and fostering a culture of ethical inquiry and debate.

Case Study

An illustrative success story from these spaces is that of the development of an open-source plate reader developed in the George H. Stephenson Foundation Bio-MakerSpace at the University of Pennsylvania. This project made use of extensive electronics, software, and mechanical design, to create an open-source version of an expensive biology testing tool. To develop the project, in addition to being well versed in building, the team had to understand the biology and chemistry, and put together the reagents to test. The team was so successful, the project was published in a scientific journal, referenced in the journal Nature, and was later built as part of an international hackathon.

Electronics

One of the most iconic images of a MakerSpace—next to a 3D printer humming away in the corner—is the familiar glow of an LED blinking on a breadboard. Electronics are a classic and foundational maker field. They empower makers to create smart, responsive, interactive objects, combining creativity with computation. From beginner-friendly blinking lights to complex systems that sense, analyze, and communicate with the world around them, electronics projects have become increasingly accessible and increasingly powerful.

The scope of what can be created in electronics MakerSpaces continues to expand rapidly. From robotic arms and environmental sensors to custom-built wearables and DIY home automation systems, electronics has grown from a hobbyist pursuit to a key skill for inventors, engineers, artists, and entrepreneurs alike.

For many people, this type of MakerSpace brings up visions of the character Tony Stark in Marvel's Iron Man movies, but in fact, they go back to Benjamin Franklin, who was a scientific hobbyist.

What Can You Make?

Electronics projects are often the "brains" of multidisciplinary maker creations. They are the invisible threads behind motion sensors in a kinetic sculpture, light displays in a fashion show, or a temperature monitor for a biology experiment. This is part of what makes electronics such a rich and rewarding field: it touches everything.

Table 3-3 below outlines some of the types of projects that can be made in an electronics MakerSpace. These range from basic circuit-building to more advanced applications in IoT, robotics, and wearable tech. As with all previous tables, this is just a starting point—many projects will span multiple categories or evolve over time from one domain to another.

Table 3-3. *Table Which Outlines Some of the Types of Projects That Can Be Made in an Electronics MakerSpace*

Electronics discipline	Project example
Circuits	Motion sensors
	Microcontroller work
	Audio filters
Robotics	Robotic arms
	Line-following cars
	Autonomous rovers
Internet of things	Smart home automation
	DIY AirTags
	Smart plant watering system
Wearables	LED-enhanced clothing
	Seizure detection watch
	Fitness trackers
Human–computer interaction	Touch-sensitive lamps
	Gesture control systems
	Capacitive sensors
Sensors and data logging	Temperature loggers
	Air quality monitors
	Physiological signal trackers
Educational kits	Arduino "Hello World" projects
	Simple breadboard games
	Sound-reactive LEDs

Just like arts and crafts or biology and chemistry, electronics making can be practiced by anyone. Beginners often start with kits or tutorials—blinking an LED, reading a button press, or printing a message to a tiny display. These small "aha!" moments build a sense of empowerment and momentum. From there, users quickly move into creating devices that react to their environment, collect data, or connect with the Internet.

One of the most exciting aspects of modern electronics making is how accessible it has become. Decades ago, building a simple sensor network or data logger required expensive tools, deep programming knowledge, and expert support. Today, many electronics MakerSpaces offer free access to open-source software and community-built libraries. Users can copy and paste code from an online tutorial, upload it to a $5 microcontroller, and watch their idea come to life in minutes.

At the same time, electronics MakerSpaces benefit from a collaborative environment. Many beginners hit a wall when debugging circuits or writing code. In a MakerSpace, other users or staff can offer tips, test components, and help troubleshoot—often unlocking a whole new level of learning.

The Space

If you've ever walked into an electronics MakerSpace, you might have noticed the compact, organized chaos: bins filled with resistors, wires, sensors, and buttons; a faint smell of solder; computers loaded with Arduino IDE or Python; and maybe a breadboard populated with blinking components whose purpose only the maker understands. It's not always a neat environment, but it's almost always filled with curiosity and invention.

Electronics MakerSpaces have become incredibly commonplace as the cost of supplies and equipment have dropped dramatically over the last few decades. The basic equipment needed for these spaces is straightforward: a multimeter for simple measurements, an oscilloscope for more complex measurements, and power supplies and signal generators for testing. In addition, soldering irons are needed for more complete prototyping and manufacturing (Figure 3-5). While traditionally, this equipment would cost tens of thousands of dollars, today, an adequate oscilloscope and signal generator can be easily generated through a PC or smartphone. Stand-alone devices can be found for under $100.

Figure 3-5. *Soldering electronics (Designed by FreePik)*

In addition, microcontrollers and development boards such as Arduino and Raspberry Pi form the core of many DIY projects. Again, decades ago, such equipment was well out of the reach of hobbyists. The development boards were often incredibly expensive, and in addition, the software to program these were an additional high cost. Also, in the past, programming microcontrollers required extensive knowledge of computer architecture and assembly programming. Debugging and support required the help of experts. Today, open-source software and hardware, combined with immense resources available online, make this work incredibly easy.

Furniture in an electronics MakerSpace should support collaboration, concentration, and comfort. Tables should be electrically grounded and easy to clean, and seating should allow for long work sessions without fatigue. Accessibility is key—users should be able to reach shared components and tools without disrupting others. Clear labeling systems for components (e.g., resistors sorted by resistance) save time and frustration.

Environmental conditions should include good lighting, especially for soldering, and sufficient ventilation to handle solder fumes. Some spaces may include fume extractors or small filtered enclosures for extended soldering sessions. Heat-resistant mats and magnifying lamps are also helpful for detail-oriented tasks.

Some MakerSpaces also offer a "checkout" system for electronics kits, allowing students to bring components to their dorms or homes and return them after completing a project. This extends the reach of the MakerSpace beyond the physical room and gives users more flexibility.

The low cost and accessibility of the material can discourage people from participating in a formal community MakerSpace since everything could be done at home. Indeed, during the COVID-19 pandemic, electrical engineering programs throughout the world realized they could duplicate their lab programs for very low costs, shipping all of the equipment to the students. However, community environments allow for a plethora of equipment and supplies, and in large quantities, encouraging creativity. In addition, having a community encourages collaboration and learning.

One of the advantages of working with these types of electronics is that safety is not as significant of a concern as in other fields. However, precautions should be taken, especially when soldering. Also, when using human physiological signals (such as electrocardiograms), extra precautions should be taken to prevent injuries. These types of measurements are easy to take, only requiring a simple electrode taped onto a human body. However, the consequences of a misplaced wire or an electric surge can be fatal. There are ways to isolate the body for protection and these methods should be considered.

Case Study

At the University of Pennsylvania, electronics plays a central role in many of the projects completed at the Stephenson Foundation Educational Laboratory and Bio-MakerSpace. One example is a student-designed seizure detection watch that uses a motion sensor, microcontroller, and vibration motor to detect potential seizure activity and alert the user. Another group developed an interactive LED display that responds to voice commands using a simple microphone array and a microcontroller-based voice recognition module.

Other institutions have seen similar projects flourish. At Yale's Center for Engineering Innovation and Design, students frequently combine mechanical and electronic systems to create prototypes for health monitoring, gaming accessories, or responsive art installations.

Mechanical

Mechanical making is often the first field that comes to mind when someone hears the word "MakerSpace." This is likely because the field of mechanical making includes many of the most visually striking and widely used tools in a MakerSpace—3D printers, CNC mills, table saws, lathes, and more. The clatter of metal against metal, the scent of sawdust, and the warmth of melted plastic from a freshly finished print all contribute to the unmistakable sensory environment of a mechanical MakerSpace (Figure 3-6).

Mechanical making involves the creation, modification, or assembly of physical components and systems, typically using a combination of additive (e.g., 3D printing) and subtractive (e.g., milling, laser cutting) techniques. Whether you're crafting architectural models, designing mechanical linkages, or prototyping furniture, mechanical MakerSpaces are where ideas are translated into tangible objects.

Figure 3-6. *Working with wood (Designed by FreePik)*

Though the perception of mechanical making is often tied to traditional shop tools, today's MakerSpaces blend manual craftsmanship with digital design, allowing users to produce parts and models with precision, repeatability, and innovation.

What Can You Make?

Table 3-4 below outlines some of the types of projects that can be made in a mechanical MakerSpace. These include prototyping, woodworking, mechanical assemblies, and scale modeling. This list serves as a reference point and should be viewed as an invitation for expansion, not limitation.

Table 3-4. *Table Which Outlines Some of the Types of Projects That Can Be Made in a Mechanical MakerSpace*

Mechanical discipline	Project example
Prototype development	CAD modeling
	Press-fit kits
	3D printing
	Laser cutting
	Milling
Woodworking design	Custom furniture
	Handcrafted organizers
	Wooden art installations
Mechanical assemblies	Gear trains
	Linkages
	Steam engine replicas
	Mechanical toys
Scale models	Architectural mockups
	Automotive models
	Marine prototypes

(*continued*)

Table 3-4. (continued)

Mechanical discipline	Project example
Kinetic objects	Marble machines
	Crank toys
	Kinetic sculptures
Structural design	Load-bearing bridges
	Truss designs
	Stress-testing rigs
Fabrication art	Parametric sculptures
	Hybrid materials assemblies

The Space

A Mechanical MakerSpaces attract a wide variety of users, from engineering students working on functional prototypes to hobbyists building custom furniture or cosplay props. While some tools require prior training due to their size, speed, or power, others—such as desktop 3D printers or laser cutters—are intuitive and safe enough for beginners after just a short orientation.

The sound of machines humming, vacuum pumps running, or the rhythmic slicing of a laser cutter offers a kind of creative energy unique to mechanical spaces. And yet, despite their reputation for being noisy or industrial, well-designed mechanical MakerSpaces are organized, approachable, and often quite beautiful in their layout.

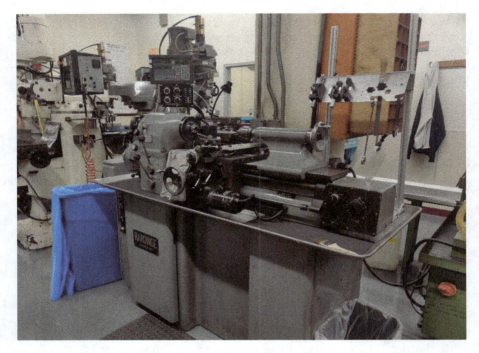

Figure 3-7. *Equipment in a typical machine shop*

The backbone of a Mechanical MakerSpace is its tools and machinery (Figure 3-7). These components are what enable enthusiasts to create their vision. These spaces often feature a diverse range of equipment, including 3D printers for rapid prototyping, CNC (Computer Numerical Control) machines such as mills and routers for precision cutting and shaping of materials, laser cutters capable of creating intricate designs on various surfaces, and a variety of hand and power tools essential for woodworking, metalworking, and mechanical assembly. This arsenal might also contain table saws, bandsaws, drills, sanders, grinders, and lathes. Outside of these larger machinery, these spaces may provide equipment for measurement and precision work, such as calipers, micrometers, and digital design software for computer-aided design (CAD).

The layout of a mechanical MakerSpace is especially important for safety, flow, and productivity. Large, open areas with appropriate clearances between machines allow for safe operation (see Figure 3-8 for a sample woodworking shop). Many of the tools used—such as table saws, CNC routers, and metal lathes—require not just training but dedicated zones to contain noise, dust, and vibration. Flooring should be non-slip and durable, and emergency stops and PPE stations should be clearly marked and easily accessible.

In most mechanical MakerSpaces, it's common to separate additive tools like 3D printers from subtractive tools like saws or mills to reduce contamination and maintain cleanliness around precision equipment. Temperature control and ventilation are also crucial—especially in areas with laser cutters or 3D printers, which can emit fumes or require enclosed, filtered environments.

One overlooked feature in some mechanical MakerSpaces is project storage. Because many mechanical projects involve large, unwieldy components or take multiple sessions to complete, having shelving or lockers available for users to store works-in-progress is essential.

Furniture in mechanical MakerSpaces should be heavy-duty and spacious. Steel-framed workbenches, pegboards for tools, and tool cabinets on wheels can help users move and adjust their workstations depending on the size or stage of their project. Comfortable stools and appropriate-height tables also support long work sessions and reduce user fatigue.

Figure 3-8. *Woodworking shop (Designed by FreePik)*

Power requirements vary considerably in this field. While a sewing machine or soldering station may run off a standard 110V outlet, tools like CNC mills, lathes, and vacuum formers often need higher-voltage lines (e.g., 220V or 240V). Planning for the electrical infrastructure ahead of time is critical to the function and growth of any mechanical MakerSpace.

While many tools in this field can be costly, open-source communities and affordable desktop machines have made it increasingly feasible to bring high-end capabilities into smaller or budget-conscious spaces. For example, a desktop CNC router can be had for under $1,000 and may be sufficient for light-duty prototyping in wood, plastic, or foam.

One example of a Mechanical MakerSpace is a Fablab (`https:// www.fablabs.io/`) or digital fabrication laboratory. Fablabs grew out of MIT and quickly became a global resource for makers across the world. Each Fablab is set up with different equipment; however, when users enter the space, they will be greeted by computer-controlled equipment, whether this be 3D printers for additive manufacturing or precision cutting machines for subtractive manufacturing. Here, users will select the proper tool/machine to take their creative vision into reality.

Case Study

One example of a mechanical MakerSpace project that combines form and function is a custom ergonomic keyboard created by a user who suffered from repetitive strain injury. After scanning hand positioning and testing several iterations using laser-cut plywood and 3D-printed keycaps, the user produced a working prototype tailored exactly to their needs. The final product was as much about design empathy as it was about mechanical precision.

Another example comes from architecture students using CNC routers and foam cutters to fabricate intricate scale models of urban developments. By combining 3D modeling in Rhino or Fusion 360 with digital fabrication, students were able to quickly iterate, test proportions, and share tangible models with their design teams and instructors.

Other Emerging Maker Fields

The Maker movement has spread beyond the fields mentioned above, as people begin to realize that there are similar possibilities in other areas. People have started to explore the vast blue ocean of new fields. In this exploration, they have noticed the myriad of benefits that come with approaching the field with a maker's attitude and perspective. As such, previous fields which were historically viewed as softer skills (such as culinary arts and jewelry making), have now been embraced by the maker community. Outside of these older fields, new and emerging technologies are also expanding what it means to be a maker, such as virtual and augmented reality.

Culinary MakerSpaces

Culinary MakerSpaces are a rising and exciting frontier within the broader maker movement. While making is often associated with technology, fabrication, or electronics, cooking is one of the oldest and most universal forms of making. Preparing food combines creativity, chemistry, culture, and craft—making the kitchen a powerful platform for innovation, learning, and collaboration.

Culinary MakerSpaces are shared kitchens designed not just for meal prep, but for experimentation, prototyping, and learning. Much like a woodshop or a biology lab, these spaces are purpose-built with tools, appliances, and safety protocols to support a range of food-based projects—from the whimsical to the high-tech.

In university settings, culinary MakerSpaces are particularly useful. Many students, especially those in dormitories, lack access to a full kitchen. Providing a shared cooking space supports not only hands-on skill development but also community, wellness, and cultural exchange. Culinary MakerSpaces can also be a launchpad for food entrepreneurship, allowing aspiring chefs or food product developers to test and refine their ideas in a semi-professional environment.

Table 3-5 below outlines some of the types of projects that can be made in a culinary MakerSpace. From traditional recipes to food science experiments and artisanal creations, the range of activities reflects the flexibility and creativity inherent to this field.

Table 3-5. *Table Outlining Some of the Types of Projects That Can Be Made in a Culinary MakerSpace*

Culinary discipline	Project example
Traditional cooking	Family recipes
	Cultural cuisine workshops
Baking and pastry arts	Custom cake designs
	Sourdough experiments
Molecular gastronomy	Spherification of juices
	Foams and gels with lecithin
Fermentation science	Kimchi
	Kombucha
	Yogurt
	Sourdough starters
Food product development	Snack bar prototypes
	Flavor emulsions
Beverage crafting	Homemade sodas
	Herbal teas
	Mocktails
Food photography and media	Recipe documentation
	Social media content

Culinary MakerSpaces can vary widely in size and sophistication. Some are designed like commercial kitchens, with industrial stoves, multiple ovens, and high-capacity mixers. Others are more casual, resembling a well-equipped home kitchen. Regardless of size, what defines a culinary MakerSpace is its focus on experimentation, shared learning, and making food as a creative process.

If you walk into one of these spaces, you may see someone frosting a cake for a friend's birthday while another team is testing homemade granola bar recipes. A student group might be running a dumpling-making night to celebrate Lunar New Year. At the same time, an aspiring entrepreneur may be working with a faculty advisor to perfect a sauce recipe for a potential product launch.

In many cases, culinary MakerSpaces become informal cultural hubs, allowing people to share food traditions, swap recipes, and learn about others through the universal language of food.

Figure 3-9 shows an example of a pizza made in a community culinary MakerSpace—an activity that's simple, social, and endlessly customizable.

Figure 3-9. *Pizza made in a culinary MakerSpace*

Culinary MakerSpaces are typically equipped with the following:

- *Basic equipment*: Ovens, stovetops, refrigerators, freezers, microwaves

- *Small appliances*: Blenders, food processors, stand mixers, air fryers, sous vide machines

- *Utensils and tools*: Cutting boards, knives, baking sheets, mixing bowls, thermometers

- *Sanitation tools*: Handwashing stations, dishwashing areas, sanitizers, cleaning supplies

- *Prep space*: Countertops with cutting mats, rolling carts, and accessible storage

Safety and hygiene are especially critical in a shared kitchen environment. Culinary MakerSpaces should follow food safety protocols, including temperature monitoring, proper storage, and regular cleaning schedules. Some institutions may require users to take a food safety certification course (e.g., ServSafe) before using the space unsupervised.

Well-designed culinary MakerSpaces should also be adaptable. Rolling tables, movable cooktops, and modular storage allow for different configurations depending on the size and nature of the group using the space. Proper ventilation is essential—not just for fire safety but also to maintain comfort and reduce odors. Adequate lighting, both for food preparation and photography, is a plus.

One successful example is Venture Lab's Test Kitchen at the University of Pennsylvania. This kitchen is used by students for cooking clubs, cultural events, and food innovation classes. It also supports ventures in Penn's entrepreneurship ecosystem, helping students prototype new food and beverage products.

Outside academia, spaces like Tinker Kitchen in San Francisco provide pay-as-you-go access to a community kitchen with professional-grade equipment. Their model supports food enthusiasts, pop-up chefs, and early-stage food entrepreneurs.

Culinary MakerSpaces are also a great fit in urban environments where housing may lack kitchen access or where co-living models are common. In these contexts, the kitchen becomes not just a place to cook, but a social and educational venue.

Beauty, Fashion, AR/VR, Gaming, and Others

Other emerging trends in MakerSpaces include beauty and fashion. For example, the company Yeleen Beauty offers the opportunity for people interested in developing new cosmetics the space to try things out. It defines itself as a "MakerSpace designed to support women and founders of color in the beauty industry." In the same way, fashion MakerSpaces are also beginning to grow, providing opportunities for people to develop their own clothing styles. As is becoming common with MakerSpaces, these facilities also offer classes. Within the area of fashion MakerSpaces, jewelry making has become a very popular field.

Finally, virtual reality (VR) and augmented reality (AR) MakerSpaces have high-performance computers, VR headsets, AR devices, and motion tracking systems, providing a haven for developers and enthusiasts to craft immersive experiences not only for practical applications but also for gaming.

For example, the Stephenson Foundation Educational Laboratory and Bio-MakerSpace at the University of Pennsylvania has several gaming consoles in the MakerSpace to encourage students to explore software ingenuity through creative hardware. The consoles can be reserved and used in the MakerSpaces by students working on interdisciplinary projects. For example, students can reserve a Microsoft Kinect. With this device students can collect point clouds of the surrounding area to track different objects as they move through space. Additionally, students can use the Kinect to create a "stick-figure" like representation of themselves in virtual space. Once students have this representation, they can start training the system to recognize different gestures or movements. Eventually this could grow into a myriad of different projects, such as a sign language interpreter, a fitness assistant which tracks a user's movements to ensure they are using the optimal form, or a simple motion-based controller.

Combination MakerSpaces

Combining different types of MakerSpaces has become increasingly common. Why restrict a MakerSpace to only one discipline when they can work so well together and allow users to better express their creativity? Perhaps the most ubiquitous combination is merging mechanical and electronics spaces together, which is what one most commonly finds in traditional college and university engineering department MakerSpaces.

Arts and mechanical MakerSpace combinations are also a relatively common type of combination MakerSpace as these two disciplines are an obvious match. However, there are truly no limitations to the types of MakerSpace that you can possibly combine!

For example, it is easy enough for a space with mechanical tools to house materials and tools for making jewelry. There may also be overlap in the tools required for different disciplines. These combined mechanical and arts and crafts facilities could easily also house other equipment like sewing machines.

In fact, the Stephenson Bio-MakerSpace at the University of Pennsylvania is an interesting example. The space houses a sewing machine with the original intent of designing "wearable" sensors, but users have gone on to use it to repair or even make outfits. In the same way, groups have used the CADing and rapid prototyping facilities to host jewelry and candle-making workshops. Another example is the Yale Center for Engineering Innovation & Design (CEID), which has also moved beyond traditional engineering and encouraged these types of creative pursuits.

Conclusion

For someone using MakerSpaces, it's important to consider the types of projects you want to work on and the tools you'll need, while exploring local MakerSpaces to see which one best fits your needs. For someone thinking of starting a MakerSpace, defining your niche and planning the necessary equipment, workflow, and community-building strategies will help you create a space that supports users' project goals. For someone running an existing MakerSpace, evaluating your space's operations, optimizing inventory and layout, and identifying the most popular user projects will allow you to improve the space and better serve the community.

Key Takeaways

- The four core maker fields are arts and crafts, biology and chemistry, electronics, and mechanical.

- There are infinite other maker fields beyond these four core fields and most MakerSpaces combine two or more fields.

- MakerSpaces provide a sanctuary for individuals of all ages and backgrounds to unleash their creative potential.

- Arts and crafts MakerSpaces offer a profound journey into human creativity and expression.

- MakerSpaces in biology and chemistry represent a significant shift in the landscape of innovation, providing hands-on opportunities for experimentation and exploration.

- By instilling a strong ethical framework, Biological MakerSpaces can ensure that scientific innovation is balanced with social responsibility and ethical integrity.

- Electronics MakerSpaces cater to a wide range of projects, from custom electronic circuits to sophisticated robotics and IoT devices. These spaces serve as incubators for innovation and learning, providing a platform for individuals to bring their electronic ideas to life with the support of a community.

- Mechanical MakerSpaces cater to a broad spectrum of projects, from intricate models and prototypes to functional machinery and complex mechanical assemblies.

- Combination MakerSpaces offer multiple maker fields in one space, allowing users to think outside the box and experiment with a variety of tools in many different ways.

CHAPTER 4

Equipment and Tools

Equipment and tools are an obvious requirement for MakerSpaces: indeed, today, MakerSpaces are typified by 3-D printers. Regardless of field, specialized equipment is necessary for MakerSpaces to thrive and meet the diverse needs of their users. This chapter will guide you through the essential considerations for selecting and managing equipment and supplies in a MakerSpace.

Laying the Groundwork

When setting up or expanding a MakerSpace, the first step is identifying the right equipment. Internet searches and searches on platforms like Amazon can help you find a variety of options to suit your needs. However, there are several critical factors to consider beyond just finding the right tools.

First and foremost, the type of equipment needed will depend on the focus of your MakerSpace. Commonly required tools include heavy-duty sewing machines for textile projects, 3-D printers for prototyping, laser cutters, and CNC machines. Each piece of equipment has its own set of requirements and uses, so it is essential to choose based on your specific needs.

Another essential aspect to consider is the throughput of each piece of equipment. High-demand tools may require multiple units to avoid bottlenecks, and assessing if you can buy in bulk can lead to cost savings

© Sevile G. Mannickarottu, Michael G. Patterson, and Carolyne Godon 2025
S. G. Mannickarottu et al., *Creating MakerSpaces*, Maker Innovations Series,
https://doi.org/10.1007/979-8-8688-1309-2_4

and ensure that you have enough supplies on hand. When evaluating equipment, it is also crucial to factor in both the initial cost and the ongoing operational costs. Some devices have high up-front costs but low operational expenses, while others might be cheaper initially but expensive to maintain. Understanding the fixed vs. variable costs will help you budget more effectively.

Lead times for ordering both supplies and equipment should also be considered. Delays in receiving critical components can disrupt your MakerSpace's operations. Additionally, it is wise to invest in equipment from established companies with good reputations. Startups might offer innovative products but also carry the risk of insolvency. For instance, there was a case with a wax printer startup that went out of business, leaving its users stranded without support or parts.

Deciding between proprietary and open-source equipment is another crucial consideration. For example, Prusa open-source 3-D printers are known for their reliability and community support, whereas MakerBot offers a proprietary system. Open-source options provide flexibility and lower costs but require more technical know-how. Additionally, evaluating whether to build or buy equipment can save money and provide custom solutions. Still, it is essential to consider the time cost and potential issues if the person who built it leaves.

Space considerations are also essential. Ensure you have enough physical space for all your equipment. This includes not only the footprint of the machines but also space for users to work comfortably and safely. Many advanced tools require specific software, so check if the software is subscription-based or requires per-user licenses. Additionally, ensure the software can be used for commercial purposes if your MakerSpace supports startups.

Lastly, look for bulk purchase discounts, educational or non-profit discounts, and opportunities for donations. Many companies offer significant discounts to educational institutions and non-profit organizations.

The following sections describe suggested equipment and supplies for equipment.

Arts and Crafts

Making arts and crafts projects can require a wide variety of equipment and tools. The landscape of arts and crafts tools and equipment spans a vast spectrum of cost and complexity, offering endless options to choose from depending on each MakerSpace's own priorities and specific constraints.

At its most simple form, an arts and crafts MakerSpace could include only the most basic and fundamental essential items: crayons, construction paper, glue, and scissors, reminiscent of the familiar supplies you might find in any kindergarten or early primary school classroom. Yet, from this humble starting point, the potential for expansion in the world of arts and crafts tools and equipment knows no bounds. Do you want to add pipe cleaners, string, aluminum foil, or yarn to your MakerSpace? Go for it! Apart from these simple items, arts and crafts, MakerSpaces can also house more extensive, complex, professional-grade electronic tools like sewing machines, vinyl cutters, kitchen-style hot plates for melting wax or heating other materials. In this section, we will describe some of the most common tools and equipment you may want to consider, including in an arts and crafts MakerSpace, and we will outline some important considerations for each. However, this list should be seen as a short list of suggestions, not a full list of requirements, and certainly not an exhaustive inventory of everything that a MakerSpace may want to provide (Table 4-1 provides a summary). What to include in an arts and crafts MakerSpace is ultimately up to the team that runs the MakerSpace and up to the users of that MakerSpace. Over time, you may find that the best MakerSpace purchases originated as user-driven suggestions based on an enthusiastic user's wants or needs. With this in mind, make sure to obtain user feedback (see Chapter 8), whether physical or digital, in your MakerSpace to collect suggestions from those who use the space about how they would like you to invest in and grow your collection of tools and equipment.

Table 4-1. *Summary of Tools and Supplies for Arts and Crafts MakerSpaces*

Category	Key equipment and tools	Important considerations
Basic supplies	Scissors, glue, tape, markers, paper, rulers, utility knives	Durable materials for repeated use; stock widely used items; low cost
Textile and fiber arts	Sewing machines, embroidery hoops, irons, knitting needles/hooks, crochet tools	Choose durable, easy-to-maintain equipment; consider check-out systems; stock a variety of sizes
Knitting machines	Consumer-grade, industrial-grade, or hybrid models	Balance cost, noise, and speed; software availability (open vs. closed); manufacturer's support reputation
Pottery and sculpting	Pottery wheels (electric/kick), kilns, modeling clay, sculpting tools	High space and cost needs; consider accessibility and training; durable tools for beginners
Drawing and painting	Sketch pads, paint brushes, acrylics, watercolors, easels, canvases	Versatile supplies; student-grade materials are space- and cost-efficient; relevant across many disciplines
Printmaking	Linoleum blocks, carving tools, inks, brayers, small printing presses	Great for creative, collaborative use; DIY or commercial presses available

(*continued*)

Table 4-1. (*continued*)

Category	Key equipment and tools	Important considerations
Paper crafting	Cardstock, origami paper, quilling tools, bookbinding supplies	Low cost and low maintenance; niche but useful for final project presentation
Digital/ software tools	Graphic tablets, design software, digital cameras, lights for photography	Useful across disciplines; invest in user-friendly, versatile tools
Jewelry making	Pliers, cutters, mandrels, files, beading needles, packaging materials	Finer tools than general metalwork; explore crossover tools for cost savings
Storage and project continuity	Storage bins, shelves, project lockers	Enable long-term projects; consider labeling and visibility of storage solutions.
User-driven additions	Any tool suggested by users.	Feedback-driven investments often have high utility; establish feedback collection mechanisms.

Textiles and Fiber Arts Tools and Equipment

Fiber arts tools and equipment and tools often represent the most significant investment of an arts and crafts MakerSpace, both in terms of monetary cost and especially storage space. Well-built, durable, professional grade sewing machines that are built to withstand wear and tear from multiple users, including many beginners who can be pretty rough on these machines when they get frustrated, can be expensive to purchase and may take up a lot of precious storage space but can be very useful in many arts and crafts or interdisciplinary projects. Multiple sewing machines, space to use them, and space to store the fabric to make sewing projects can quickly take over even a good-sized MakerSpace.

Knitting Machines

Consider whether your MakerSpace is best suited for a consumer or industrial grade knitting machine. These are distinguished by cost, throughput speed, and loudness. Consumer machines will be slower, often quieter. Industrial machines will be much larger, but also much faster, and much louder, since they are designed for commercial use, not for use in someone's home. There are also some new options that fit in the space between those two categories, for heavy home use or light industrial use, and appear to be well suited for MakerSpace applications. However, when looking into a knitting machine, make sure to consider the manufacturer's reputation and longevity. Use caution if buying from a smaller, newer company, especially if their funding situation is precarious or uncertain. Larger, more established companies, while maybe not always offering the most innovative products, typically offer better post-purchase support. Another thing to keep in mind is the software that is needed to use these machines. Is it open or closed source? If closed source, does purchasing the machine give you unrestricted forever access to its accompanying software, or do you need to buy a subscription to keep using the machine?

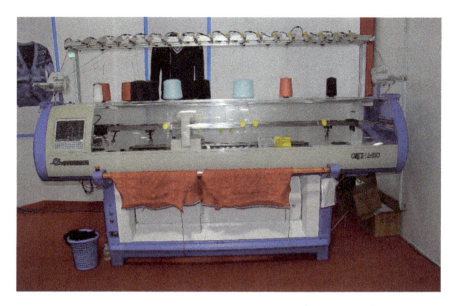

Figure 4-1. *Automatic computerized knitting machine (Courtesy:* `https://commons.wikimedia.org/wiki/File:Automatic_ Computerized_Flat_Knitting_Machine.jpg)`

There are smaller more accessible knitting machines, such as by the company Sentro (`https://www.sentroknittings.com/`).

Sewing Machines

Sewing machines come in different varieties. Define how often and how hard you think the sewing machine will be used in your MakerSpace. What kind of fabric will be sewn? Consider sticking to established, reputable brands that have strong support for spare parts and repairs (see Figure 4-2). Well-cared-for sewing machines can last a very long time. Many grandmothers all over the world use decades-old sewing machines without any issues. For cost savings, buying a used sewing machine might be all you need.

Figure 4-2. *Sewing machine in a MakerSpace*

Iron

Getting a clothes iron is essential to flatten fabric to work on sewing and quilting projects. Also, it is helpful for ironing patches onto fabric or melting bead projects, among many other applications that creative MakerSpace users will find. Fortunately, these are quite inexpensive.

Embroidery Supplies

Embroidery supplies include hoops, cloth, thread, and needles. Embroidery is an excellent complement to any textile project, in any medium. Users can also dabble in embroidery to customize clothing items they own, adding embroidery to caps, jackets, shirts, and bags. Buy solid wood embroidery hoops that can be reused, not the flimsy ones that break with the first project. Also, sturdy needles. While maybe less critical for an individual at home, anything in MakerSpace needs to be chosen to be used and abused by many people over and over again.

Knitting Needles and Crochet Hooks

Both wood and metal work for knitting needles since users' needs may vary depending on preference. You should aim to get a variety of single-pointed, double-pointed, and circular needles in a variety of different sizes. Completing a knitting project often takes time, so assume users won't finish a project in just one session. Consider having the option for users to "check out" equipment and take it home, like borrowing books from the library. If stocking yarn, make sure to get knitting needles in the appropriate size for the yarn that you are stocking. You should consider the same for crochet hooks. Ideally, if cost is not a significant concern, you should try to prioritize metal needles or hooks over plastic and make sure they fit the yarn that is stocked. Unlike knitting needles that remain in the project while it is underway and can't readily be removed from the project without compromising it, crochet hooks can be very easily removed from projects without any issues. That means that users won't be monopolizing crochet hooks the entire duration of their project, the way knitters would monopolize knitting needles. Therefore, fewer crochet hooks could possibly be stocked. If planning to include crochet, make sure also to stock stuffing, thread, beads, and buttons for amigurumi. These are great MakerSpace project options since they can be completed pretty quickly and are accessible to beginner crocheters.

Pottery and Sculpting Tools

Equipping a MakerSpace for pottery and sculpting involves a notable investment in both finances and space. Durable, professional-grade kilns and pottery wheels are essential, especially considering the wear and tear from frequent use by newcomers who may not always handle the equipment gently. These pieces of equipment are often pricey and require significant space for both operation and storage. Accommodating multiple kilns and wheels, as well as providing ample room for clay and sculpting tools, can quickly fill even a generously sized MakerSpace. However, the benefits of having such resources are immense, as they enable a variety of creative and interdisciplinary projects to flourish.

Modeling Clay

As a highly versatile material, modeling clay is vital to stock in any arts and crafts MakerSpace. If space allows it, get a variety of colors and types of clay. Outside of pure arts and crafts projects, it can also be used to mockup other 3D projects and can be used for 3D animation projects. Another underrated use of clay is to keep track of small parts, such as tiny screws. Sticking them in clay can help prevent them from being blown off or knocked off the work surface.

Pottery Wheels

If space allows it, consider getting a pottery wheel for your arts and crafts MakerSpace. Pottery wheels are available in a wide range of sizes, types, and features, each suited to different skill levels and purposes (see example in Figure 4-3). Choosing the right pottery wheel for your MakerSpace is an important decision that requires careful consideration of various factors to ensure it meets the needs of the space and its users. First, you should decide between an electric wheel and a kick wheel. Electric wheels, as the name indicates, are powered by electricity. They provide consistent speed control and are suitable for both beginner and more experienced potters. Kick wheels, as their name suggests, are operated manually by kicking a foot pedal to rotate the wheel. They provide a much more traditional and rustic pottery experience and can be appealing to those interested in a more hands-on approach. However, they offer less consistent results and may be more frustrating to use for beginner potters, especially for perfectionists. Kick wheels may also be less accessible to makers with disabilities. The next important feature is the size and capacity of the wheel. This is very important as space is a crucial constraint for many

MakerSpaces. Larger wheels offer more workspace and can accommodate larger chunks of clay, making them suitable for creating large items like bowls and vases. Smaller wheels are more compact but can only be used to make smaller scale projects. It's a lot to think about, but as with any piece of equipment, you can always start with a smaller less costly option and upgrade or add a new larger piece later if your needs change.

Figure 4-3. *Pottery Wheel (Courtesy:* https://www.pexels.com/photo/bowl-being-made-with-potters-wheel-18798250/)

Sculpting Tools and Carving Tools

Hand tools for sculpting and carving are essential for a pottery or sculpture working space. Like anything, they can vary greatly in complexity, quality, and cost. Luckily, they are often sold as sets, so if you are new to this field, a basic set of clay sculpting tools built out of sturdy materials is a great place to start. They are widely available at crafting supply stores and online. Metal tools are generally easier to clean and maintain than wooden or plastic-handled tools. While metal may be more expensive, it is likely a better choice for a highly trafficked MakerSpace with primarily beginners. Different tools are suitable for different materials so make sure you pick something that works with the materials you will be supplying in your MakerSpace.

Drawing and Painting Supplies

Some of the most common arts and crafts tools and equipment are drawing and painting supplies. These supplies can include sketch pads, drawing paper, paint brushes, acrylic paints, watercolors, oil paints, palettes for mixing colors, easels for painting, canvas boards, stretched canvases, rolls of canvas and wood to DIY stretched canvases, palette knives, etc. Though the costs of these supplies can vary, while professional-grade supplies can be very expensive, there are plenty of student-grade supplies widely available that can easily be cost-effective and don't take up very much space. Painting and drawing supplies are also incredibly versatile and great for interdisciplinary projects. Even if you do not consider your MakerSpace to have anything to do with arts and crafts, you should consider stocking some basic painting and drawing supplies for use in other types of projects. For example, paint can be applied both to paper and to 3D printed robot parts. Drawing tools can also be used to help draft design projects in different disciplines. Many colors of pens, markers, pencils, paper, and tape can help makers label parts of their mechanical or electronic projects.

Printmaking Tools and Equipment

Printmaking equipment and supplies are a great addition to an arts and crafts MakerSpace. These tools are not very common but can be used to make very interesting creative projects, making them a great fit for a shared collaborative space like a MakerSpace. Having printmaking equipment could be a strong selling point to attract users to a MakerSpace. Types of equipment and tools to consider for printmaking include linoleum blocks, carving tools, printing inks, brayers, printing rollers, and printing presses. Printing presses come in all sizes and price points. Small-scale printing presses can also be DIYed; there are free video tutorials online, and there are even commercially available kits to build and assemble your own printing press. An interested Maker could feasibly build their own printing press that could then be used by others in the MakerSpace, truly embodying the spirit and meaning of MakerSpaces.

Paper Crafting

Paper crafting tools and supplies could also be found in an arts and crafts MakerSpace. These would include card stock, colored paper, paper cutters, punches, origami paper, tissue paper, quilling tools, and bookbinding supplies. Although a fairly niche discipline, paper crafting is low maintenance, and the supplies don't take up too much space so the cost of having these products in your MakerSpace is relatively low. Paper-making supplies can also help put the finishing touches on other things that users make, such as creating custom wrapping paper to gift an electronic project to a friend or family member for their birthday.

Computer and Software Tools

In addition to physical tools and supplies, computer and software tools are also relevant to arts and crafts MakerSpaces. These can include computers with graphic design software, graphic tablets for digital drawing, 3D printers, CAD software, digital cameras for documenting projects, and product photography supplies such as backgrounds and lights. Like many other types of arts and crafts tools and equipment, these computer and software tools can also be applied to other types of MakerSpace projects.

Jewelry Crafting

Jewelry crafting tools and supplies can also be within the scope of an arts and crafts MakerSpace. These may include different types of pliers (round-nose, chain-nose, flat-nose, needle-nose, etc.), wire cutters, jewelry hammers, jeweler's saw, jeweler's blades, metal files, jewelry mandrels, ring sizers, beading needles, wire needles, jewelry display cases, jewelry stands, jewelry busts, gift boxes, and packaging materials. Jewelry crafting tools share some common tools with metalworking tools, but tend to be finer and smaller than most metalworking tools, since jewelry is often more delicate than most other types of metalwork. If space and cost is a concern, consider getting tools that work for both applications. Being able to make simple rustic jewelry with standard metalworking tools is better than not being able to make any jewelry at all. MakerSpace users interested in jewelry making may also want to experiment with casting and forging their own metals or using CNC machines to make custom computer-guided designs. Laser cutters could also be used to make jewelry such as earrings. These pieces of equipment are covered in more detail in the mechanical section.

Basic Arts and Crafts Tools and Supplies

Finally, no arts and crafts MakerSpace would be complete without an assortment of basic arts and crafts tools and supplies such as scissors, paper, rope, utility knives, cutting mats, rulers, measuring tools, pens, markers, permanent markers, pencils, erasers, sharpeners, various types of adhesive tape, glue guns, super glue, glue sticks, etc. Anything that you may find in a pencil case or in an office supply cabinet should be well stocked in any arts and crafts MakerSpace.

Biology and Chemistry

MakerSpaces related to biology and chemistry can perhaps be the most expensive to set up and operate, depending on the type and level of work envisioned. These spaces often require specialized workstations with proper surfaces (typically not wood), enhanced ventilation, and more extensive personal protective equipment (PPE), such as lab coats, gloves, and safety goggles. At their core, these MakerSpaces support experiments and investigations in life and physical sciences by providing access to equipment like microscopes, PCR machines, centrifuges, and spectrophotometers.

While some of these tools—such as gel electrophoresis systems or basic incubators—can be implemented cost-effectively using DIY approaches, others, like CO_2 incubators or autoclaves, may fall outside the feasible scope for many educational or community MakerSpaces. As with all MakerSpace fields, careful consideration should be given not only to the selection of equipment but also to the needs, skill levels, and safety of the users. This section describes a range of tools and equipment that support biology and chemistry projects, with notes on costs, capabilities, and practicality for different MakerSpace contexts (see Table 4-2 for a summary). Whether you're launching a space from scratch or expanding your capabilities, this guide can help you prioritize equipment that offers the most impact for your community.

Table 4-2. *Summary of Tools and Supplies for Biology and Chemistry MakerSpaces*

Category	Key equipment and tools	Important considerations
Microscopes	Compound, stereo, and smartphone microscopes	Magnification needs and portability
Centrifuges	Benchtop and floor centrifuges	Balancing needs; maintenance requirements
CO2 incubators	Controlled environments for cell culture	Typically beyond scope for DIY spaces
PCR machines	Standard and real-time thermal cyclers	Essential for DNA amplification work
Gel electrophoresis	Agarose gel units, power supplies, imaging	Can be inexpensive; core bio tool
Autoclaves	High-pressure steam sterilizers	Costly; avoid with disposable alternatives
Incubators	Temperature-controlled culture environments	Affordable options exist
Pipettes and pipetting systems	Manual, electronic, and multichannel pipettes	Accuracy and compatibility with tips
Fume hoods	Ventilated workspaces for chemical safety	Critical for hazardous material handling
Cell culture hoods	Sterile, filtered environments for cultures	Not required but enhances sterility
Spectrophotometers	UV-Vis, fluorescence, and absorbance units	Precision measurement for assays
Balances and scales	Analytical and top-loading balances	Essential for quantitative experiments

(continued)

Table 4-2. (*continued*)

Category	Key equipment and tools	Important considerations
Glassware and labware	Beakers, flasks, test tubes, petri dishes	Various sizes/materials needed
Serological Pipettes	Graduated pipettes for liquid transfer	Used for precise measurements
Image analysis software	ImageJ and similar software tools	Free and open source, for example, ImageJ
General laboratory Supplies	Gloves, lab coats, tubes, reagents	Daily essentials for safety and workflow

Microscopes

Microscopes are essential tools in biology, allowing scientists to magnify and visualize tiny structures such as cells, tissues, and microorganisms (see Figure 4-4 for an example of a microscope with imaging tools). There are various types of microscopes available, including compound microscopes, stereo microscopes, and electron microscopes, each with its specific applications and magnification capabilities. Traditional microscopes for biological work are pricey, but inexpensive versions exist, including decent microscopes, which are attachments to a smartphone. For sophisticated biological applications, usually a fluorescent microscope is needed, but they can be quite expensive.

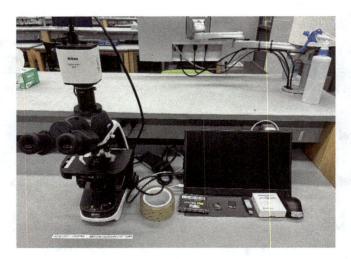

Figure 4-4. *Microscope with a display to view in the Stephenson Foundation Bio-MakerSpace at the University of Pennsylvania*

Centrifuges

Centrifuges are used to separate components of biological samples based on their density through high-speed spinning. They are commonly used in applications such as cell fractionation, DNA extraction, and protein purification. Centrifuges come in different sizes and capacities, including benchtop and floor models, to accommodate various sample volumes and types. Almost universally, centrifuges are expensive as they need to be properly balanced and maintained.

CO2 Incubators

CO2 incubators provide a controlled environment for cell culture experiments by maintaining optimal temperature, humidity, and CO2 levels. These incubators are essential for cell growth, maintenance, and experimentation in fields such as mammalian cell biology, microbiology, and tissue engineering. For most DIY-type biology and chemistry laboratories, this type of work is often outside the scope of what can be done.

PCR Machines

PCR (Polymerase Chain Reaction) machines are used to amplify DNA segments through repeated cycles of heating and cooling. They are indispensable tools for molecular biology research, diagnostics, and genetic engineering applications. PCR machines come in different formats, including standard thermal cyclers, real-time PCR instruments, and digital PCR systems.

Gel Electrophoresis Systems

Gel electrophoresis systems (see Figure 4-5 for an example) are used to separate and analyze DNA, RNA, and proteins based on their size and charge. These systems are crucial for molecular biology research, genetic analysis, and diagnostic testing. Gel electrophoresis systems include agarose gel units, power supplies, and imaging equipment for visualizing the separated molecules. The systems can be very sophisticated but can easily be done through DIY methods and can thus be inexpensive.

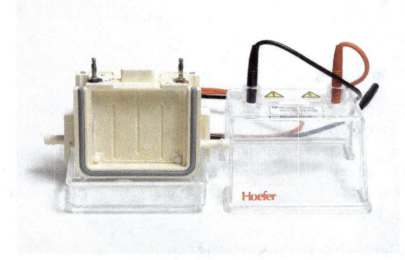

Figure 4-5. *Sample electrophoresis system (Courtesy:* `https://`
`commons.wikimedia.org/wiki/File:Polyacrylamid_gel_`
`electrophoresis_apparatus-02.jpg)`

Autoclaves

Autoclaves are used to sterilize laboratory equipment, media, and
biological waste by exposing them to high-pressure steam. They play a vital
role in maintaining aseptic conditions in microbiology, biotechnology, and
medical laboratories to prevent contamination and ensure experimental
reproducibility. Oftentimes, labs avoid autoclaves by focusing more on
disposable supplies, but this can become quite expensive.

Incubators

Incubators are used to culture and grow microorganisms, cells, and
tissues under controlled conditions of temperature, humidity, and
sometimes CO_2 levels. They are essential for a wide range of biological and

biomedical research applications, including microbial fermentation, cell proliferation assays, and stem cell culture. Traditional incubators, unlike CO_2 incubators, are often quite affordable.

Pipettes and Pipetting Systems

Pipettes are precision instruments used to measure and transfer small volumes of liquids in laboratory settings. They come in various designs, including manual, electronic, and multichannel pipettes, to accommodate different experimental needs (see Figure 4-6 for a sample). Pipetting systems may also include accessories such as pipette tips, reservoirs, and dispensers for efficient liquid handling.

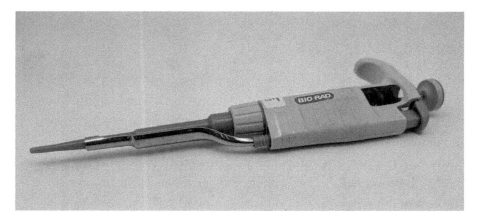

Figure 4-6. A pipette

Fume Hoods

Fume hoods are enclosed, ventilated workspaces designed to protect laboratory personnel from exposure to hazardous fumes, vapors, and airborne particles generated during experiments. They are essential for working with chemicals, solvents, and biological agents that may pose health risks if inhaled or absorbed through the skin. This is most critical in labs focused more on chemistry but can be helpful in work related to proteins and tissues.

Cell Culture Hoods

Cell culture hoods, also known as laminar flow hoods or biosafety cabinets, provide a sterile environment for handling cell cultures and biological samples. They use HEPA filters to remove airborne contaminants and maintain aseptic conditions necessary for cell culture work in fields such as cell biology, immunology, and tissue engineering. While not absolutely necessary for biological work with bacteria, it can be helpful to have one to guarantee a sterile environment.

Spectrophotometers

Spectrophotometers are instruments used to measure the absorbance or transmission of light by a sample as a function of wavelength. They are widely used in biochemical assays, molecular biology experiments, and analytical chemistry to quantify biomolecules, assess sample purity, and perform spectral analyses. Spectrophotometers may include UV-Vis, fluorescence, and absorbance spectrometers, among others. The cost of these can vary significantly depending on the quality and precision needed.

Balance and Scales

Balances and scales are used to measure the mass or weight of samples and reagents in laboratory experiments. They come in various types, including analytical balances, precision scales, and top-loading balances, with different capacities and levels of accuracy to suit specific measurement needs. Balances and scales are essential for preparing solutions, dosing reagents, and conducting quantitative analyses in biological research and chemical analysis.

Glassware and Labware

Glassware and labware are essential tools for conducting experiments and performing analyses in biology and chemistry laboratories. They include items such as beakers, flasks, test tubes, pipettes, petri dishes, and microplates, which are used for mixing, storing, and containing liquids and solids during various laboratory procedures. Glassware and labware are available in different materials, sizes, and shapes to accommodate diverse experimental requirements.

Serological Pipettes

Serological pipettes are graduated pipettes used for precise measurement and transfer of liquids in biological and biochemical applications. They feature a tapered tip and a bulbous portion for aspirating and dispensing liquids accurately. Serological pipettes are commonly used in cell culture, molecular biology, and clinical diagnostic laboratories for tasks such as media dispensing, sample dilution, and reagent preparation.

Image Analysis Software

Image analysis software such as ImageJ is used for processing, analyzing, and quantifying images obtained from microscopy, gel electrophoresis, and other imaging techniques. These software tools provide features for image enhancement, segmentation, measurements, and statistical analysis, facilitating data interpretation and visualization in biological and chemical research. Unlike so much in the biological sciences, ImageJ is open source and freely available.

General Laboratory Supplies

In addition to specialized equipment, biology and chemistry laboratories require various general supplies for routine operations and experiments. These may include consumables such as gloves, lab coats, filters, centrifuge tubes, PCR tubes, microcentrifuge tubes, syringes, needles, and molecular biology reagents. These supplies are essential for maintaining laboratory safety, hygiene, and workflow efficiency.

Electronics

Electronics MakerSpaces offer a compelling combination of accessibility and innovation, making them ideal environments for learners and inventors alike. Much like arts and crafts MakerSpaces, electronics spaces can be highly cost-effective to launch, with basic tools and supplies available at relatively low prices. What was once the exclusive domain of advanced engineering labs is now within reach for hobbyists, students, and community makers. Breadboards, multimeters, soldering tools, and power supplies form the foundation of many electronics projects, while microcontrollers like Arduino and Raspberry Pi introduce programming and interactivity in tangible, approachable ways.

As the needs of your MakerSpace evolve, you can scale up with tools like oscilloscopes, signal generators, and reflow ovens to support more sophisticated projects. The possibilities are expansive and interdisciplinary—touching everything from wearable tech to robotics to smart home devices. In this section, we highlight a range of equipment and supplies to consider for an electronics MakerSpace (see Table 4-3 for a summary). However, this is not an exhaustive list. As always, what you choose to include should be shaped by your space, your budget, and most importantly, your users. Be sure to gather feedback and remain open to expanding or refining your offerings based on their interests and aspirations.

Table 4-3. *Summary of Tools and Supplies for Electronics MakerSpaces*

Category	Key equipment and tools	Important considerations
Power supplies	Battery packs, wall-powered DC supplies	Low-cost options suffice for most projects
Soldering tools	Soldering irons, stands, fume extractors	Ventilation and safety glasses needed
Multimeters	Digital multimeters for basic measurements	Inexpensive; essential for diagnostics
Oscilloscopes	Analog and digital oscilloscopes	High cost for high-frequency; consider needs
Signal generators	Basic AC signal sources; microcontroller-generated signals	Often replaceable with microcontrollers
Virtual test systems	USB-powered tools like Digilent Analog Discovery	Cost-effective and compact for learning
Software tools	TinkerCad, Eagle, Altium, Arduino IDE	Balance between accessibility and depth
Basic Supplies	Breadboards, jumper wires, resistors, sensors	Starter kits are affordable and versatile
Microcontrollers	Arduino Uno, Nano, etc.	Great for learning coding and physical computing
Single-board computers	Raspberry Pi, Pi Zero	Supports full Linux OS; enables complex projects

Power Supplies

Perhaps the most ubiquitous equipment needed in the world of electronics is the power supply, which provides direct current (DC) power to your system. Power supplies can range from just a basic alkaline battery to large variable supplies which plug into a wall outlet. The significant features which affect the cost of your power supply are voltage variability and current output. Fortunately, for most electronics work, these expensive features are not needed, and low-cost options, as in Figure 4-7, would work.

Figure 4-7. *A low-cost power supply*

Soldering Tools

Another important tool for electronics would be soldering irons (see Figure 4-8 for an example) and related accessories. These are hand tools that can heat and melt solder (a metal) in order to connect electronic components together. These, too, can be purchased very cheaply. In addition, soldering stands and solder-removing tools are needed. For more sophisticated projects, a reflow oven could be implemented, which can be used to quickly solder printed circuit boards (PCBs). Traditionally, solder was made with lead, but lead solder is being phased out due to its adverse health effects. It would be best to avoid it as well.

Good ventilation is needed for soldering as it produces a lot of fumes. Small exhaust fans can be purchased to help with this. It's always good practice to wear safety glasses when soldering.

Learning how to solder is straightforward, and there are many tutorials available online.

Figure 4-8. *Soldering station (Courtesy: https://commons. wikimedia.org/wiki/File:Soldering_Station_Weller_2.jpeg)*

Multimeters

Multimeters are the primary measurement tool in electronics, allowing users to measure voltage, current, resistance, and sometimes other measurements. This is important for identifying problems (debugging) with electronic systems. These can be incredibly inexpensive and an important tool for any MakerSpace using electronics.

Oscilloscope

Oscilloscopes are measurement tools meant primarily for measuring variable voltage signals, which cannot be adequately measured with traditional multimeters. Traditional oscilloscopes (see Figure 4-9 for an example) were analog and fired an electron beam to a display and were quite large (about the size of a 1990s desktop computer). Today, digital oscilloscopes have become commonplace, but they can be quite expensive. The cost is tied to the upper limits of the frequencies that can be measured. Again, typically, these high frequencies are relevant to complex analog systems, which are generally outside the scope of most MakerSpaces.

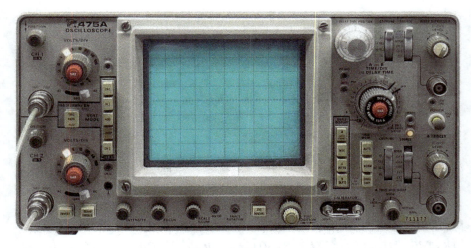

Figure 4-9. An Analog oscilloscope (Courtesy: https://commons.wikimedia.org/wiki/File:Tektronix_Oscilloscope_475A_%28cropped,_without_oscillogram%29.jpg)

Signal Generators

Signal generators provide low-current AC signals to test electronic systems. Signal generators are useful tools, but normally only needed when working with analog systems, something which hobbyists rarely do. Similar to oscilloscopes, they can be quite expensive, but today, there are many cheaper options available. Electronic designers often just use a microcontroller with an analog output to create the signals needed.

Virtual Electronic Test Systems

A number of options exist to create virtual systems for electronics. These often use USB power to drive a small device, which, when accompanied by software, can turn a computer into a sophisticated electronics testing system. For example, Digilent's Analog Discovery is less than $400, but it is incredibly powerful and is used by many engineering colleges.

Interestingly, it is possible to use the microphone input of a computer, combined with custom software, to create an oscilloscope. However, this can be risky as it could damage your computer. Also, similar to oscilloscopes, the speaker output of a computer can serve as a signal generator.

Software

There are plenty of excellent software tools for electronics work, many of which are generally free or low-cost to use. Many web applications, such as TinkerCad, provide great ways to learn basic electronics. In addition, there are software packages for printed circuit board design that range from free (Eagle) to professional quality software (Altium).

Supplies

There are a variety of supplies which are helpful, the most critical being breadboards, wires, and a variety of components. You can often find kits at very low costs that include all of these, in addition to a variety of sensors and actuators. Many suppliers, such as Sparkfun and Adafruit, specialize in the DIY hacker world. More traditional suppliers include Digikey and Jameco.

Most people tend to work with microcontrollers, which are simple computers to control sensors, using packages such as Arduino. The Arduino platform is great because there are many resources available to learn how to use it, both free and paid. Using a microcontroller requires some coding, which can also be learned relatively quickly. The basic "Arduino Uno" is often a great way to start, but more advanced devices exist that come with built-in Wi-Fi and Bluetooth connectivity.

In the same manner, the Raspberry Pi computer (Figure 4-10) is also popular among hobbyists and DIY-ers. The Raspberry Pi is a single-board computer that can operate like a personal computer, with HDMI and USB ports, and can thus be connected to a monitor, keyboard, and mouse. The Pi can be programmed using a variety of languages and can also be used to read sensor data and control systems.

Figure 4-10. *Raspberry Pi computer board*

Mechanical

Mechanical MakerSpaces form the backbone of many traditional making environments, enabling users to cut, shape, mill, and assemble physical objects with precision. From 3D printers and laser cutters to mills, lathes, and drill presses, the mechanical field offers a range of tools to support prototyping, fabrication, and testing. These spaces often require more robust equipment and infrastructure compared to other fields and can be more costly to set up. However, there are definitely cost-effective options that makers can use to get the ball rolling in the mechanical space. Typically, makers can find a tool or piece of software in their price range by isolating the key features they need from the nice-to-have features. If constrained by a budget, accept that you will not be able to afford a piece of equipment that does exactly everything that you are looking for and focus on the aspects that matter the most to your MakerSpace and its users. Many expensive mechanical tools can also be found on the secondhand market, so consider approaching other local workshops, schools, or MakerSpace that may be looking to offload or upgrade some of their current equipment. In fact, shop tools such as mills and lathes are often decades old, even in highly funded prestigious university settings, as with proper maintenance, these tools may outlive many of us. Alternatively, once mechanical MakerSpaces are up and running, makers can explore customizing tools to better meet their needs by creating their own attachments for different pieces of equipment.

Computer-Aided Design (CAD) software plays a central role in this environment, allowing users to create digital models that can be turned into physical products. Tools like 3D printers (using additive manufacturing) and laser cutters (for subtractive work) provide accessible entry points, while more advanced equipment like tensile testing machines, CNC mills, or metalworking tools can support sophisticated engineering and product design efforts. As always, space and safety considerations are critical because these tools are large, heavy, and potentially hazardous if not properly managed.

This section outlines key tools and equipment commonly used in mechanical MakerSpaces, with practical considerations about their use, maintenance, and selection (see Table 4-4 for a summary). Like other sections, it is not meant to be exhaustive. Instead, it serves as a foundation for developing your space based on user needs, available resources, and the types of projects your community is most excited to pursue.

Table 4-4. *Summary of Tools and Supplies for Mechanical MakerSpaces*

Category	Key equipment and tools	Important considerations
CAD software	AutoCAD, Fusion 360, SolidWorks, Onshape	License cost and learning curve; compatibility with hardware
3D printers	FDM, SLA, SLS printers; open vs. closed source	Match printer type to user needs and material compatibility
Laser cutters	Vector/raster engraving and cutting machines	Ventilation and safety protocols are critical
Slicing software	Software to translate CAD models into printer commands	Ease of use vs. control; community support matters.
Testing machines	Tensile and compression testers (e.g., Instron)	Great for material science; attachments expand use
Mills	Vertical and CNC mills with attachments	High precision; training and maintenance required
Lathes	Manual and power lathes for shaping materials	Essential for round/cylindrical parts; needs training
Drill presses	Stationary machines for accurate drilling	Accuracy and depth control; safety procedures
Woodworking tools	Table saws, bandsaws, routers, sanders, etc.	Maintenance access, dust collection, user skill level
Fasteners	Screws, nails, bolts, nuts in various sizes	Stock based on typical projects; match materials

CAD Software

One of the most critical decisions for a mechanical MakerSpace is the choice of CAD software and license. In today's day and age, Computer-Aided Design (CAD) dominates how people create new things and share their mechanical insights with others. Some of the most common companies in this space include AutoDesk (AutoCAD 360, Fusion 360, and Tinkercad), Dassault Systèmes (SolidWorks and DraftSight), and PTC (Creo and Onshape)

3D Printers

3D printers allow makers to take the CAD models they create into the physical world. They operate under the principles of additive manufacturing, building an object one layer at a time. The main styles of 3D printers are Stereolithography (SLA), Selective Laser Sintering (SLS), and Fused Deposition Modeling (FDM), the form of 3D printer with which most people are familiar.

Figure 4-11. *A low cost 3D printer by Prusa (Designed by Freepik)*

Open-Source vs. Closed 3D Printers

Outside of the different styles of 3D printers, MakerSpaces should be conscious of open-source vs. closed companies. Both open-source and closed 3D printing companies, for example, Prusa (Figure 4-11) and MakerBot, each have their own set of advantages and drawbacks. Open-source printers foster community collaboration through helpful support forums, allowing users to troubleshoot issues collectively. They also offer customization options, enabling users to freely modify or print different parts of the printer to suit their specific needs. Transparency is another key benefit, as users can easily understand the purpose of every component and learn how the device operates. Additionally, open-source printers tend to be more affordable, making them accessible to a broader audience. However, they require diligent quality control and servicing by end users, which can be time-consuming and complex, particularly for those delving into customization. Furthermore, their throughput may be limited, as they are primarily geared toward hobbyists and low-throughput applications. On the other hand, closed printers offer ease of use, coming fully assembled and tuned for minimal setup. They boast reliability, undergoing rigorous quality control checks to ensure optimal performance. Moreover, they provide robust support and warranty options, assisting users with troubleshooting when issues arise. Integration is another advantage, as closed companies have control over both hardware and software, ensuring seamless compatibility. However, closed printers have limited customization options, as users are confined to choices made by the company. Additionally, they tend to be higher in cost up-front due to the added benefits of ease of use, reliability, and support. Ultimately, the choice between open-source and closed-source 3D printer companies depends on the MakerSpace's preferences, priorities, and technical expertise, as well as their specific requirements in terms of cost, customization, reliability, and support.

Slicing Software

When selecting a 3D printer slicer program, it's essential to consider several factors to ensure compatibility with your printer and desired output quality. Some 3D printer companies will have their own slicing software for the printers they make, but not all of them. This begs the question: Should you use a generic slicer or a dedicated slicer for each printer? The easiest way to begin this decision is to see what type of slicer your printer needs, as not all slicers are created equally, and some might not work with your printer. You should also consider the ease of use of each slicer program. You want to strike a balance between software that gives you control of each print and one that is not overly complicated. If you can get detailed control of the settings, you can optimize all your prints; however, you do not want to spend too much time fiddling with settings, especially if a print fails. Lastly, you should consider community support for your slicer, as you will inevitably face some challenges as you operate the MakerSpace. You want to find a slicer that either has good customer support or has a community of people or online resources you can go to in order to fine-tune your printer. By carefully weighing these factors, you can choose a 3D printer slicer program that best suits your needs and preferences.

Laser Cutter (Subtractive Manufacturing)

Laser cutters are precision cutting tools that are vital to rapid prototyping and operate through subtractive manufacturing, that is, removing material to create a finished product. Laser cutters (Figure 4-12) can either be used to vector cut through a material, vector etch a sketch, or raster etch a design by focusing a high-intensity beam of light. When vector etching, a laser will have a consistent beam that is lower powered than the vector cut, such that it etches the sketch into the top couple layers of the material but does not completely sever it from the rest of the material. In a raster etch, the laser pulses its beam to vaporize the first couple of layers, leaving a shaded region behind. With a combination of these three types of cuts, laser cutters enable makers to combine 2D drawings/panels together to make 3D structures. Additionally, laser cutters can work with a variety of materials, including wood, acrylic, paper, fabric, and certain types of metals, making them versatile tools for various applications.

Figure 4-12. *Laser cutter*

When considering purchasing a laser cutter, operators of a MakerSpace should evaluate several factors to ensure they make the best choice for their needs. Firstly, the staying power and reputation of the company providing the laser cutter is crucial, as a reliable company offers better support, warranty services, and updates, which can be essential for long-term operation. Secondly, it is vital to consider the safety hazards associated with operating a laser cutter. Proper ventilation systems must be installed to handle fumes and particles generated during the cutting and engraving processes. Lastly, operators should also ensure that users are trained in safety protocols, such as wearing appropriate protective gear and knowing emergency procedures.

Tensile and Compression Testing Machines

Another essential machine for a mechanical MakerSpace is a controlled testing machine for tensile and compression testing. The most widely known example of this type of machine is made by Instron (see Figure 4-13 for an example). Makers can use these machines to determine the material properties of their creations. When testing your own creations on a tensile or compression testing machine, sometimes makers need to use specialty attachments, which can either be purchased from the company or created in-house by the maker.

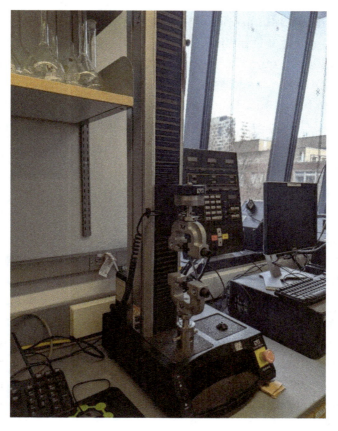

Figure 4-13. Tensile and compression testing machine by Instron

Mills

Mills are valuable assets in mechanical MakerSpaces, offering unparalleled precision and versatility in material removal and shaping processes. These machines operate by rotating a cutting tool against a stationary workpiece to carve out intricate designs, contours, and features. Mills can execute a wide range of machining operations, including face milling, end milling, slot milling, and profile milling, allowing makers to fabricate components with exceptional accuracy and repeatability. Additionally, mills can be equipped with various accessories and attachments, such as rotary tables and indexing heads, to enable the machining of complex geometries and angles. By harnessing the capabilities of mills, users can realize their creative visions, from precision parts and mechanical assemblies to intricate sculptures and artistic masterpieces.

Lathe

Lathes are indispensable tools in mechanical MakerSpaces, as they offer precise shaping and turning capabilities for a wide range of materials. These machines operate by rotating a workpiece on its axis while various cutting tools are applied to the material to create intricate designs, contours, and threads. Additionally, lathes can be used for facing, boring, drilling, and tapering operations, allowing makers to create complex geometries with high accuracy. By combining different cutting tools and techniques, lathes enable users to transform raw materials into finished components, contributing to the fabrication of mechanical assemblies, precision parts, and artistic creations.

Drill Press

Drill presses (Figure 4-14) are essential tools in mechanical MakerSpaces, providing precise and efficient drilling capabilities for a wide range of materials and applications. These machines operate by vertically advancing a rotating drill bit into a stationary workpiece, allowing users to create clean, accurate holes with consistent depth and alignment. Drill presses excel in various drilling tasks, including through-holes, countersinking, and boring large-diameter holes, making them versatile for both simple and complex projects. Equipped with adjustable speed settings, depth stops, and a stable worktable, drill presses offer enhanced control and repeatability for high-quality results. Additionally, various accessories, such as vises, clamps, and specialized drill bits, can be used to expand the functionality of the drill press, enabling users to tackle diverse tasks with precision and ease.

Figure 4-14. *Drill press (Designed by Freepik)*

Woodworking Supplies

Woodworking tools are the backbone of any mechanical MakerSpace. Among the essential tools are table saws, which enable makers to make precise and straight cuts on wooden boards. Bandsaws are versatile, allowing intricate curved cuts, resawing, and creating irregular shapes. For shaping and smoothing, woodworkers turn to planers and jointers to refine the thickness and straightness of boards. Additionally, routers add finesse by hollowing out areas or creating decorative edges. Sanders play a crucial role in achieving a smooth finish, ranging from belt sanders for rapid material removal to detail sanders for intricate work. Carving tools, such as chisels and gouges, allow for detailed sculpting. Wood lathes open up possibilities for crafting turned items like table legs or intricate bowls. A dust collection system is paramount to maintaining a clean workspace. Power tools such as drills, routers, and jigsaws provide efficiency and accuracy in cutting, drilling, and shaping wood. Additionally, Dremel rotary tools offer versatility, enabling makers to carve, engrave, sand, and polish wood with ease. Maintenance is vital for all these woodworking tools, so be sure to keep maintenance access in mind when setting them up in your space.

Fasteners

Fastening materials together is another critical aspect of woodworking. Without any fasteners to assemble parts together, a woodworking project is just a pile of nicely shaped wood, and its only practical use may be as a door stopper or firewood. Therefore, it is important to stock different types of fasteners to enable users to complete the final steps of assembling their various woodworking or mechanical projects in your MakerSpace. Screws and nails provide solid and reliable joints, with screws offering the advantage of being removable and providing greater holding power. Nuts and bolts are essential for creating secure yet adjustable connections, especially in more complex assemblies where parts may need to be disassembled or adjusted. Consider keeping different sizes of fasteners in various quantities based on the types of projects your MakerSpace users typically choose to make. Is your MakerSpace more focused on electronics, and are your woodworking supplies primarily used to make boxes or enclosures for small items? You may not need screws longer than 1 inch or wider than ¼ inch. Are your users more interested in building rustic outdoor furniture that needs to be sturdy and support a person's weight? Then, you may want to stock larger fasteners in materials that are suitable for outdoor conditions.

Other Useful Tools

While items like 3D printers, laser cutters, and soldering stations tend to draw the spotlight in a MakerSpace, there are many other tools and features that are just as critical to consider—if not more so—for creating a safe, functional, and inclusive environment. These tools may not have the same "wow factor," but thinking intentionally about work surfaces, chairs, storage systems, waste management, and computing equipment can make the difference between a chaotic workspace and a thriving one.

This section covers those often-overlooked but absolutely essential elements: sturdy tables and ergonomic chairs that support long hours of work, monitors that improve productivity, whiteboards for collaboration, computers loaded with the right software, and robust storage solutions to keep everything organized (see Table 4-5 for a summary). These components form the backbone of any successful MakerSpace, supporting users and staff alike in their day-to-day activities. While they may not be flashy, they're what help everything else run smoothly. Don't underestimate their impact—planning for these elements up front will pay dividends in safety, efficiency, and overall user satisfaction.

Table 4-5. *Summary of Other Things Needed for a MakerSpace*

Category	Key equipment and tools	Important considerations
Computers and software	Computers with CAD, coding tools, Internet access	Ensure adequate specs; install versatile software; consider accessibility
Tables and chairs	Workbenches, ergonomic chairs, stools	Match height and materials to use cases; prioritize comfort and safety
Monitors	Stand-alone high-resolution monitors	Improve visibility and workflow; support detailed work like CAD or coding
Whiteboards	Wall-mounted or mobile dry-erase boards	Encourage collaboration and planning; keep markers and cleaners stocked
General supply storage	Bins, drawers, shelves, cabinets, organizers	Use labeled, visible containers; support reorganization and inventory checks
User storage	Lockers, cubbies, under-desk storage	Support multi-session projects; promote user trust and comfort
Trash cans and waste management	Bins for general waste, recycling, hazardous materials	Strategic placement; proper disposal protocols for safety and cleanliness

Computers and Specialized Software

Computers are essential in a MakerSpace, particularly for running specialized software and programming languages. Whether for coding, CAD design, or other technical tasks, having computers readily available can significantly enhance the capabilities of the space. The cost and specifications of these computers can vary widely, but even budget-friendly models can be sufficient for many applications. Ensuring that the computers have enough processing power and memory to run the required software efficiently is key. Additionally, a variety of programming languages and development environments, such as Python, C++, Java, and MATLAB, as well as CAD software, should be installed to meet diverse user needs. While MATLAB can be expensive, Python is a free alternative. Similarly, there are many free or low-cost options for CAD software, as described above. Making sure the computers are accessible to all users, possibly with adjustable desks and chairs to accommodate different needs, is also essential.

Tables and Chairs

The choice of tables and chairs can significantly influence the usability and comfort of a MakerSpace. Sturdy, spacious workbenches capable of supporting heavy equipment are ideal for most tasks. Height-adjustable tables can accommodate a variety of tasks and user preferences, while larger collaborative tables can facilitate group work and discussions. Depending on the type of work being done, the table surface needs to be chosen. For more mechanical work, wood surfaces work well; however, if you are using liquids or working with chemicals, high-pressure laminate is a good choice. A "sacrificial" wood piece can be placed on top when using drills and such to protect the table surface.

Ergonomic chairs provide comfort and support for extended periods of use, and stools are useful for high workbenches or areas where mobility is needed. Adjustable chairs with customizable height and back support can suit different users and tasks, enhancing overall productivity and comfort. In specialized environments such as a biological area within a MakerSpace, it's crucial to select chairs and stools with non-porous, easy-to-clean fabrics. Materials such as vinyl or antimicrobial-coated fabric can withstand frequent cleaning and disinfection, reducing the risk of contamination and maintaining hygiene standards essential for biological work. These materials are also resistant to chemicals and spills, which make them ideal for environments where exposure to various substances is common.

Monitors

Having stand-alone monitors in the MakerSpace can enhance productivity, especially for detailed work like coding or design. Larger monitors with high resolution improve visibility and ease of use. Monitors with adjustable stands allow users to set the optimal height and angle.

Whiteboards

Whiteboards are invaluable for brainstorming, planning, and collaboration. Large whiteboards provide ample space for group work and should be installed in accessible locations where they can be easily seen and used. Providing markers, erasers, and cleaning supplies helps keep the whiteboards in good condition, ensuring they remain a useful tool for all users.

General Supply Storage

Regardless of the type of MakerSpace, supply storage is critical (see Figure 4-15). This can be used to store anything, such as paper for arts and crafts, cables for electronics, screwdrivers for mechanical, or microcentrifuge tubes for biology.

Figure 4-15. *Storage variety in a MakerSpace*

Nesting bins are convenient to store unused bins; however, they cannot be stacked on the same shelf for users to gain access to the contents (see Figure 4-16). Another consideration is accessibility: do you want users to easily access the supplies, or do you want them to open a lid? Finally, do you want the bins to be see-through or opaque? Often, stackable bins are ideal for shelves that are easily reachable, while nesting bins can be placed up high since they would have to be pulled down regardless of the situation.

Figure 4-16. *Nested bins (left) vs. stacked bins (right)*

Drawers and cabinets also work well for storage. However, bins are convenient as things can be reorganized and moved quickly. See-through and open bins are convenient for the MakerSpace staff to quickly see if items are running low. If you do use drawers, you can use small bins to organize it (Figure 4-17); alternatively, you can 3D print your own organization (Figure 4-18)! This is helpful for customizing the bins to meet your needs.

Figure 4-17. *Drawer with small bins for organization*

161

Figure 4-18. *3D printed drawer organization for custom fits*

Finally, for really small items, small parts bins and drawer organizer bins can work incredibly well (Figure 4-19). Examples of these are sewing needles, electronic components, and screws.

Figure 4-19. *Bins for organizing small components*

Storage for Users

Adequate storage solutions are crucial for keeping the MakerSpace organized and ensuring that users have a place to store their belongings. Secure lockers for personal items like coats and bags can be helpful so users can move around the space without worrying about their personal items. On the other hand, storage for bags and coats can be designed under desks (Figure 4-20) to maximize space.

Figure 4-20. *Sample under-desk storage for bags and coats*

In addition, storage lockers (Figure 4-21) for projects can be helpful. So many MakerSpace projects require multiple sessions, so the opportunity of storing the work in progress can be incredibly beneficial.

Figure 4-21. *Samples of lockers available at a MakerSpace*

Trash Cans and Waste Management

Proper waste management is often overlooked but essential for maintaining a clean and safe MakerSpace. Providing separate bins for general waste, recyclables, and hazardous materials helps in the proper disposal of different types of waste. Ensuring that trash cans are conveniently located throughout the MakerSpace and establishing protocols for the proper disposal of waste, particularly hazardous materials, are important steps in maintaining a safe and efficient environment.

Conclusion

As someone using MakerSpaces, you should consider the types of projects you want to accomplish, the required skills and tools for those projects, and what your local MakerSpace offers, whether that's arts and crafts equipment like sewing machines, scientific instruments like microscopes and PCR machines, or technical tools like 3D printers and oscilloscopes. As someone thinking of starting a MakerSpace, you need to carefully plan and prioritize equipment based on anticipated user needs and project types, evaluate demand to avoid bottlenecks with high-use tools, and decide between proprietary vs. open-source equipment based on your technical capabilities and budget. As someone running an existing MakerSpace, you should regularly assess which tools are most popular, consider reallocating resources to better serve constituents, and continuously explore new tools and technologies rather than becoming complacent with your current setup.

Key Takeaways

- **Arts and Crafts**:

  - *Diverse Tools*: Offers a wide array of tools from basic crafting supplies to advanced equipment like laser cutters and 3D printers.

  - *Creative Expression*: Encourages customization and innovation, fostering creativity and skill development.

  - *Safety and Maintenance*: Emphasizes proper tool use, maintenance, and safety measures for long-term usability.

- **Biology and Chemistry**:

  - *Specialized Equipment*: Includes microscopes, PCR machines, and fume hoods for precise biological and chemical experiments.

  - *Sterile Environment*: Maintains aseptic conditions crucial for working with microorganisms and sensitive biological materials.

  - *Quality Control*: Utilizes spectrophotometers and balances for accurate measurements and data interpretation.

- **Electronics**:

  - *Affordable Setup*: Provides cost-effective entry-level equipment for learning and experimentation in electronics.

- *Key Tools*: Includes power supplies, soldering tools, and oscilloscopes for basic to advanced electronic projects.

- *Software Integration*: Supports programming languages like Python, CAD software, and microcontrollers for diverse project needs.

- **Mechanical**:

  - *Cost-Effective Options*: Balances setup costs by exploring secondhand tools and customized attachments for optimal functionality.

  - *CAD Design*: Utilizes CAD software for precise mechanical design and prototyping.

  - *Fabrication Tools*: Incorporates 3D printers and laser cutters for additive and subtractive manufacturing, enhancing design versatility and material options.

  - *Testing Capabilities*: Integrates tensile and compression testing machines for evaluating material properties and ensuring project durability.

  - *Woodworking Expertise*: Provides a range of woodworking tools and fasteners for detailed mechanical projects, with an emphasis on safety and maintenance practices.

- **Other Useful Tools**:

  - *Computers and Specialized Software*: Equips MakerSpace with computers running programming languages and CAD software, enhancing technical capabilities and accessibility.

- *Tables and Chairs*: Choose sturdy workbenches, adjustable tables, ergonomic chairs, and stools tailored to different tasks and user needs, ensuring comfort and productivity.

- *Monitors*: Installs stand-alone monitors for detailed work like coding and design, enhancing visibility and usability.

- *Whiteboards*: Provide large whiteboards for brainstorming and collaboration, equipped with markers, erasers, and cleaning supplies for user convenience.

- *Storage Solutions*: Install secure lockers, shelves, and labeled bins for organizing supplies and personal belongings, maintaining order and accessibility within the space.

- *Waste Management*: Establishes proper disposal protocols with separate bins for general waste, recyclables, and hazardous materials, ensuring a clean and safe MakerSpace environment.

CHAPTER 5

Organizing MakerSpaces

While Chapter 4 focused on tools, a MakerSpace is more than that. It's an environment intentionally designed to support creativity, exploration, and community. The way a MakerSpace is organized has a profound impact on how users interact with tools, how they learn new skills, and how they connect with one another. Organization, in this context, is not just about keeping the space clean; it's about fostering accessibility, promoting safety, enabling self-directed learning, and ensuring the space can adapt and grow over time.

Laying the Groundwork

Effective organization involves both physical and strategic thinking. It means considering how people enter the space and how they find their way once inside. It includes determining where staff should be stationed to support users and monitor tool use. It requires planning the layout so that tools, materials, and utilities are accessible where and when they are needed—without creating bottlenecks or safety risks. It means anticipating how different activities will coexist, from quiet design work to noisy, messy fabrication. Whether a MakerSpace serves artists, engineers, scientists, or all three, its layout must reflect the range of work being done.

© Sevile G. Mannickarottu, Michael G. Patterson, and Carolyne Godon 2025
S. G. Mannickarottu et al., *Creating MakerSpaces*, Maker Innovations Series,
https://doi.org/10.1007/979-8-8688-1309-2_5

Organization also includes infrastructure. Power, ventilation, lighting, and Internet connectivity must all be planned with intention, ideally built into the space from the start. Thoughtful infrastructure planning helps ensure that a MakerSpace runs smoothly day to day, and that it can evolve to support new tools or user needs in the future.

Just as important as the physical space is the virtual space. A well-structured digital presence—especially in the form of a website—serves as the first point of contact for many users. It communicates who can use the space, how to get started, and what to expect. It provides training materials, tool documentation, inventory systems, and event calendars. A strong website empowers users to learn independently, find what they need quickly, and reduce unnecessary demands on staff. It can also reflect and reinforce the values of the MakerSpace, whether that's safety, sustainability, collaboration, or innovation.

This chapter explores what it takes to organize a MakerSpace effectively. It begins with the entry zone, where first impressions are made and expectations are set. It moves through layout design, flexible work areas, and the integration of specialized zones for tasks like electronics, woodworking, and wet lab work. It examines how to support staff through space design, how to plan for utilities and waste, and how to future-proof the layout for emerging technologies. The final sections focus on digital organization, exploring how websites and other online tools can help MakerSpaces operate more efficiently and support their communities more fully. Along the way, case studies and examples illustrate how these ideas come to life in real spaces.

A well-organized MakerSpace doesn't just function well: it becomes a place where people feel confident, creative, and supported in their work. Whether you're designing a new space or improving an existing one, this chapter provides the tools and frameworks to build a space that works now and continues to grow over time.

Space Organization

One of the biggest challenges for MakerSpace design is the organization. With the rapid development and changes to tools and resources. In Chapter 4, we enumerated a variety of equipment and tools for various MakerSpaces. Where would one keep everything? Whether you're designing a MakerSpace from scratch or improving an existing one, the way equipment, furniture, and tools are arranged can profoundly affect user behavior, workflow, and creativity. While the tools themselves may be cutting-edge, their placement and the logic of movement within the space often determine whether they're used efficiently—or at all. Table 5-1 provides a summary.

Unlike traditional classrooms or laboratories, MakerSpaces must accommodate a wide range of activities—from soldering circuits and laser cutting, to sewing fabric or editing digital media. That means your layout must balance flexibility with structure, and safety with accessibility. The layout needs to support individual work as well as group collaboration. It also needs to evolve over time, adjusting to the emergence of new technologies or changes in your user base.

In this section, we explore strategies for organizing your MakerSpace layout to foster creativity, ensure safety, and maximize space efficiency. We'll examine how different tools and activities can be zoned, how to integrate specialized spaces like wet labs or electronics rooms, and how simple infrastructure choices—like the placement of outlets and storage—can enhance usability. We'll also look at real-world examples from successful MakerSpaces, offering practical insights and design principles you can adapt to your own environment.

Table 5-1. *Summary of Considerations for the Entrance of a MakerSpace*

Element	Purpose	Examples/features
Defined point of entry	Establishes a clear and welcoming entrance to the space	Reception desk, digital kiosk, badge scanner, directional signage
Check-in system	Tracks usage, enforces training access, and logs entry	iPad or tablet kiosk, Radio Frequency Identification (RFID) badge reader, QR code scanner (see Chapter 6 for details)
Orientation resources	Helps users understand expectations and find what they need	Posters, safety signs, digital displays, QR codes linking to guides or training
"Start here" station	Supports first-time or infrequent users with onboarding guidance	Touchscreen intro, printed pamphlets, greeter during peak hours
Navigation cues	Directs users toward key zones and staff support	Floor tape, wall signage, digital wayfinding screens
Culture and community display	Reinforces identity and promotes engagement	Bulletin board, project showcase, welcome message board, photos of past events

Entry, Check-In, and Orientation Zones

The entrance to your MakerSpace sets the tone for everything that follows but is, unfortunately, often an afterthought. Oftentimes, the MakerSpace can appear overwhelming to visitors. A well-designed entry zone welcomes users and establishes expectations for safety, access, and community participation. Whether your space is hosted in a university, library, school, or independent building, creating a clear check-in and orientation flow is essential for smooth operations.

At minimum, every MakerSpace should have a clearly defined point of entry. This could be as simple as a reception desk or a digital kiosk, or as advanced as a badge-scanning access point tied to a training management system. When users enter the space, they should know where to go, what is expected of them, and how to get help. A simple visual flow—via floor markings, signage, or screens—can guide both new and returning users toward workstations, storage, and staff support.

Check-in systems (see Chapter 6 for more details) help track usage, enforce training requirements, and reinforce a culture of responsibility. For example, a digital check-in kiosk (using tools like iPads or badge readers) can log user attendance, verify tool access eligibility, and even prompt reminders for expiring certifications. These systems can also help you collect data about peak usage times and inform staffing or maintenance schedules. In some cases, RFID or QR-based access tied to training completion can control entry into specific rooms or enable machines.

The entry zone is also the ideal location for orientation resources. Posters, screens, or QR codes (Figure 5-1) can point users to training modules or how-to guides, lab rules and safety expectations, upcoming events or workshops, equipment availability, and reservation portals.

Figure 5-1. *Lab safety sign with QR code at the entrance to a MakerSpace*

For spaces that serve the public or have many first-time users, consider adding a "Start Here" station—this could be a touchscreen, a printed booklet, or a friendly staff member posted during busy hours. This not only enhances safety but reduces user anxiety and helps build a sense of community.

Beyond safety and logistics, the entrance area is an opportunity to express the culture of the space. Consider featuring a rotating display of user projects, a welcome message board, or photos from recent events (Figure 5-2). This turns the entry zone from a transactional point into an invitation to create and collaborate.

Figure 5-2. *The entrance of the George H. Stephenson Foundation Bio-MakerSpace showcases user accomplishments and publications*

Staff Workspace and Oversight Areas

Another overlooked feature of MakerSpaces is staff areas. Creating intentional spaces for staff helps ensure they can do their jobs effectively, sustainably, and with a sense of professional belonging.

There are two primary functions of staff space: oversight and operations (see Table 5-2 for a summary). Oversight means placing staff in visible, accessible locations where they can support users and monitor activity. For example, positioning an electronics technician within or adjacent to the electronics zone allows them to provide quick assistance while passively observing tool usage. This "embedded expertise" model reduces bottlenecks and increases safety by aligning staffing with technical areas.

Operationally, staff also need space for administrative work, tool maintenance, and rest. This includes access to computers, storage for tools and personal items, and room for documentation and planning. A small staff desk or workstation can often serve multiple functions— updating training records, coordinating events, or logging equipment issues. In smaller spaces, a desk near the entrance or in a central location can also double as an info/help station. There might also be spaces where equipment or supplies can be "checked out." A staff desk and appropriate equipment should be available there.

Importantly, MakerSpace staff—especially in high-traffic or high-stakes environments—need a place to step away. Providing a small, dedicated break area allows staff to recharge, make a private phone call, or eat lunch away from machines and users. This is especially important for MakerSpaces with areas that cannot allow food or drinks. Figure 5-3 shows the staff space at the George H. Stephenson Foundation Educational Laboratory and Bio-MakerSpace at the University of Pennsylvania. Since the MakerSpace was not purpose-built, the staff area was combined with storage. This is a food-approved zone, and thus has a microwave and refrigerator.

Figure 5-3. *Staff area for the Stephenson Foundation Bio-MakerSpace at the University of Pennsylvania*

While not every MakerSpace has room for private offices or full staff suites, including even minimal accommodations—like lockable drawers, shared storage closets, or corner workbenches—sends a message: staff matter. When staff feel supported, their ability to support others improves.

Table 5-2. *Summary for Staff Workspaces and Oversight Areas*

Staff space	Primary purpose	Examples/features
Embedded oversight station	Monitor tool usage and assist users within specific zones	Desk or stool placed near equipment; staff stationed within electronics, woodshop, etc.
Central staff desk/help station	Provide user-facing support and operational presence	Located near entrance or central area; includes computer, signage, equipment checkout
Administrative workspace	Conduct recordkeeping, planning, and coordination of operations	Desk with computer access, secure file storage, access to task lists and training logs
Tool maintenance area	Perform equipment repair, calibration, and parts organization	Workbench, shelving for parts, ESD mat, tools for upkeep and troubleshooting
Break area	Offer staff a private space to rest, eat, or make calls	Small table, chairs, microwave, water station; ideally separated from active zones
Shared staff storage	Secure personal belongings and shared supplies	Lockable drawers, cabinets, closets, or modular bins for shared materials and tools

Flexible Workspaces and Open Layouts

Unlike traditional classrooms or labs with fixed functions, MakerSpaces must support everything from brainstorming and sketching to soldering and fabrication. A well-planned open layout (Table 5-3 provides tips) enables these diverse activities to happen simultaneously and safely, empowering users to shape the space around their needs.

Tables should be large enough for collaborative projects but lightweight enough to rearrange. Adjustable-height tables and stools offer ergonomic benefits and make the space more accessible to users of different ages or physical abilities. Surface materials matter too: laminate tops are affordable and easy to clean, while butcher block surfaces are ideal for woodworking or general-purpose use. In heavier-duty zones, steel-topped tables may be appropriate for metalwork or equipment maintenance. Regardless of material, work surfaces should be durable and easy to repair or replace.

Flexibility comes not just from individual pieces of furniture but from the entire environment's ability to reconfigure. Many MakerSpaces use mobile furniture—rolling whiteboards, carts, tool racks, and tables on wheels—to define temporary zones or support different kinds of programming. These modular elements make it easy to switch between individual work, group projects, and event hosting without disruption. Simple tools like floor tape or signage can help provide structure while maintaining openness. Figure 5-4 illustrates a sample layout showing how modular elements can be used to define work areas while keeping the space open and responsive to change.

Figure 5-4. *The prototyping lab in the Engineering Studios @ Venture Lab at the University of Pennsylvania*

Storage plays a key role in these environments. Open shelving, pegboards, and wall-mounted tool holders are popular in many MakerSpaces because they keep tools visible and accessible. However, wall-mounted systems can limit layout flexibility by locking tool zones to fixed walls. Over time, this can constrain how furniture and equipment are rearranged, especially if electrical access or space requirements change. For highly flexible spaces, consider using rolling tool carts, mobile cabinets, or freestanding vertical storage that can move with the layout.

Equipment placement should be guided not just by space or safety needs, but also by how users actually work. Group tools in ways that support natural project workflows—such as arranging cutting tools near sanding stations, or placing soldering irons close to component storage. This reduces backtracking and tool transport, especially in high-traffic areas. For larger tools or machines, locating them along the perimeter can preserve open floor space while maintaining clear access.

Finally, as new technologies and project types emerge, your layout should evolve with them. A modular approach gives you the freedom to adapt to future needs without requiring major renovations.

Table 5-3. *Summary for Flexible MakerSpaces*

Feature	Purpose	Examples/considerations
Lightweight, modular tables	Enable rearrangement for different group sizes and activities	Foldable or wheeled tables; clustering for team work; quick reconfiguration
Adjustable-height furniture	Increase accessibility and ergonomic comfort	Supports both seated and standing work; accommodates a wider range of users
Durable work surfaces	Withstand varied tool use and wear	Laminate for general use; butcher block for woodworking; steel for heavy-duty work
Mobile furniture elements	Support layout reconfiguration and zone definition	Rolling whiteboards, tool carts, mobile cabinets, freestanding vertical storage
Flexible zoning aids	Maintain order without rigid boundaries	Floor tape, signage, movable dividers
Storage solutions	Keep tools accessible while preserving layout flexibility	Favor mobile or freestanding storage over fixed pegboards or wall-mounted systems

Zoned Areas for Specialized Activities

While open, flexible workspaces serve as the central hub of many MakerSpaces, designated zones for specialized activities are essential for supporting high-risk, high-skill, or equipment-intensive work. These zones help manage noise, safety, cleanliness, and access—ensuring that advanced tools and materials can be used appropriately while maintaining a safe and productive environment for all users. Table 5-4 provides an overview of different types of zones.

A common strategy is to create enclosed or semi-enclosed rooms for specialized functions such as woodworking, electronics, metalworking, or biological prototyping. These rooms provide physical separation from the general workspace, allowing for more controlled use of tools and materials. For example, a woodworking room might house saws, sanders, and dust collection systems, while an electronics room may include soldering stations, microscopes, and ESD-safe benches. In addition, any specialized Personal Protective Equipment (PPE) can be kept at the entrance.

Roll-up garage doors offer an effective way to separate specialized rooms from the main workspace. When open, they promote visual and spatial continuity. When closed, they help contain dust, fumes, and noise while signaling that access is restricted. Many spaces also include a walk-through door with controlled access—ideal for staff or trained users who need to enter when the main garage door is closed. These walk-through doors can be outfitted with badge readers or keypad locks to enforce training requirements and promote accountability.

This zoning strategy is particularly useful when combined with expertise-based staffing. For example, an electronics expert might be stationed in or near the electronics room, supporting users, maintaining tools, and ensuring safety. This model, sometimes referred to as embedded expertise, improves response time, reduces tool misuse, and fosters informal mentorship.

Specialized rooms can also house dedicated infrastructure that is impractical or too expensive to distribute throughout the entire MakerSpace. Wet labs may include fume hoods, gas lines, eye wash stations, and sinks. If the space supports biological prototyping or chemical handling beyond typical classroom materials, it may need to meet Biosafety Level 1 (BSL1) or Level 2 (BSL2) standards, especially if users are working with microorganisms, reagents, or live cell lines. These requirements impact everything from waste handling to training protocols and should be incorporated early in the planning process.

Some MakerSpaces also include digital media zones, such as podcasting booths, video editing suites, or sound-isolated rooms for voiceovers and interviews. These areas typically require acoustic treatment, cable management, and controlled lighting. Though they may not involve physical fabrication, they are increasingly important in entrepreneurial or storytelling-focused spaces where makers document and share their work.

In educational settings, specialized rooms may also serve as instructional zones for focused workshops or smaller courses where environmental control and tool access are essential.

Table 5-4. *Typical Zones for a MakerSpace*

Zone type	Primary activities	Key features	Design considerations
Electronics	Soldering, circuit design, PCB assembly	ESD mats, fine-tip tools, microscopes, oscilloscopes	Quiet environment, ESD-safe workstations, adjustable lighting
Woodworking	Cutting, sanding, shaping wood-based materials	Table saws, band saws, drill presses, dust collection system	Dust control, noise isolation, PPE storage, supervised access
Metalworking	Grinding, cutting, welding, machining metals	Welding booths, grinders, CNC mills, fume extraction	Fire safety, heat-resistant surfaces, ventilation, restricted access

(*continued*)

Table 5-4. (*continued*)

Zone type	Primary activities	Key features	Design considerations
Textiles/soft goods	Sewing, embroidery, wearable electronics prototyping	Sewing machines, sergers, ironing stations, pattern storage	Bright lighting, clean surfaces, layout for soft material handling
Wet lab/bio	Biological prototyping, pipetting, reagent use	Fume hoods, eye wash stations, sinks, refrigeration, sharps/biohazard disposal	May require BSL1 or BSL2 compliance, bio-waste protocols, trained user access only
Digital media/ AV	Podcasting, video editing, 3D modeling	Soundproofing, green screen, microphones, high-performance computers	Acoustic isolation, equipment booking, clutter-free workspace

Utilities and Core Infrastructure

Often invisible to users but critical to safe and effective operation are utilities. Electrical systems, ventilation, plumbing, and data infrastructure are critical for tool usage, comfort, and safety. If these elements are underbuilt or poorly placed, the flexibility and scalability of the entire space can be compromised. Table 5-5 provides a summary of various considerations.

Power distribution is one of the most important and frequently underestimated aspects of infrastructure planning. MakerSpaces should offer power access that supports both high- and low-voltage tools across different zones. For general-purpose work tables, suspended extension reels or ceiling drops are often more flexible than floor outlets, especially when the layout changes frequently. However, floor outlets (especially flush-mounted) may still be useful in semi-permanent tool locations where trip hazards or ceiling obstructions are a concern. In high-load zones—like 3D printing banks, CNC equipment, or laser cutters—dedicated 220V circuits or isolated power lines may be required.

Plumbing needs will vary by space type but are essential in wet labs, arts and crafts areas, and any zone involving adhesives, resins, or biological materials. At minimum, MakerSpaces should include one or more deep utility sinks with splash guards for tool cleaning and handwashing. If biological or chemical work is planned, additional features like eyewash stations, fume hoods, and emergency showers may be required. These should be located in easy-to-access, well-marked areas near where risky work occurs.

Ventilation and air quality control are especially important in spaces with soldering, woodworking, or chemical processes. Local exhaust systems, fume extractors, or room-wide HVAC upgrades can reduce exposure to particulates and fumes. Some tools (such as resin 3D printers or laser cutters) must be vented directly to the outside or passed through filtration units that meet local safety codes.

While not always visible, data and connectivity infrastructure also play a critical role. MakerSpaces benefit from high-speed Internet, strong Wi-Fi coverage, and ample Ethernet access in zones that rely on cloud-based design software, machine controls, or live-streaming digital media. If users are expected to bring their own devices or control tools via laptops, accessible outlets with USB charging or surge-protected power strips should be integrated into the workstations.

In some cases, infrastructure must also support institutional or safety protocols. For example, some spaces must have real-time environmental monitoring (e.g., CO_2 levels, fume detection), integration with facilities reporting systems, or remote control of tool power based on user training status (see Chapter 6). Anticipating these needs early during planning will reduce costly retrofits later.

Above all, utility infrastructure should be built with growth in mind. As the toolset expands or as new maker fields emerge—such as food tech, biotech, or clean energy prototyping—the demands on power, ventilation, and water will increase. Overbuilding infrastructure may seem expensive at first, but it offers the flexibility needed to evolve alongside your community's ambitions.

Table 5-5. *Utilities and Infrastructure Considerations*

Zone / Function	Key Infrastructure Elements	Considerations
General Work Areas	Standard electrical outlets, ceiling drops or floor boxes, Wi-Fi, task lighting	Flush-mounted outlets to reduce tripping; overbuild power access for flexibility
Electronics	ESD-safe outlets and mats, anti-static flooring, climate control, task lighting	Low-noise environment; ventilation for soldering fumes
Woodworking	High-power circuits, dust collection system, local exhaust or air filtration	Noise control; outlet placement for large equipment
Metalworking	Dedicated 220V circuits, grounding, heat-resistant surfaces, welding ventilation	Fire safety protocols, PPE storage
Wet Lab / Bio	Plumbing (sinks, eyewash, emergency showers), fume hoods, gas lines, ventilation, cold storage.	May require BSL1 or BSL2 compliance; biohazard disposal systems

(continued)

Table 5-5. (*continued*)

Zone / Function	Key Infrastructure Elements	Considerations
Digital Media / AV	Soundproofing, power/data drops, hardwired Ethernet, acoustic treatments	Noise isolation; climate control for sensitive equipment
Tool Control / Access	RFID readers, badge-controlled doors, digital signage, real-time monitoring (CO_2, VOCs, tool status)	Integrate with training database; ensure visibility and redundancy
User Comfort	HVAC, air filtration, water fountains, accessible power and charging stations	Design for ADA compliance and general comfort

Waste Management and Sustainability Integration

Another common afterthought in MakerSpaces is waste management. Because users often work with a wide range of materials, from scrap wood and solder to PLA filament and biohazards, planning for proper disposal and recycling needs to be incorporated into the physical design of the space from the outset (see Table 5-6 for a summary).

At the most basic level, every zone should include clearly labeled bins for general trash and recycling. Bins should be placed where waste is generated—not just near exits or break areas. For example, sanding stations should have trash and dust collection nearby, electronics zones may need bins for wire trimmings or failed PCBs, and 3D printing areas often generate failed prints and support material waste. Including disposal options at the point of use encourages proper sorting and reduces cleanup bottlenecks.

More advanced waste streams—such as biohazards, chemicals, adhesives, solvents, or electronic waste—require specialized infrastructure and protocols. Wet labs may require sharps containers, biohazard bins, and chemical waste disposal processes in alignment with biosafety level requirements. Electronics labs might benefit from a dedicated e-waste drop zone, where users can place damaged components or retired boards for later safe disposal or harvesting (see Figure 5-5 for an example of multiple waste streams).

Figure 5-5. *Samples of waste management at the Stephenson Foundation Bio-MakerSpace. Options are available for regular waste, multi-stream recycling, pen and marker recycling, electronic waste, and biohazard waste*

Ventilation and airflow planning also intersect with waste management. Areas that produce airborne particulates (e.g., sanding, laser cutting, soldering) should be located near or within zones with local exhaust systems or filtered ventilation. Waste management is not only about solids and liquids—it includes planning for fumes, dust, and airborne residues that accumulate over time.

To reinforce sustainable behavior, consider incorporating signage and just-in-time education at disposal sites. QR codes linking to material-specific disposal guidelines, visual sorting posters, or mini-infographics showing how waste is reused or recycled within the space can all help shape user habits. Spaces that operate within university or municipal buildings should also align with institutional Environmental Health and Safety (EH&S) guidelines and partner with campus sustainability teams when possible. For example, the University of Pennsylvania George H. Stephenson Foundation Educational Laboratory & Bio-MakerSpace has guidelines published on their website here: `https://belabs.seas.upenn.edu/resources-tutorials/waste-disposal`. Before using the lab, students are required to read the guidelines and must pass an assessment.

In some MakerSpaces, waste can also be repurposed as a resource. Offcuts from wood or acrylic projects might be made available in a scrap bin for prototyping. Failed prints or electronics may be harvested for reusable components. Encouraging a culture of creative reuse not only supports sustainability but can also lower material costs for early-stage projects.

Another way of managing waste is to reduce waste! Generating less waste is better for the planet and also means less waste to manage.

Table 5-6. *Waste Management*

Waste type	Typical sources	Recommended disposal method	Infrastructure/signage tips
General trash	Packaging, food wrappers, small debris	Standard waste bin	Place bins near desks and entry/exit points
Recyclables	Paper, cardboard, plastics, aluminum	Recycling bin based on local guidelines	Use clear signage; align with institutional recycling policies
3D printing waste	Failed prints, rafts, support material	Trash or specialty recycling (if offered for PLA/ABS)	Provide scrap bins near printers; label clearly
Wood/ acrylic offcuts	Laser cutting, CNC, hand tools	Scrap bin for reuse or trash if too small	Encourage reuse for prototyping; monitor for dust/fire risks
Electronics waste	Dead PCBs, wire clippings, failed sensors	E-waste bin; periodically collected and processed	Secure collection zone; staff-monitored or behind counter
Chemical waste	Adhesives, resins, solvents	EH&S-approved chemical waste containers	Partner with institutional EH&S; label with pictograms
Biohazard waste	Wet lab waste, sharp tools, biological samples	Red biohazard bins, sharps containers, liquid disposal protocols	Follow BSL1/BSL2 compliance; signage and restricted access required

(continued)

Table 5-6. (*continued*)

Waste type	Typical sources	Recommended disposal method	Infrastructure/signage tips
Dust/ particulates	Sanding, routing, grinding	Vacuum systems, dust collection units	Provide PPE and local exhaust; clean filters regularly
Reusable materials	Large offcuts, failed but usable components	Scrap/reuse bin	Label as "Free to Use"; position near prototyping areas

Future-Proofing the Space

One of the most common mistakes in designing a MakerSpace is planning too specifically for what users need today. While it's important to respond to current demands, it's even more critical to design a space that can adapt to new technologies, workflows, and ways of learning. Whether you're building from scratch or renovating an existing facility, future-proofing should be a guiding principle throughout your design process (see Table 5-7 for a tip summary).

Future-proofing is not about predicting exactly what tools or fields will emerge—it's about building flexibility into the space itself. Physical layout, utilities, infrastructure, and digital systems should all be planned with growth and change in mind. The cost of "overbuilding" in a few key areas is often lower than the cost of modifying or retrofitting a space that wasn't designed for evolution.

Avoid designing for specific technologies—today's cutting-edge tools are tomorrow's relics. Instead, focus on versatile infrastructure: adjustable furniture, modular partitions, extra conduit for electrical or data lines, and ceiling-mounted utility drops that can serve a variety of functions. Consider including more power and network access points than are currently needed, and build in accessible pathways for future plumbing or HVAC additions.

As new Maker Fields emerge—such as bioengineering, robotics, AI hardware, and sustainable materials—the physical and digital needs of your user base may shift dramatically. Space that is too tightly tied to a single discipline may end up underused or functionally obsolete. If your MakerSpace is affiliated with a school or institution, consider aligning your planning horizon with broader trends in curricula or research. What fields are your students entering now? What kinds of interdisciplinary work are being encouraged?

While it's impossible to plan for everything, future-proofing your MakerSpace means giving yourself room to grow.

Table 5-7. *Future Proofing Considerations*

Strategy	Purpose	Examples/implementation Tips
Design for flexibility	Adapt to changing needs over time	Use mobile furniture, modular partitions, open floor layouts
Avoid tool-specific fixtures	Prevent early obsolescence	Don't embed docks or mounts for current tech (e.g., phones, tablets)
Overbuild core infrastructure	Reduce need for expensive retrofits	Add extra power/data outlets, reserve capacity in HVAC and plumbing
Use versatile utility access	Support evolving equipment and layouts	Include ceiling drops, conduit, and accessible service panels
Plan for Emerging Fields	Support long-term relevance of space	Allocate zones that can flex between disciplines (e.g., bio, AI, robotics)
Align with institutional trends	Match space design to future academic or research directions	Consult strategic plans, new degree programs, and interdisciplinary goals

Case Studies in Layout Design

While each MakerSpace is shaped by its community, budget, and institutional context, existing spaces offer valuable insights into how layout decisions support flexibility, safety, creativity, and community. The following case studies highlight different approaches to spatial organization, illustrating how principles like zoning, modularity, visibility, and infrastructure planning can be implemented in practice. They show that there is no one-size-fits-all layout—but successful spaces are intentional. They use physical design to signal values, guide behavior, and adapt to the evolving needs of their communities. Whether you're planning a 500-square-foot classroom lab or a 20,000-square-foot innovation hub, there's always something to learn from the way others have shaped space for making.

Artisan's Asylum

Artisan's Asylum in Somerville, Massachusetts, spans over 40,000 square feet and is organized using a zone-based layout. The space features distinct areas for metalworking, woodworking, digital fabrication, electronics, textiles, and bike repair—each with its own tools and safety protocols. Spaces are physically separated but visually open, creating a sense of flow while maintaining structure. Artisan's model is particularly strong in embedding expert users within zones and balancing openness with accountability.

Chattanooga Public Library MakerSpace

Housed on the fourth floor of the Chattanooga, Tennessee, downtown public library, this MakerSpace blends open access with managed programming. The layout combines open worktables, digital fabrication stations, and media labs with community meeting areas. Key features include clear zoning for equipment-intensive activities and strategic

193

placement of staff desks for visibility and assistance. As a public institution, the library has emphasized signage, self-guided learning, and safety systems that do not rely solely on staff presence.

The Yale Center for Engineering Innovation and Design

Designed as a university-wide, multidisciplinary space, the Yale Center for Engineering Innovation and Design (CEID) at Yale University in New Haven, CT, blends making with social engagement. The two-floor layout includes prototyping areas, a wood shop, a machine shop, a biological work space, and flexible meeting spaces—all flowing into one another with minimal physical barriers. Emphasis is placed on transparency. The CEID demonstrates how space design can support spontaneous collaboration and integrate creativity into daily campus life.

Digital Organization

A well-designed website is not an add-on to a MakerSpace—it is core infrastructure. Just as power distribution, ventilation, and tool storage are essential to how a physical space functions, a thoughtfully built digital presence is critical to how people find, access, and engage with the MakerSpace. It's the first thing many users encounter, the place they return to for answers, and a key support system for working independently.

A website can do far more than post open hours or showcase recent projects. It can help users navigate the space, complete required training, locate tools and supplies, troubleshoot problems, and connect with the community. It can reduce confusion, minimize unnecessary staff intervention, and reinforce a culture of openness and shared responsibility.

When developed with care, a MakerSpace website supports users at every stage of engagement—from orientation and tool access to advanced project work and documentation. It can house

- *Basic operational information*: location, hours, policies, and who can use the space

- *Joining procedures*: how to gain access, complete training, or get certified

- *Tool documentation and tutorials*: guides for using equipment safely and effectively

- *Inventory and lab maps*: searchable lists and location references for tools and supplies

- *Protocols and safety guidelines*: covering usage, waste disposal, and emergencies

- *Community-building tools*: announcements, project showcases, event calendars, and shared resources

A good website (see Table 5-8 for a summary) is intuitive, up-to-date, and aligned with the culture of the space. Whether it's a simple page built in Google Sites or a full-featured custom platform, its primary job is to make the space easier to navigate and more welcoming to all users.

The following sections break down the core components of a strong MakerSpace website—from the basics of access and hours to systems for learning, sharing, and growing a vibrant user community.

Table 5-8. Website Components

Component	Purpose	Key features
General info and access	Introduce the space and explain how to get started	Hours, location, who can join, how to gain access, FAQs, contact details
Inventory tools	Help users locate tools and materials	Searchable item list, location tags, lab maps, photos, storage references
Tool documentation	Support safe and independent use of equipment	Safety guides, setup instructions, maintenance checklists, training links
Tutorials and Protocols	Enable learning and reduce reliance on staff	How-to guides, project-based tutorials, debugging manuals, printable formats
QR code integration	Provide just-in-time access in physical space	Codes on tools and stations linking to guides, inventories, or booking systems
Events and scheduling	Communicate programming and support structured use	Calendar of workshops, orientations, tool reservation links
Announcements and updates	Share timely info and changes	Closures, new tools, policy updates, system alerts
Community features	Foster engagement and ownership	Project showcases, user submissions, suggestion forms, feedback channels
Collaborative editing	Keep content relevant and inclusive	Google Docs/Sheets, editable tutorials, TA/staff curation
Accessible design	Ensure usability across devices and audiences	Mobile-friendly layout, clear navigation, plain language, ADA considerations

Website Basics

For many users, the website is the first touchpoint with a MakerSpace. Whether they're students, staff, or members of the broader community, visitors often go online to find out what the space is, who can use it, and how to get started. A clear, friendly, and well-structured homepage can demystify the space and make it easier for new users to engage (see Table 5-9 for a summary).

Table 5-9. *Overview of Basic Information for a MakerSpace Website*

Element	Purpose	Suggestions
Hours and location	Let users know when and where to access the space	Include semester hours, breaks, maps, and building info
Eligibility	Clarify who can use the space	Note differences for students, staff, faculty, public
Access instructions	Guide users through onboarding	Step-by-step guides, orientation signup, training requirements
Contact info	Provide a direct path to help	List staff emails, help desks, or request forms
FAQs	Reduce repetitive questions	Focus on first-time user concerns

The most essential role of the website is to communicate basic operational information. This includes

- Location and contact information

- Open hours, including variations for semesters, breaks, or holidays

- Who can use the space (e.g., enrolled students, faculty, staff, community members)

- What to expect upon arrival—whether walk-in use is allowed, whether there's a check-in process, or if orientation is required

- Equally important is outlining how to join or gain access to the space. Depending on the MakerSpace, this might include

  - *A step-by-step guide to onboarding*: attend orientation, complete training, sign safety agreements, etc.

  - Access tiers (e.g., general access vs. tool-specific access)

  - Links to training modules, registration forms, or intake surveys

  - Information about membership fees or course enrollment (if applicable)

  - Details about ID card activation, keycodes, or badge readers if access is controlled

This section of the website should be written in plain, welcoming language, avoiding jargon and assumptions about prior experience. It's also helpful to include FAQs that address common beginner questions like

- "Do I need to know how to use tools before joining?"

- "Can I use the space if I'm not taking a course?"

- "How long does training take?"

- "Is help available during open hours?"

In more complex or high-traffic spaces, the homepage might also highlight

- Announcements or closures

- A live calendar of upcoming workshops, trainings, or staffed hours

- A link to a tool or room reservation system

The goal is to reduce ambiguity and anxiety—especially for first-time users—by making it clear that the space is welcoming, structured, and navigable. A good landing page lowers the barrier to entry and helps new users understand how to become active participants.

Inventory and Location Systems

One of the most consistent barriers to productivity in a MakerSpace is not a lack of tools—but a lack of knowing where they are. Whether it's a specific sensor, an obscure connector, or a roll of masking tape, users frequently lose time and momentum searching for items that are technically available but practically hidden. A well-structured inventory and location system helps mitigate this by making tools, supplies, and equipment legible, accessible, and searchable (see Table 5-10).

Table 5-10. *Inventory and Location System Summary*

Element	Purpose	Suggestions
Inventory list	Help users find tools/ supplies	Use searchable format (Google Sheets, Airtable, etc.)
Location codes	Direct users to exact storage spots	Label drawers, cabinets, shelves clearly
Lab maps	Reduce user confusion and improve navigation	Post static or clickable maps with cross-referenced zones
Visual aids	Support different learning styles	Include item photos or videos of tools in use
Update system	Keep data current and usable	Assign staff or student editors; embed live spreadsheets

At the most basic level, an inventory system should allow users to know what exists and where to find it. This might be a simple spreadsheet or a more advanced database, but the key is consistency and clarity. Each item should be listed with

- A name or description

- A location reference (e.g., cabinet number, drawer label, shelf code)

- Notes on use, access restrictions, or alternatives

- Optional: quantity, photo, link to a datasheet, or tutorial

Spaces that invest in digitally accessible inventories—whether through a Google Sheet or a web-based database—create opportunities for faster onboarding, less staff interruption, and a smoother user experience. These systems can be displayed on a public screen in the space or accessed via the website. When paired with physical signage (e.g., clearly labeled drawers or color-coded storage areas), users can navigate the lab with greater confidence.

A complementary tool is the lab map—a visual or schematic representation of the space that links location codes to specific rooms, cabinets, or benches. When combined with an inventory system, a lab map can greatly reduce the cognitive load of finding supplies, especially for first-time users or those unfamiliar with technical language. Users may not know to search for "hook-up wire (22 AWG, solid core)," but they can find "wire" on the map and go directly to the labeled drawer.

Some MakerSpaces build in redundancy by also including photos of the items and storage units in the inventory—this supports visual learners and helps users confirm they're in the right place. Others include QR codes inside drawers or on storage bins that link directly to reordering info, instructional videos, or related tutorials.

Maintaining a clean, accurate inventory requires upkeep and user buy-in. Labeling systems should be intuitive and resilient to wear. Item names should use common, user-facing terminology. Staff or trained student workers can perform regular audits or restocking, and experienced users may be empowered to suggest edits or corrections through shared platforms.

For high-volume or high-value items, some spaces may implement check-out systems or integrate inventory tracking with tool reservation platforms. Even without full automation, visibility into tool availability and location can drastically reduce friction in the making process.

Tutorials, Protocols, and Documentation

Tutorials, protocols, and documentation form the backbone of user learning, enabling newcomers to gain confidence and returning users to deepen their expertise. When delivered digitally and integrated into daily workflows, these resources make the MakerSpace safer, more accessible, and more empowering for everyone (see Table 5-11).

Table 5-11. *Adding Supporting Material to a Website*

Element	Purpose	Suggestions
Tool guides	Teach users how to safely operate tools	Step-by-step instructions, checklists, images/videos
Protocols	Standardize procedures for specific tasks	Include safety, material prep, and post-use cleanup
Troubleshooting guides	Help users resolve issues independently	Use flowcharts or common error lists
Printable resources	Support offline or low-connectivity access	Keep PDFs or one-page quick references available
Editable format	Allow for continuous updates and contributions	Use collaborative tools like Google Docs

In many spaces, technical knowledge is stored informally—in the heads of experienced users or passed along through quick verbal instructions. While that culture of peer-to-peer support is important, relying solely on oral tradition leads to gaps, inconsistency, and frustration. Codifying knowledge into written or visual tutorials helps ensure that all users receive accurate, up-to-date, and standardized guidance.

Tutorials and protocols can take many forms:

- Step-by-step instructions for using tools (e.g., laser cutters, oscilloscopes)

- Material handling guides (e.g., adhesives, textiles, biohazards)

- Safety checklists and maintenance procedures

- Troubleshooting and debugging flowcharts

- Project-based guides (e.g., building an amplifier or prototyping with Arduino)

These resources are most effective when they are embedded in the user's environment. Many MakerSpaces place QR codes near tools or on equipment that link directly to tutorials or datasheets (Figure 5-6). Others mount printed guides in tool zones or post video walkthroughs on their website. Using collaborative platforms like Google Docs allows these materials to evolve over time, incorporating edits from staff, teaching assistants, or experienced users.

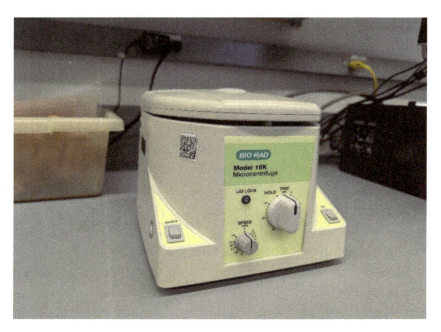

Figure 5-6. *A microcentrifuge with a QR code taped onto it. The QR code directs to the user manual on the MakerSpace website*

Just-in-time access is essential. Users are most likely to engage with documentation when they need it—right before powering up a machine, or while troubleshooting an unfamiliar issue. This is why digital access via phones or laptops is often more effective than relying solely on binders or handouts. Providing mobile-friendly or printable formats ensures users can refer to the material even in low-connectivity zones.

Beyond helping individuals, documentation plays a key role in preserving institutional memory. When a staff member leaves or a tool is replaced, knowledge doesn't vanish with them. Archived protocols can also serve as training templates for new staff or a reference point for refining safety practices.

MakerSpaces can take this even further by encouraging users to contribute back. Advanced students or project teams may be invited to write tutorials for tools they've mastered or to improve outdated documentation. This builds a participatory knowledge base that reflects the evolving reality of the space.

Finally, documentation can also help build community identity. A shared troubleshooting guide becomes a record of collective learning. A growing repository of protocols reflects a vibrant, experimental culture.

Building Community Through Digital Tools

When thoughtfully integrated into the life of a MakerSpace, websites, tutorials, inventories, and feedback platforms can reinforce a culture of openness, collaboration, and shared ownership (see Table 5-12 for tips). A strong digital presence helps build community, making the space feel more accessible, inclusive, and alive.

Table 5-12. *Community Building Tips*

Element	Purpose	Suggestions
Project showcases	Celebrate and inspire creativity	Feature builds on homepage, newsletter, or social channels
Announcements	Keep users informed	Post lab closures, tool changes, or event reminders
Feedback tools	Gather input and improve space experience	Use suggestion forms or QR-coded feedback links
Community calendars	Share upcoming opportunities	Include workshops, training sessions, social events
Group communication	Support collaboration and questions	Use Slack, Discord, or mailing lists as extensions of the space

At their best, digital platforms reflect and amplify the core values of the MakerSpace. A website that is welcoming, well-organized, and transparent sends a message: you belong here, and you have what you need to get started. Online documentation and searchable inventories don't just support tool use—they signal that knowledge is meant to be shared. When users see that the space is organized with them in mind, they're more likely to take initiative, care for tools, and contribute to the culture of the space.

Community-building through digital tools can take many forms:

- Project showcases or "Featured Builds" on the website or screens in the space

- A shared troubleshooting wiki or FAQ that users contribute to over time

- Announcements of upcoming workshops, talks, or project milestones

- A user feedback form that invites suggestions and highlights needs

- Internal or public-facing newsletters featuring staff picks, project highlights, or tool updates

- Integration with community platforms like Slack, Discord, or group chats for organizing builds, coordinating teams, or asking questions

These platforms don't need to be high-tech to be high-impact. A Google Form embedded on the homepage can surface useful suggestions. A monthly email update can keep people in the loop. A shared image folder can make it easy to document and celebrate the work happening in the space.

Users who are new to making—or to the community—can access information and participate in ways that aren't always possible in busy, in-person environments. Quiet users can ask questions asynchronously. First-time visitors can explore what the space offers before ever stepping inside. The website can help a first-time visitor to become more comfortable with the space prior to visiting it physically.

As your MakerSpace grows, these tools can help scale the sense of connection. Instead of relying on a few staff members or regulars to carry the culture, digital infrastructure distributes that work—preserving institutional memory, inviting participation, and making the space more welcoming to newcomers.

Case Study: The Stephenson Foundation Bio-MakerSpace

The George H. Stephenson Foundation Educational Laboratory & Bio-MakerSpace at the University of Pennsylvania provides a compelling example of how a well-designed website can serve as the digital backbone of a complex, interdisciplinary learning environment. Originally developed to support undergraduate bioengineering lab courses, the website has since evolved into an independent, self-guided resource hub that empowers users to work safely, creatively, and with minimal staff intervention.

At the core of the site is a searchable inventory that lists hundreds of tools, supplies, and reagents—each tagged with storage location codes that match a physical lab map (Figure 5-7). This mapping system, supported by photos and signage, enables students to find everything from pipette tips to soldering irons quickly and confidently. The inventory is maintained via a Google Sheet that feeds directly into the public-facing website, allowing staff and teaching assistants to update in real time.

Figure 5-7. *Lab Map for the Stephenson Foundation Bio-MakerSpace showing location numbers*

Beyond inventory, the site houses a robust library of protocols, tutorials, and project guides. These include lab-specific workflows (e.g., how to dispose of biohazardous waste), user-generated guides (e.g., how to use an Arduino to measure temperature), and a comprehensive debugging manual for electronics projects. QR codes throughout the space link directly to these resources, reducing the need for staff to answer repetitive questions and allowing users to get help in the moment (Figure 5-8).

Figure 5-8. *QR code at every station in the George H. Stephenson Foundation Bio-MakerSpace. This QR code directs users to the lab website which provides access to inventory lists*

The digital infrastructure also supports the lab's training model. While high-risk equipment still requires in-person verification, many tools are paired with self-paced online tutorials and quizzes. Staff can check a user's training status before granting access, and students can review materials at their own pace.

Importantly, the website helps build a culture of independence and innovation. In user surveys, over 75% of respondents reported that the site made it easier to solve problems on their own, encouraged them to try new tools, and helped them feel more confident working independently. By making documentation visible, searchable, and student-centered, the space reinforces its values of openness, learning, and shared responsibility.

Conclusion

As someone using MakerSpaces, you should follow safety procedures, wear proper PPE, complete required training, and make use of available resources like signage, QR codes, and the MakerSpace website while respecting booking systems and lab etiquette to keep the space efficient and equitable for everyone. As someone designing a new MakerSpace, you need to plan a thoughtful layout, considering circulation, noise control, and visibility with flexible infrastructure that can support evolving tools, while planning early for power, ventilation, and data access needs and creating a strong digital presence through a website for training, inventory, and user onboarding. As someone operating an existing MakerSpace, you should balance flexibility with structure by maintaining tools regularly, enforcing training and safety policies, keeping digital systems updated and navigable, planning proactively for emerging technologies and user needs, and fostering a culture of shared responsibility to create an environment where creativity thrives.

Key Takeaways

- *Space Organization*: MakerSpaces should be laid out with flexibility in mind. Mobile furniture, clear work zones, and access-controlled areas for high-risk tools help support diverse user needs and safe collaboration.

- *Infrastructure Planning*: Power, ventilation, lighting, data, and plumbing should be planned early and built into the layout. Well-integrated infrastructure supports long-term adaptability and smooth day-to-day operations.

- *Entry and Orientation*: The entrance sets the tone for the space. A clear check-in process, visible signage, and introductory resources help users navigate confidently and safely.

- *Staff Support*: Staff play a key role in safety and community-building. Embedding staff in technical zones and providing administrative and break spaces improves oversight and sustainability.

- *Zoned Work Areas*: Specialized workspaces—such as those for electronics, woodworking, wet labs, or digital media—should be separated and outfitted with the right utilities and access controls.

- *Future-Proofing*: Layouts should be designed with adaptability in mind. Overbuilding infrastructure and avoiding tech-specific furniture allows the space to grow with new tools and user needs.

- *Waste Management*: MakerSpaces generate varied waste streams. Point-of-use disposal stations with clear signage help users safely and sustainably manage electronics, chemicals, and biohazards.

- *Digital Infrastructure*: A well-designed website is essential. It should include onboarding info, tool documentation, searchable inventory, training links, and calendars—all easy to navigate and regularly updated.

- *Culture and Community*: Good organization reflects and reinforces culture. Signage, tutorials, documentation, and community showcases support a space that feels welcoming, empowering, and user-driven.

CHAPTER 6

Operating a MakerSpace

In this chapter, we will explore how to operate a MakerSpace. While the previous chapter focused on the end user experience, this chapter will focus on the behind-the-scenes activities, starting with funding. This chapter continues by exploring staffing models and training, user training, operational consideration, and equipment and supply maintenance and supply management.

Laying the Groundwork

Operating a MakerSpace is about far more than keeping tools in working order. Behind every 3D print, group project, or soldered circuit lies an intricate network of systems, people, and processes that make those moments possible. A MakerSpace that feels open, safe, and creative is the product of careful planning, thoughtful infrastructure, and day-to-day work that often goes unseen. This chapter explores the operational foundations that support vibrant MakerSpaces—from staffing and scheduling to maintenance and inventory to safety, policy enforcement, and digital systems that keep everything aligned.

© Sevile G. Mannickarottu, Michael G. Patterson, and Carolyne Godon 2025
S. G. Mannickarottu et al., *Creating MakerSpaces*, Maker Innovations Series,
https://doi.org/10.1007/979-8-8688-1309-2_6

In contrast to the previous chapter, which focused on space layout and physical organization, this chapter focuses on how those spaces are activated, sustained, and improved over time. It provides a framework for building and refining the operational infrastructure necessary to support a wide range of users and activities. Whether a MakerSpace serves a university course, a public library, a K–12 classroom, or a local nonprofit community, its success depends on how well its operations support its mission and users.

Each section of this chapter offers tools, examples, and strategies that help answer questions like: What kind of staff do you need? Who keeps the space running day-to-day? How are staff trained and users onboarded? What routines and systems prevent breakdowns, burnout, or safety incidents? How can technology—often taught in the MakerSpace itself—be used to streamline access, supply tracking, and communication?

You'll find guidance on defining staff roles and scheduling coverage; onboarding new users and reinforcing safety protocols; managing consumables and maintaining tools; and creating systems for knowledge retention, task management, and accountability. We also examine how automation can be applied to simplify repetitive tasks like approving 3D prints or logging equipment access—especially helpful in high-traffic university and K–12 settings.

Finally, we end the chapter with one of the most important and often overlooked elements of operation: fostering a culture of safety, accessibility, and shared responsibility. Policies and procedures are only effective when paired with an inclusive environment where users feel empowered to take care of the space and each other.

Whether you're launching a new MakerSpace, refining a growing one, or simply hoping to strengthen existing systems, this chapter offers practical approaches and adaptable models to help your space run more smoothly, safely, and sustainably.

Funding Models

Sustaining a MakerSpace requires a well-thought-out funding strategy that balances accessibility with financial stability. Unlike traditional businesses, MakerSpaces often operate within a hybrid model—blending revenue from memberships, grants, sponsorships, and educational partnerships. The right funding approach depends on the space's mission, target audience, and available resources. This section explores various funding models, and examines strategies to maintain financial health while keeping the space accessible and innovative. Table 6-1 provides a summary.

Table 6-1. *Summary Overview of Funding Models*

Model	Description	Best for	Key benefits
Subscription model	Users pay a recurring fee (monthly or annually) for access, similar to a gym membership. Tiers may offer different levels of access and benefits.	Commercial MakerSpaces, professional users, and those needing a steady revenue stream.	Predictable revenue, scalable pricing, incentivizes long-term engagement
One-time use model	Users pay per visit or per use of specific equipment. Ideal for occasional users, tourists, or those testing the space before committing to membership	Urban MakerSpaces, casual users, and spaces serving transient populations	Flexible, attracts a broad range of users, complements other funding models

(continued)

Table 6-1. (*continued*)

Model	Description	Best for	Key benefits
Donations model	Relies on donations from individuals, businesses, or grants. Often used by community-focused or non-profit MakerSpaces. May include "pay-what-you-can" pricing	Community-driven MakerSpaces, non-profits, and organizations focusing on accessibility	Encourages community involvement, increases accessibility, allows flexible pricing.
University or area-funded model with paid materials	Institution covers operational costs, allowing free or subsidized access. Users typically pay for consumables like 3D printing filament or laser-cut materials.	University-affiliated or government-supported MakerSpaces that aim to foster education and innovation.	Supports hands-on learning without financial barriers, promotes research and innovation.
Corporate or sponsorship model	Companies provide financial support in exchange for branding, recruitment, or innovation opportunities. Common in startup-friendly MakerSpaces.	MakerSpaces with strong industry ties, those supporting startups, and those seeking alternative revenue sources.	Provides financial stability, access to cutting-edge equipment, and industry connections.
Hybrid or tiered models	Combines multiple revenue streams, such as free access for students, paid memberships for professionals, and corporate sponsorships.	Large or diverse MakerSpaces needing a flexible, inclusive funding approach	Diversifies revenue streams, ensures accessibility while maintaining financial health.

Subscription Model

The subscription model for MakerSpaces is a popular funding mechanism, particularly among commercial spaces like NextFab. In this approach, users pay a recurring fee—monthly or annually—in exchange for access to the space and its resources. This model is reminiscent of gym memberships. Subscription tiers are often structured to provide different levels of access based on user needs. For example, a basic tier might offer access to only certain tools or limited hours, while premium memberships could include access to specialized equipment, classes, and dedicated workspace. This model ensures a steady revenue stream for the MakerSpace, which can be used to maintain equipment, hire skilled staff, and upgrade facilities. The subscription model is particularly attractive for individuals or small businesses who use the space regularly, as it offers predictable costs and often comes with value-added services such as networking events or training. MakerSpaces like NextFab successfully implement this model by balancing accessibility with premium offerings that justify higher-tier subscriptions.

One-Time Use Model

The one-time use or pay-per-use model is designed to attract occasional users who may not require ongoing access to the MakerSpace. In this system, users pay a fee each time they access the space or specific equipment. Fees can vary based on the type of tools used, the amount of time spent, or the complexity of the project. This model is especially beneficial for users who only need the space for a single project or for tourists and casual makers who do not want a long-term commitment. It also works well for MakerSpaces that serve a large, transient population or those located in urban centers where many visitors may want to "try out" the space before committing to a subscription. One-time use fees, while more variable in terms of revenue, can complement other funding models by filling in gaps during slower membership periods or appealing to a broader audience.

Donations Model

A donation-based funding model is another option, often utilized by community-focused or non-profit MakerSpaces. In this model, the MakerSpace relies on donations from individuals, businesses, or grant-making organizations to cover operational costs. Donation campaigns can be launched for specific needs, such as purchasing new equipment, or for ongoing operational expenses like rent and utilities. This model can foster a sense of ownership and community among users, as they feel directly responsible for the space's success. In addition, MakerSpaces that operate on a donation model often encourage volunteerism and offer public programming to increase visibility and attract donors. While donations may not provide the consistent revenue stream of subscriptions or pay-per-use models, they allow for greater flexibility in pricing for users, enabling access for individuals who may not be able to afford traditional fees. Some spaces also incorporate a "pay-what-you-can" model, ensuring that the space is open to a broader range of economic demographics.

University or Area-Funded Model with Paid Materials

In many academic- or government-supported MakerSpaces, the institution covers the costs of maintaining the space, making it free or highly subsidized for users. In this model, students, faculty, or members of the community can access the MakerSpace without a fee, but they are typically responsible for the materials they use, such as 3D printing filament, laser-cutting wood, or electronics components. This model aligns with the goals of many educational institutions to foster innovation and hands-on learning without placing a financial burden on users. By covering operational costs, universities or local governments can promote entrepreneurship, research, and interdisciplinary collaboration. While users may pay out of pocket for materials, this is often seen as more manageable than full subscription fees or other cost-prohibitive pricing structures. Moreover, this model can be combined with other revenue streams, such as donations, grant funding, or corporate sponsorships, to ensure long-term sustainability (Figure 6-1).

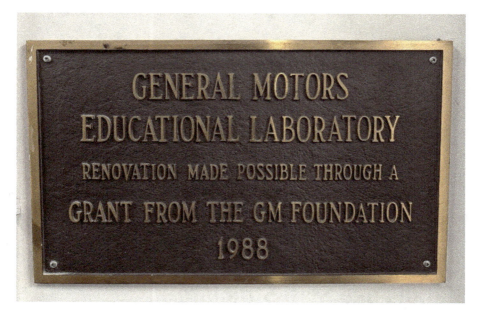

Figure 6-1. *Plaque to recognize the donation to support an educational laboratory/MakerSpace*

Corporate or Sponsorship Model

Another funding approach is through corporate sponsorships or partnerships. In this model, companies provide financial support to the MakerSpace in exchange for branding opportunities, recruiting pipelines, or access to talent and innovation. This model is especially popular with MakerSpaces that cater to startups or individuals in technology and design fields. Corporate sponsors may donate equipment, offer workshops, or provide financial backing for specific programs or competitions. In return, the MakerSpace can offer corporate partners the opportunity to test new products, scout potential employees, or gain insights into emerging trends and technologies. This symbiotic relationship benefits both parties: the MakerSpace gets much-needed financial support and resources, while the company gains visibility and access to a highly creative community.

Hybrid or Tiered Models

Finally, a hybrid or tiered model can combine multiple funding approaches to meet the needs of different user groups. For example, a MakerSpace might offer free access to students or community members while charging businesses or professional users for membership or equipment rental. This ensures broad access while still generating revenue from users who can afford to pay more. A hybrid model could also combine elements of donation-based funding, grants, and subscriptions to build a diverse and stable financial base.

Staffing and Staff Structure

Too often, MakerSpaces are launched with energy and enthusiasm, but without a fully developed plan for how day-to-day operations will be sustained. Staffing is frequently an afterthought—positions are defined loosely, roles overlap inconsistently, and critical functions like training, maintenance, and community engagement are left to whoever happens to be available. This lack of intentional structure can lead to inefficiencies, burnout, and a diminished experience for users.

A successful MakerSpace requires a clear staffing strategy that aligns with the space's mission, supports its operations, and evolves with its community. This section outlines key staff roles, how they work together, and the importance of thoughtful planning in building a team that can support not just the equipment but the people who use it.

Staffing

Not surprisingly, identifying the correct staff is important for a MakerSpace. Staff members not only maintain equipment and enforce safety protocols but also serve as educators, mentors, and community builders. The right mix of technical expertise, administrative support, and instructional staff ensures that users have access to both the tools and the guidance they need to succeed. This section outlines key staff roles, responsibilities, and how to structure a team that balances efficiency, expertise, and engagement. While different roles are provided, many can be combined into one individual, depending on the size of the MakerSpace. In addition, if the MakerSpace is part of a larger organization, for example, a library or University, certain roles will be taken up by the larger entity. Table 6-2 provides a summary.

Table 6-2. *Summary of Staff Roles for a MakerSpace*

Position	Description	Key responsibilities
MakerSpace director	Oversees overall strategy, operations, and financial sustainability of the MakerSpace. Ensures alignment with mission and long-term goals.	Strategic planning, financial oversight, staff supervision, partnerships, innovation and growth
Technical lead	Manages all equipment, ensures maintenance and repairs, develops technical training for staff and users, and evaluates new tool acquisitions.	Equipment maintenance, safety oversight, technical training, vendor coordination
Facilities lead	Oversees the physical infrastructure, ensuring safety, cleanliness, and efficient layout. Handles compliance with building codes and emergency protocols.	Space organization, facility maintenance, compliance, security planning
Financial and purchasing coordinator	Manages budgeting, purchasing, and financial tracking. Secures funding through grants, sponsorships, and membership revenue.	Budget management, expense tracking, purchasing, funding strategy
Staffing coordinator	Recruits, hires, and schedules staff. Oversees onboarding, training, and professional development to ensure effective team performance.	Staff hiring, training, scheduling, conflict resolution

(*continued*)

Table 6-2. (*continued*)

Position	Description	Key responsibilities
Membership coordinator	Handles member recruitment, onboarding, engagement, and retention. Manages access control, membership tiers, and member support.	Member services, engagement programs, membership policies, customer support
Marketing coordinator	Develops and executes marketing campaigns. Manages social media, branding, event promotion, and public relations.	Marketing strategy, outreach, digital content, event promotion, sponsorships
Events coordinator	Designs and delivers events that engage the MakerSpace community and support learning, outreach, and collaboration.	Event planning, logistics coordination, workshop development, community outreach, feedback collection

MakerSpace Director

The MakerSpace Director or Manager is responsible for ensuring that the space remains financially sustainable, operationally efficient, and aligned with its mission—whether that mission is education, research, entrepreneurship, or community engagement. As the senior leader, the Director oversees all aspects of the MakerSpace, from staffing and budgeting to programming and facility management, ensuring that it remains a thriving environment where innovation and collaboration can flourish.

A core part of the Director's role is strategic leadership and vision. This position defines the long-term direction of the MakerSpace, working closely with institutional leaders, advisory boards, and key stakeholders to ensure that the space continues to evolve and serve its community effectively. Whether the MakerSpace is part of a university, a nonprofit, or a corporate innovation hub, the Director must stay ahead of industry trends and emerging technologies, ensuring that the space adapts to meet new challenges and opportunities. The Director also plays a key role in program development, collaborating with marketing and membership staff to expand outreach efforts, build partnerships, and create training programs that add value to the MakerSpace's users.

The Director is ultimately responsible for the day-to-day operations of the MakerSpace, policies and procedures, hiring, facility and equipment maintenance, and user experience.

Beyond the internal operations of the space, the Director serves as the public face of the MakerSpace, building relationships with external partners, engaging with universities, businesses, government agencies, and local maker communities to expand the MakerSpace's reach. Whether speaking at conferences, forming strategic partnerships, or advocating for the role of MakerSpaces in education and entrepreneurship, the Director plays a crucial role in ensuring that the space remains relevant and well-connected within its ecosystem.

Looking ahead, the Director must always be focused on innovation and growth. They continuously seek opportunities to expand the MakerSpace's impact—whether by developing new programs in cutting-edge fields like artificial intelligence or sustainability, forging collaborations with startups and R&D labs, or implementing diversity and accessibility initiatives to welcome a broader audience. By staying forward-thinking and adaptable, the Director ensures that the MakerSpace remains a valuable resource for its community well into the future.

Technical Lead

The Technical Lead is responsible for overseeing all equipment within the MakerSpace, ensuring that tools, machinery, and digital fabrication resources are operational, well-maintained, and safe for use. Traditional titles for this role include "Lab Engineer" or "Technical Director," though the specific designation may vary depending on the size and structure of the MakerSpace.

This position plays a critical role in the daily operations of the space by managing preventive maintenance schedules, troubleshooting mechanical and software issues, and coordinating repairs when necessary. The Technical Lead also ensures that proper safety protocols are in place, minimizing risks associated with high-powered tools, hazardous materials, and specialized machinery.

Beyond maintenance, this individual serves as the primary point of contact for evaluating new equipment acquisitions, ensuring that any new tools align with the MakerSpace's mission and user needs. The role collaborates with vendors and manufacturers for support, repairs, and warranty claims, keeping the space's infrastructure up-to-date and functional.

When developing training processes for staff and users, the Technical Lead must be closely involved to ensure that best practices for machine operation, troubleshooting, and safety are effectively communicated. This position may design or oversee the development of training materials, conduct hands-on instructional sessions, and certify staff members before they train others. Additionally, the lead provides critical input on user access policies, ensuring that only properly trained individuals operate specialized equipment.

Given the technical complexity of MakerSpaces, the Technical Lead serves as both a problem solver and an educator, bridging the gap between technical expertise and user accessibility.

Facilities Lead

The Facilities Lead is responsible for overseeing the physical environment of the MakerSpace, ensuring that the space remains safe, organized, and conducive to creative and technical work. This role may also be referred to as "Facilities Manager" or "Operations Coordinator," depending on the structure of the MakerSpace.

This position maintains the space's infrastructure, including HVAC systems, electrical setups, lighting, storage areas, and general cleanliness. The Facilities Lead ensures that workspaces remain functional and accessible, addressing issues such as overcrowding, inefficient layouts, and wear and tear on commonly used areas. The position coordinates with custodial services, manage waste disposal (including hazardous materials, if applicable), and ensures that shared areas remain clutter-free and safe for all users.

Safety is a core responsibility of this position. The Facilities Lead ensures compliance with fire codes, emergency evacuation plans, OSHA regulations, and local building codes. This includes conducting routine inspections of the space to identify potential hazards, such as blocked emergency exits, improper tool storage, or ventilation issues in areas handling fumes or particulates. In collaboration with the Technical Lead, this role would ensure that safety signage, first-aid stations, fire extinguishers, and emergency stop buttons are properly placed and maintained.

Another critical responsibility of the Facilities Lead is space optimization and workflow efficiency. This role would assess how users move through the space and adjust layouts accordingly to prevent bottlenecks and maximize accessibility. This can include optimizing storage solutions, defining designated work zones, and coordinating with staff to ensure that different user groups (e.g., students, hobbyists, professionals) have the appropriate workspaces available.

When planning renovations, expansions, or space modifications, the Facilities Lead plays an integral role in the design and implementation process, working with administrators, architects, and contractors to ensure that facility improvements align with the needs of users while staying within budget and safety regulations.

Additionally, the Facilities Lead must be involved in scheduling space usage—ensuring that workshops, classes, and general member access are balanced effectively. This can include overseeing reservation systems, coordinating facility access policies, and managing after-hours security protocols.

Financial and Purchasing Coordinator

The Financial and Purchasing Coordinator is responsible for managing the financial health of the MakerSpace, overseeing budgeting, purchasing, and resource allocation to ensure smooth operations. Depending on the size and structure of the MakerSpace, this role may also be referred to as "Finance Coordinator," or "Procurement Specialist."

This position ensures that the MakerSpace operates within its financial means while still providing high-quality tools, materials, and programming. The Coordinator develops and oversees the annual budget, tracking expenses related to equipment maintenance, facility upkeep, staff salaries, consumables, and event programming.

A key aspect of this position's responsibilities is purchasing and procurement. The Coordinator researches vendors, negotiates contracts, and maintains relationships with suppliers to ensure that the MakerSpace has access to reliable, high-quality equipment and materials at competitive prices. This includes purchasing everything from high-cost machinery (e.g., CNC routers, 3D printers) to everyday consumables (e.g., filaments, wood, adhesives, safety gear). The position also tracks inventory levels, ensuring that frequently used supplies are always stocked while preventing unnecessary overspending.

The Financial and Purchasing Coordinator must also manage funding sources, whether through memberships, grants, sponsorships, or institutional support. The position may also be responsible for grant writing and reporting, working with leadership to secure funding for new initiatives, equipment, or facility upgrades. This can include coordinating with external funders, university departments, or local government agencies to ensure compliance with grant requirements.

Additionally, this role includes overseeing financial policies and transactions to ensure compliance with organizational guidelines and financial best practices. The Coordinator may handle membership payments, invoicing for services, and tracking revenue streams from classes, workshops, or corporate partnerships. If the MakerSpace offers paid services such as fabrication consulting or prototyping, the Financial and Purchasing Coordinator ensures proper billing and cost recovery.

Beyond finance, this role requires collaboration with the Technical Lead and Facilities Lead to prioritize spending. For example, the Coordinator might help decide whether to repair vs. replace equipment, optimize supply orders based on usage trends, and allocate funds for infrastructure improvements.

Staffing Coordinator

The Staffing Coordinator is responsible for managing the recruitment, scheduling, and professional development of MakerSpace staff, ensuring that the space operates efficiently with a well-trained and engaged team.

A core responsibility of the Staffing Coordinator is hiring and onboarding new employees, ensuring that the MakerSpace attracts individuals with the necessary technical expertise, instructional skills, and community engagement abilities. This includes writing job descriptions, conducting interviews, and overseeing the orientation process to ensure new hires understand safety protocols, equipment policies, and organizational culture.

Beyond recruitment, this position is responsible for staff scheduling and shift management. MakerSpaces often have varying traffic patterns, with peak usage times requiring more staff coverage. The Staffing Coordinator ensures that shifts are properly staffed to balance technical support, instructional needs, and front-desk operations while preventing staff burnout. This role may also manage on-call or part-time staffing models, ensuring flexibility without sacrificing operational effectiveness.

Another critical function is staff training and development. The Staffing Coordinator collaborates with the Technical Lead to ensure that all staff receive technical training on equipment maintenance and operation, as well as safety procedures. Additionally, this position works with the

Facilities Lead to ensure staff understand their roles in maintaining an organized and accessible workspace. This role may also coordinate professional development opportunities, such as sending staff to external workshops, organizing peer training, or implementing certification programs for key technical skills.

For MakerSpaces that incorporate volunteers, student workers, or interns, the Staffing Coordinator manages these individuals, ensuring they receive proper training and are assigned meaningful tasks. This individual may also develop recognition programs to retain long-term volunteers and keep engagement high.

In addition to direct staffing management, the Staffing Coordinator may also handle conflict resolution, performance evaluations, and team-building initiatives, ensuring a positive work environment. This position serves as the primary point of contact for staff concerns, helping to mediate issues and improve workplace culture.

Membership Coordinator

The Membership Coordinator is responsible for managing the MakerSpace's membership program, ensuring a seamless experience for members while maintaining strong engagement and retention. This role, sometimes referred to as "Community Manager" or "Member Services Coordinator," serves as the primary point of contact for new and existing members, handling everything from onboarding to renewals and ongoing support.

A key responsibility of the Membership Coordinator is managing member recruitment and onboarding. This role develops outreach strategies to attract new members, whether through university partnerships, local maker communities, or corporate engagements. Once members join, the Membership Coordinator ensures they receive a comprehensive orientation, covering MakerSpace policies, safety procedures, and available resources. This may include leading facility tours, distributing welcome materials, and coordinating introductory training sessions.

Beyond initial onboarding, the Membership Coordinator is responsible for member engagement and retention. This includes creating and managing programs to keep members active, such as exclusive workshops, networking events, or member spotlights. The Coordinator may also facilitate mentorship or peer collaboration opportunities to strengthen the community within the space.

The administrative side of the role includes handling memberships, payments, and renewals. The Membership Coordinator tracks expiration dates, sends renewal reminders, and ensures that membership tiers (e.g., student, professional, corporate) align with user needs. This role may also manage access control systems, ensuring that only active members can enter the space during designated hours.

Another critical function of the role is member support and conflict resolution. The Membership Coordinator serves as the first point of contact for members who have concerns, whether it's about space access, equipment reservations, or interpersonal conflicts.

In MakerSpaces with a tiered or structured membership system, the Membership Coordinator may also oversee corporate or institutional memberships, coordinating special access, private workshops, or partnership agreements. This role ensures that membership policies are clearly communicated and that all members, from casual users to long-term professionals, understand their benefits and responsibilities.

Marketing Coordinator

The Marketing Coordinator is responsible for promoting the MakerSpace, increasing public awareness, and attracting new members, partners, and participants. This role, sometimes referred to as "Communications

Manager" or "Outreach Coordinator," plays a key role in shaping the MakerSpace's brand identity and ensuring that its offerings are effectively communicated to both internal and external audiences.

A primary responsibility of the Marketing Coordinator is developing and executing marketing strategies to grow membership, promote events, and showcase the space's impact. This includes creating promotional materials, managing social media accounts, updating the website, and crafting email newsletters. They ensure that branding is consistent across all platforms and that messaging aligns with the MakerSpace's mission.

The Marketing Coordinator is also responsible for event promotion and outreach. Whether it's a new workshop, an open house, or a large-scale maker fair, they create and distribute marketing campaigns to drive attendance. This role collaborates with instructors and staff to ensure that classes and programs receive adequate promotion and that event participation meets expectations.

Another key aspect of the role is community and media engagement. The Marketing Coordinator builds relationships with local organizations, schools, industry partners, and media outlets to increase visibility. This individual may coordinate press releases, interviews, and sponsorship opportunities, positioning the MakerSpace as a key hub for innovation and creativity. In university-affiliated MakerSpaces, this role may also liaise with institutional communications teams to align with broader outreach efforts.

The Marketing Coordinator works closely with the Membership Coordinator to support recruitment and retention efforts. This includes developing targeted campaigns to attract specific user groups, such as students, professionals, hobbyists, or corporate partners. This can also include analyzing user engagement metrics and adjust marketing approaches based on data-driven insights.

Another critical function of this role is managing digital content creation. The Marketing Coordinator may be responsible for producing blog posts, videos, member success stories, and project showcases to highlight the impact of the MakerSpace. This content not only promotes the space but also fosters a sense of community by celebrating members' work and achievements.

In addition, the Marketing Coordinator may oversee fundraising campaigns and sponsorship initiatives, collaborating with the Financial and Purchasing Coordinator to secure funding from donors, grant opportunities, or corporate sponsors.

Events Coordinator

The Events Coordinator plays a vital role in making the MakerSpace more than just a facility—it becomes a vibrant community through their efforts. Responsible for designing, organizing, and executing events, the Events Coordinator helps activate the space and build a sense of belonging and engagement among members. Events may include everything from hands-on workshops and skill-building sessions to open houses, guest speaker talks, hackathons, and collaborative design challenges.

A key aspect of the role is developing a consistent and strategic calendar of programming that reflects the MakerSpace's mission and the interests of its user base. This requires close collaboration with other staff members, particularly the Technical Lead and Membership Coordinator, to ensure the events meet users' needs and are well integrated with the technical and community aspects of the space. The Marketing Coordinator is also a critical partner, helping to promote events effectively through newsletters, social media, and outreach campaigns.

The Events Coordinator is responsible not just for ideation and planning but also for logistics—scheduling rooms, registering participants, coordinating supplies, and managing setup and cleanup. This can include coordinating with volunteers or student assistants to support event execution.

Structuring the MakerSpace Team

For a MakerSpace, the right staffing model ensures that equipment is properly maintained, members receive the support they need, finances are managed efficiently, and the space continues to grow in alignment with its mission. Whether the MakerSpace is a small, community-run facility or a large, university-affiliated lab, structuring the team effectively requires careful planning around roles, responsibilities, scheduling, and long-term scalability.

How the various roles in a MakerSpace are structured depends on the organizational model adopted. A traditional hierarchical model provides clear reporting lines, with department leads reporting to the MakerSpace Director, who in turn reports to an advisory board or institutional leadership. This structure is effective in large MakerSpaces with multiple teams, ensuring accountability and specialization. However, for smaller MakerSpaces, a flat organizational model may be more practical. In this setup, staff members share multiple responsibilities and work collaboratively, without rigid reporting lines. This flexible approach encourages innovation and adaptability, making it easier to shift priorities based on user needs. However, it can also create challenges in accountability, requiring strong communication and clear role definitions to ensure smooth operations.

One of the most important aspects of team structuring is staff scheduling and coverage. To ensure that members receive adequate support, staffing levels should be adjusted based on peak and off-peak hours. During high-traffic periods, such as evenings and weekends, additional staff—especially technical and membership support—should be present to assist users. Off-peak hours may require minimal staffing, with volunteers or interns providing supplementary support. Additionally, cross-training staff across multiple roles can enhance flexibility, ensuring that no single department is overwhelmed while allowing for emergency coverage when key personnel are unavailable.

As the MakerSpace grows, its staffing needs will evolve. Scaling the team strategically is key to maintaining efficiency while expanding services. A new MakerSpace may start with a small, multitasking team, with one or two full-time staff members handling multiple responsibilities. As membership increases, it becomes necessary to introduce dedicated roles for membership services, marketing, and finance. Over time, as the MakerSpace reaches full capacity, additional specialists may be required to support new initiatives and ensure continued sustainability.

Regardless of the team structure, effective communication is critical. Weekly staff meetings can help ensure that operations remain aligned with goals, while project management tools such as Slack, Trello, or Asana can streamline collaboration. Additionally, fostering cross-departmental cooperation—such as the Technical Lead working with the Membership Coordinator on training programs or the Financial Coordinator collaborating with Marketing on sponsorships—ensures that every aspect of the MakerSpace functions as a cohesive unit.

Staff Visibility and Identification

To ensure that users can easily locate and identify MakerSpace staff, all employees—including full-time staff, student workers, and volunteers—should wear clearly visible identification, such as lanyards, name badges, or branded jackets. This policy helps improve user experience by making it easier for members to seek assistance, ask technical questions, or report issues.

Identification protocols may include using lanyards (Figure 6-2) or name tags. This is perhaps the cheapest option. All staff should wear a designated lanyard or badge with their name and role, making it clear who is available to assist users.

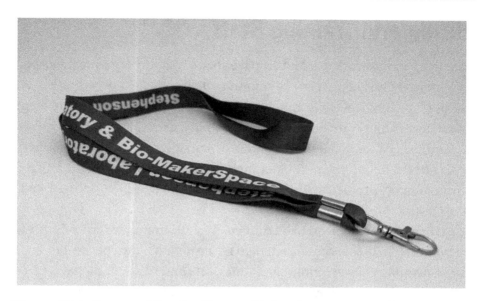

Figure 6-2. *Lanyard for the George H. Stephenson Foundation Educational Laboratory & Bio-MakerSpace*

Another option is branded jackets, shirts, or aprons. In larger MakerSpaces, staff may wear specific apparel (such as lab coats, branded T-shirts, or aprons) to further distinguish themselves from general users.

MakerSpaces could consider using color-coded identification. This helps differentiate between staff roles (e.g., blue lanyards for technical staff, red for safety officers, green for membership support).

This approach ensures that users always know who to approach for assistance, reducing confusion and improving overall efficiency. Secondly, employees who are not "on the clock" and might be users of the space can remove the identifier. Finally, having a visible staff presence helps reinforce safety and ensures that MakerSpace policies are consistently enforced.

Hiring and Training Staff

The people who work in a MakerSpace shape its culture, define the user experience, and keep the space running safely and effectively. Unlike traditional technical environments, MakerSpaces demand a unique blend of skills: technical proficiency, teaching ability, a service mindset, and an enthusiasm for making. Whether it's a staff member troubleshooting a 3D printer, helping a user solder their first circuit, or leading a group through safety protocols, the impact of well-trained, well-supported staff is enormous.

Once hired, staff need to be trained. At a minimum, it's crucial to train staff in the basics of each field represented in the space—be it woodworking, 3D printing, electronics, arts and crafts, or digital fabrication. This foundational knowledge allows staff to assist users effectively, ensuring they can safely operate equipment and understand the fundamental principles of their projects. General staff training sets the minimum bar for what a fully trained MakerSpace staff member should be able to offer.

In addition to requiring basic competency training across all the disciplines available in your MakeSpace for every staff member, having a resident expert in each of these Maker fields is ideal and can truly help elevate your MakerSpace experience. Staff members who are experts in a designated field can provide deeper insights to MakerSpace users, help them troubleshoot complex problems, and help guide users through the exploration of more advanced techniques. The presence of expert staff members not only enhances the quality of learning and innovation within your MakerSpace but also builds a supportive community where the users feel confident to push the boundaries of their creativity and feel supported in exploring more advanced projects. Skilled expert staff members are invaluable in creating a space that is not just a workshop, but a thriving hub of knowledge exchange and innovation.

Experts in this context are not just instructors; they act as mentors and facilitators who can inspire and challenge users to grow. They are coach-players who can both walk a user through how to accomplish their project but also jump in and get in the weeds of their code or circuits to help them troubleshoot a problem and take their project to the finish line. Their in-depth knowledge and genuine personal interest in their area of expertise also ensures that the MakerSpace remains up-to-date with the latest technologies and practices, which is crucial in fields that evolve rapidly. An expert staff member is one who will approach the MakerSpace leaders about a new 3D printer that has just gone on pre-sale and share rumors about initial testing results. They may be active on social media, open-source projects, or forums related to their area of expertise and get early information and rumors about upcoming new product releases. A well-trained and knowledgeable staff is the backbone of a successful MakerSpace, making it a dynamic environment where creativity and technical proficiency flourish

This section explores how to build a capable and cohesive team—from hiring individuals who align with the mission of the space, to developing onboarding systems that prioritize safety and operations, to nurturing long-term growth and expertise. It covers best practices for staff training, including peer-to-peer instruction, skill tracking, and validation methods. It also emphasizes the importance of cultivating a workplace culture that supports both professional development and community-building.

By investing in thoughtful hiring and comprehensive training, MakerSpaces can create an adaptable and resilient staff capable of supporting a wide range of users, technologies, and programs.

Hiring Staff

The staff hired to work in the MakerSpace are the people who spend the most time in the MakerSpace; their near-constant presence means that they have an outsized impact on shaping the culture. Unlike traditional workplaces, MakerSpaces thrive on creativity, collaboration, and technical expertise. The team will not only be responsible for maintaining equipment and ensuring safety but also for fostering an environment that encourages innovation, learning, designing, and inventing. Hiring the right staff for a MakerSpace requires careful consideration of both technical skills and personal qualities that align with the collaborative, community-driven nature of these environments. Table 6-3 below provides key things to consider when hiring staff for a MakerSpace. The list is not definitive or exhaustive and each MakerSpace will have their individual needs.

In many cases, it can be best to hire a customer service-focused individual with the understanding that the person can be technically trained. In the process of hiring the candidate, you should gauge the desire for the individual to learn and explore on their own, which can inform you on whether or not the candidate will be able to develop the necessary technical skills.

Table 6-3. *Considerations When Hiring MakerSpace Staff*

Considerations for hiring MakerSpace staff
Technical Expertise
Teaching and Mentorship Skills
Problem-Solving and Troubleshooting
Customer Service and Community Engagement
Safety Awareness
Passion for Creativity and Innovation
Project Management and Organization Skills
Experience with Diverse Populations
Administrative and Operational Skills
Alignment with the Makerspace's Mission and Values

For cultural fit, it is best to have the candidate interview with many members of the staff. It is often ideal to have two people interview the candidate at a time as it can make the interview more relaxed and conversational.

Depending on the level of technical expertise needed, it is also worthwhile to include technical components in the interview process.

Staff Training

A successful MakerSpace requires staff who are not only skilled in technical areas but also adept in soft skills and committed to safety practices. Building a well-rounded team involves providing initial training in safety and operations, followed by technical tutorials tailored to the most relevant tools and equipment. To ensure staff are capable of supporting the space's wide-ranging projects, a structured, staged approach to training is essential. This section will outline best practices for developing such a system, including the importance of tracking skills and encouraging peer training. Safety and operational training are always prioritized first, followed by skills-based training aligned with upcoming projects or labs. Table 6-4 shows a sample training structure and Figure 6-3 shows an image of a checklist used by a MakerSpace.

Table 6-4. *Sample Training Structure*

Training type	Timing
Safety Training	First scheduled shift
Operations Training	First scheduled shift
Familiarity with Systems	First two weeks, ongoing refresher
Skills-Based Training	Scheduled as per project demands; prioritize high-use equipment like 3D printers, then specific tools like sewing machines based on MakerSpace needs.

Training Guidelines

Before Starting

- [ ] Complete all paperwork
- [ ] Schedule First Day w/ Lab Coordinator

First Day

- [ ] Get Materials
    - [ ] Key for Lab Office
    - [ ] Lanyard
    - [ ] Whistle
- [ ] Online Onboarding - Confirm Access to Following:
    - [ ] Main Lab Website Intro
    - [ ] Notion
        - [ ] Review 👫 Student Employee Guide
        - [ ] Review 🍀 General Lab Rules
    - [ ] Internal Website Intro
    - [ ] Student Employee Drive
    - [ ] Slack
        - [ ] Lab Staff
        - [ ] Scheduling
        - [ ] Listserv
    - [ ] Student Employee Calendar
- [ ] Lab Tour
    - [ ] Lab Office
    - [ ] Main Lab
    - [ ] Projects Room
    - [ ] Basement
    - [ ] Towne 143
- [ ] Give Patagonia Size

First week

- [ ] Order Form (Confirm Access)
    - [ ] Ordering
    - [ ] Receiving
    - [ ] Student Orders
    - [ ] Package Pickup
- [ ] S Drive Overview
- [ ] Card Reader
    - [ ] Borrowing Equipment
    - [ ] Laser cutter
    - [ ] Extended Hours
- [ ] Task Sheets
    - [ ] Morning + Evening
    - [ ] Weekly Tasks
- [ ] Check for Swipe Access:
    - [ ] Main Lab
    - [ ] Autoclave

Training

- [ ] 3D Printing
    - [ ] Review 3D printer notion page 🧶
    - [ ] Confirm access to google sheet
    - [ ] 3D printer and Prusa overview 💼
    - [ ] Test print 💼
- [ ] Electronics Tutorial (AD2) 🧶
- [ ] Laser cutting & CAD
    - [ ] SolidWorks Tutorials (3 tutorials when you open the program) 🧶
        - [ ] Design Nametag 🧶

Figure 6-3. *Sample training checklist at a MakerSpace using Notion*

Foundational Training—Safety and Operations First

To establish a safe and effective MakerSpace environment, all staff members should begin their onboarding with basic safety training on their first scheduled shift. Safety protocols for handling equipment, emergency procedures, and lab cleanliness are prioritized, equipping staff to respond to incidents and create a secure environment for all users. Following safety training, staff should undergo operations training, familiarizing themselves with the basic systems of the MakerSpace, such as equipment sign-out procedures, access control, and supply restocking. This sequence—safety first, operations second—builds a foundational understanding that supports all other functions within the MakerSpace. The initial focus on safety not only mitigates risks but also sets a precedent for professionalism and responsibility within the space. Clear and consistent onboarding protocols reduce incident rates and help staff become reliable points of contact for user safety questions.

Technical Skills Development—Tailored and Progressive

After the foundational training, staff should begin building their technical skills through beginner tutorials on essential MakerSpace tools and software. Examples of critical skills include familiarity with software like SolidWorks or CAD, as well as hands-on equipment such as 3D printers, CNC machines, and sewing machines. In this phase, training should be tailored based on the space's needs and user demands. For instance, staff in a Bio-MakerSpace may first prioritize learning to operate PCR thermocyclers or laser cutters. At the same time, those in a more general-purpose MakerSpace may focus on prototyping tools like 3D printers or laser engravers (Figure 6-4).

Figure 6-4. *Staff training for a 3D pPrinter (Designed by Freepik)*

To support a well-balanced staff capable of meeting a variety of MakerSpace needs, it is critical to track who has been trained on each piece of equipment, their skill level, and any specialties. Keeping a centralized skills log enables managers to monitor proficiency across disciplines and avoid unintentional skill gaps, such as having no staff familiar with textiles or only having electronics experts. In addition to training logs, assigning staff to areas where they have foundational knowledge encourages an even distribution of skills and makes the MakerSpace more versatile for user projects. By using a skill-tracking system, MakerSpaces maintain a flexible staffing structure that supports interdisciplinary work, ensuring the space's resources are accessible to students from all fields.

Training Validation and Testing

To validate that training has been effective, consider incorporating testing or skill assessments after each training module. For example, staff members might complete a short quiz after safety training or demonstrate proper equipment setup and basic troubleshooting after technical tutorials. Figure 6-5 is a sample result of training staff to learn how to use CADing software as well as to use the laser cutter. The employee first has to draw out and dimension the box to be press-fit, and then use the laser cutter to cut the box, and ultimately demonstrate that the pieces fit together properly. Testing encourages accountability and confirms that staff can perform critical tasks independently. Referencing previously developed user training materials may offer consistency and insight into expected skills for both staff and users, ensuring alignment between staff capabilities and user support needs.

Figure 6-5. *Training to demonstrate the ability to create a press fit box*

An alternative suggestion would be to have the staff member mock-train another fully trained member. In this fashion, the fully trained member would be able to identify any holes in the new staff member's understanding of the procedure. A peer-training model leverages experienced staff to train new hires, creating a collaborative learning environment that strengthens team skills while promoting leadership. Assigning experienced team members to teach specific tools or procedures not only reinforces their own knowledge but also fosters a team-based approach to training. For instance, staff who are proficient in CAD or CNC machining can mentor new employees, helping to reduce the training burden on management and encouraging a culture of skill-sharing. Peer training also ensures continuity; even with turnover, knowledge is transferred organically among staff, preserving institutional memory and enhancing the MakerSpace's adaptability. By investing in peer-led instruction, MakerSpaces can create a sustainable training model that empowers staff to become both learners and teachers, contributing to a more versatile and resilient environment.

Staff Development

Finally, developing staff skills can have great benefits for both the individual staff members and the MakerSpace as a whole. Staff members can develop great organization and customer service skills, in addition to phenomenal technical expertise. In addition, it is well worth hosting activities and celebrations for staff members to help strengthen the sense of community and has the secondary benefit of improving customer service. Along with this, regular reviews should be held to make sure staff are content and meeting their responsibilities. Feedback through surveying customers and asking other staff will be helpful here. By following these methods, staff members can grow in their careers, whether at the MakerSpace or in other places.

User Onboarding and Training

In addition to training staff, it is just as important to train users on the proper use of the MakerSpace facility, in addition to the equipment. Users must be adequately trained to use high-risk tools and equipment in the MakerSpace to avoid risks of injury or other hazards due to improper use by untrained individuals. Training can be completed in many different ways and can be conducted either fully in person, fully remotely, or in a hybrid fashion (e.g., self-study online quiz followed by in-person assessment). Training should be adaptable and administered in a way that corresponds to the risk of improper use. For example, different parts of the same MakerSpace may require different types of training based on different levels of risk. Online self-paced assessments are quick and inexpensive to administer, but they are not the best at assessing full comprehension and are very easy to cheat on. They are generally suitable for low-risk equipment and procedures, where improper use may result in less-than-ideal results but poses no risk of injury or hazard to anyone or anything. Any equipment or procedures that have a risk of injury if used incorrectly should have some element of in-person training or validation.

Orientation and Onboarding

For a new user, entering a MakerSpace can feel both exciting and intimidating. The space may be filled with unfamiliar tools, experienced users, and an unspoken rhythm that's not immediately clear to a first-time visitor. A thoughtful orientation process can ease that transition by making expectations explicit, safety non-negotiable, and the culture of the space welcoming and accessible. Orientation is not just about rules and checklists—it's the first opportunity to communicate what it means to be part of the MakerSpace community.

A strong onboarding experience introduces users to both the physical environment and the values that guide it. This includes how to navigate the space, how to treat tools and other users with respect, and how to ask for help. Through short presentations, interactive walkthroughs, videos, or staff mentoring, the goal is to create confident, safety-minded users who understand that participation comes with shared responsibility. This can be validated either through agreements or short online quizzes.

Equipment and Procedures Training

Once a user is oriented, the next phase, depending on the type of MakerSpace, is training the user to use equipment in the space, or proper procedures to use the space. For example, using a laser cutter might require training; on the other hand, if laser cutting is done by the staff, users may need to train on how to submit a design to be cut. Both of these are important, and there are different methods to approach this. It is important to note that the choice of training should depend on the equipment or the procedure rather than using a blanket training method for all things in the MakerSpace. It is also important to recognize that different training methods can be combined as well.

A summary of the different training methods discussed in this section can be seen below in Table 6-5.

Table 6-5. *Training Summary*

Training method	Pros	Cons	Comparison to other methods
In-person staff-guided training	Personalized attention	Resource intensive	Best for individual attention and deep skill development but requires significant staff time.
	Immediate feedback	Limited availability	
	High engagement	Higher costs	
	Thorough assessment		
Self-paced courses with quizzes	Flexible scheduling	Limited personalization	Good for mass training but needs validation steps to ensure comprehension.
	Scalable for many users	No immediate feedback	
	Cost-effective	Engagement challenges	
	Frees up staff	Verification required	
In-person on-demand quizzes	Immediate feedback	Time-consuming for staff	Ensures understanding but requires staff availability and can be stressful for users.
	Interactive assessment	Resource intensive	
	Enhances accountability	Potential user anxiety	
	Personalized attention	Logistical challenges	

(*continued*)

Table 6-5. (*continued*)

Training method	Pros	Cons	Comparison to other methods
Training expiry and renewal	Ensures ongoing competence	Time-consuming for users	Helps maintain long-term competency but requires effort to manage
	Keeps users updated	Administrative burden	
	Reinforces learning	May frustrate users	
	Maintains quality control	Requires resources	

In-Person Staff-Guided Training

The best way to train users in a MakerSpace in an ideal world would be to have in-person 1:1 training sessions with a fully trained expert staff member. This is the best way to tailor the training to the user's experience level and test their understanding and competency. With a 1:1 training session, the user needs to be fully attentive, and the staff member is actively assessing their skill for the entire duration of the session. The user can't tune out the training and can't cheat (at least not easily) on the assessment. For instance, if a user is learning to operate a laser cutter, a staff member can provide personalized guidance on setting up the cutter, selecting appropriate settings, and troubleshooting common issues (see Figure 6-6 for a sample training guide for users).

Pros of In-person staff-guided training:

1. *Personalized Attention*: The training can be customized to the individual's skill level and learning pace.

2. *Immediate Feedback*: Users receive direct and immediate feedback, which helps them correct mistakes and understand the equipment better.

3. *Enhanced Engagement*: The user is more likely to stay engaged and focused during the session, leading to better retention of information.

4. *Thorough Assessment*: The trainer can thoroughly assess the user's competency and provide certification or approval based on actual performance.

Cons of In-person staff-guided training:

1. *Resource Intensive*: It requires a significant amount of time and effort from the staff, which can be a constraint if the number of users is high.

2. *Limited Availability*: Not all users can be accommodated quickly, leading to potential delays in training new users.

3. *Higher Costs*: More staff hours are needed for 1:1 training, which can increase operational costs.

However, in the real world, staff limitations and time constraints mean that not all training can be conducted this way. If you have the staff, go for it for all the training! But if staff time is limited and you have many users needing to be trained, consider some of the other options for user training detailed in the next few sections.

Laser Cutter Training

General Information

Before you can get access to the laser cutter in the lab, you first need to be in a Bioengineering class which requires laser cutting as defined by the Lab Director. Next, you will need to complete a two-stage process to be completely trained on the laser. The two stages CANNOT be completed on the same day.

Training certifications last through May of each year. Users will need to retrain after each May.

Stage 1

Note: This procedure is identical to that used by MEAM. If there is a discrepancy, please inform the Bioengineering Lab Staff immediately. You can use your object drawing to gain access to MEAM's RPL lab.

1. Use OnShape or SolidWorks to create a model for this shape. You must add a couple of other things to your part. Use Arial font with 18 point size (for SolidWorks) and Allerta Stencil font with the largest dimension of 1.25" (for onshape) to:

   - Write your **Full First Name** centered on the top left-hand corner, 0.25" away from the top edge, and your **Full Last Name** in the bottom left-hand corner, 0.25" from the bottom edge.
   - Write your **PennCard Number** centered on the top right-hand corner, 0.25" away from the top edge.
   - Centered underneath your PennCard Number, put your Penn Card Version. This is the two-digit number following your ID number and should generally start with a '0'.
   - Write your **PennCard Expiration Date** centered on the bottom right-hand corner, 0.25" away from the bottom edge. Note: Expiration date is NOT the day that you will be attending the cutting session, or "today's" date...

2. Once you are done with your model, **convert it into a 2D file.**

   - Use the following color code:
     1. Set the outline of your shape to RED
     2. Set your name and PennCard info to YELLOW
     3. Create a GREEN hatch for the raster area in the middle
   - In the end, your DWG file should look like this image.

3. Review the **"BE Labs Laser Cutter Usage" Document**.

4. Save the file onto a flash drive or to your Penn Engineering Google Drive (NOT S DRIVE)

5. ONLY once you have completed steps 1 through 4 completely, you may go to the lab during normal or extended hours (with your flash drive or SEAS Google Drive). Request to the lab staff (wearing lab lanyards) that you would like your training object cut on the laser cutter. Lab Staff will confirm that you have reviewed the laser cut usage document and that your part is correctly colored- if your knowledge seems lacking or your part is incorrectly colored, you will be asked to review the document and/or color code your file and return at a later date.

When you complete the training, Lab staff will review your part, and if you are successful, enter your successful completion of stage 1 into the laser cutter access list

Figure 6-6. *Sample image for laser cutter training (Available at:* `https://belabs.seas.upenn.edu/equipment-inventory/equipment/laser-cutter-training`*)*

Self-Paced Courses with Quizzes

Self-paced courses are a great way to train many users in little time. Depending on how the courses are set up, users could even complete the self-paced training at home in the middle of the night while the MakerSpace is closed and be able to access the relevant tools and equipment as soon as the MakerSpace opens again.

Pros of Self-Paced Courses:

1. *Flexibility*: Users can complete the training at their own pace and on their own schedule, making it convenient for those with busy or irregular schedules.

2. *Scalability*: A large number of users can be trained simultaneously without the need for multiple staff members.

3. *Cost-Effective*: Reduces the need for staff involvement in the training process, which can save on operational costs.

4. *Resource Availability*: Frees up staff to focus on other tasks and responsibilities within the MakerSpace.

Cons of Self-Paced Courses:

1. *Limited Personalization*: The training is not tailored to the individual user's skill level or specific needs, which might result in less effective learning for some users.

2. *Lack of Immediate Feedback*: Users may not receive immediate answers to their questions or corrections for their mistakes, potentially leading to misunderstandings.

3. *Engagement Challenges*: Some users might struggle to stay motivated and engaged without the structure and accountability of in-person training.

4. *Verification Needs*: Additional steps might be required to ensure users have actually completed the training and understood the material, such as follow-up assessments or practical demonstrations.

Compared to in-person staff-guided training, self-paced courses save user and staff time. Typically, only a quick verification or validation of training completion is required, which often involves simply checking if the user has completed training by looking up the log of trained users.

In-Person On-Demand Quizzes

In-person on-demand quizzes are an effective way to ensure users understand and retain the training material before using the MakerSpace tools and equipment. These quizzes can be administered quickly by staff members whenever a user is ready to be assessed, providing immediate feedback and reinforcement of key concepts. For instance, after attending a group workshop on CNC milling, users could take a quiz to test their knowledge of safety protocols and machine operations before being granted access to the equipment.

Pros of In-Person On-Demand Quizzes:

1. *Immediate Feedback*: Users receive instant feedback on their performance, allowing them to quickly understand and correct any mistakes.

2. *Interactive Assessment*: The quiz can be tailored to address specific areas of concern, ensuring a thorough understanding of the material.

3. *Enhanced Accountability*: Users are more likely to take the training seriously, knowing they will be quizzed on it immediately.

4. *Personalized Attention*: Staff can provide additional support and clarification based on the user's quiz performance.

Cons of In-Person On-Demand Quizzes:

1. *Time-Consuming*: Administering and grading quizzes can be time-consuming for staff, especially if the number of users is high.

2. *Resource Intensive*: Requires the availability of staff to administer the quizzes, which can be a constraint during busy periods.

3. *Potential for Anxiety*: Some users may feel anxious about being tested, which could affect their performance and overall learning experience.

4. *Logistical Challenges*: Coordinating quiz sessions can be challenging, especially if users have varying schedules and availability.

Compared to self-paced courses, in-person, on-demand quizzes provide a more interactive and immediate form of assessment, ensuring users have a solid understanding of the training material before they proceed. However, they require more time and resources from staff, which can be a limitation in a busy MakerSpace environment.

Training Expiry and Renewal

Training expiry and renewal is an important mechanism to ensure that users maintain up-to-date knowledge and skills in a MakerSpace, particularly when operating complex or potentially hazardous equipment. Under this system, users are required to renew their training at regular intervals, such as every six months or annually, depending on the tool or process. For example, a user who was trained on a laser cutter a year ago might need to retake a brief refresher course or pass a re-certification quiz to continue using the machine. This approach helps ensure that users remain competent and aware of any new safety protocols or updated equipment features.

Pros of Training Expiry and Renewal:

1. *Ensures Ongoing Competence*: Regular renewal helps ensure that users maintain their skills and knowledge, reducing the risk of accidents or equipment misuse.

2. *Adapts to Updates*: Users stay informed about any changes or updates to equipment, software, or safety protocols that may have occurred since their initial training.

3. *Reinforces Learning*: Periodic renewal reinforces the training material, helping users retain important information over time.

4. *Quality Control*: Helps the MakerSpace maintain high standards of safety and equipment use, as only those current in their training can access certain tools.

Cons of Training Expiry and Renewal:

1. *Time-Consuming*: Users must allocate time to renew their training, which can be inconvenient, especially for those who use the MakerSpace infrequently.

2. *Administrative Overhead*: Managing and tracking training expirations and renewals requires additional administrative effort, including maintaining records and notifying users.

3. *Potential User Frustration*: Some users may find the renewal process burdensome, particularly if they feel confident in their skills and knowledge.

4. *Resource Demands*: Depending on the frequency and format of the renewal process, it may place additional demands on staff and resources, particularly if in-person components are required.

Compared to one-time training, training expiry and renewal provides a mechanism to ensure that users' knowledge and skills remain current, contributing to a safer and more efficient MakerSpace environment. However, it requires careful management and can be seen as an added hurdle for users, particularly if the renewal process is not streamlined.

Timing of Training

The timing of training sessions and how they are spaced out is a critical factor in ensuring effective learning and retention for users in a MakerSpace. Properly timed training can help users retain information better and feel more confident in their abilities. For instance, a new user might first receive an introductory session on basic safety and tool operation, followed by more advanced training sessions after they've had some time to practice and become familiar with the space. Spacing these sessions out over a few weeks allows users to absorb and apply the knowledge gradually, reducing the likelihood of overwhelm and improving long-term retention.

Research on cognitive load theory suggests that the brain has a limited capacity for processing new information. For example, after two or three intense training sessions, users might struggle to absorb and retain additional information, especially if the sessions cover complex or technical material. It's also important to account for mental and physical fatigue, particularly in a hands-on environment where users are learning to operate machinery or tools.

When planning training sessions in a MakerSpace, it's important to consider how many sessions a user can effectively complete in one day. While it's tempting to maximize efficiency by scheduling multiple sessions back-to-back, there's a risk of diminishing returns if users are overloaded with information. Cognitive fatigue can set in, leading to decreased attention, retention, and overall learning effectiveness.

Learning skills as they are needed is a good way to space out training; however, sometimes users feel that everything is needed at once. Staff should keep an eye out for such users and encourage them to slow down.

Training Enforcement

Training requirements are meaningless without enforcement. All users, whether trained or untrained, should be made aware of which tools or equipment require training for operation. Floor tape, child gates, or any other form of visual marker or physical barrier can be used to demarcate spaces in a MakerSpace that require different levels of training to access. For example, laser cutters can be kept in a separate room with a low gate that requires proper training to access. Be mindful to make sure that no physical barriers obstruct emergency egress paths and end up adding to risk rather than removing it. When in doubt, use simple, non-obstructive measures such as bright, large font signage and floor tape.

The unique features of a MakerSpace might need to be emphasized when enforcing training. Sometimes users feel that because they might have trained somewhere else, they do not need training in the current space. Staff should stay firm, recognizing that the processes and safety protocols are different for different places, and users should respect these requirements.

Digital enforcement mechanisms can further support training requirements. Implementing RFID-based access control, where only trained users have the ability to activate or unlock certain machines, ensures that unqualified individuals cannot use restricted tools. Badge systems and digital logging can track when and how often equipment is used, providing insight into usage patterns and potential risks.

Additionally, a certification system can be introduced to formalize training enforcement. Users can receive a digital or physical certificate after completing training, which must be presented before accessing restricted equipment. Regular refresher courses and re-certifications ensure that users maintain competency over time, particularly for high-risk tools.

Mentorship programs can also play a crucial role in training enforcement. Pairing newer users with experienced makers for an initial period ensures hands-on guidance and oversight. Encouraging a culture of peer accountability helps reinforce training expectations organically, reducing reliance on direct staff intervention.

Running the MakerSpace

Running a MakerSpace requires careful planning, efficient systems, and consistent execution to ensure smooth operations and high user satisfaction. A well-run MakerSpace must balance the upkeep of equipment, the management of consumables, the organization of workspaces, and the training of staff, all while supporting the users. By incorporating tools such as Standard Operating Procedures (SOPs), internal websites for knowledge management, and task management software like Notion, MakerSpaces can create a sustainable operational model that supports both day-to-day functions and long-term growth.

Policy Definitions

A successful MakerSpace requires well-defined policies that govern access, safety, equipment use, and community conduct. These policies serve as the backbone of operations, ensuring that users understand their responsibilities while helping staff maintain a safe, efficient, and welcoming environment. Without clear guidelines, inconsistencies in enforcement and misunderstandings among users can create unnecessary risks and operational challenges. By establishing structured policies, MakerSpaces can foster a culture of responsibility, inclusivity, and shared ownership of the space.

One of the most fundamental policy areas concerns access and membership. It is essential to define who is eligible to use the space, whether it is open exclusively to students and faculty, to the general public, or to industry partners. Membership policies should clearly outline the different tiers of access, including any required training, pricing structures, and user privileges. Additionally, access control mechanisms, such as keycard systems, check-in procedures, or restrictions for minors, must be established to prevent unauthorized use and ensure security.

Beyond access, safety and risk management policies play a critical role in preventing injuries and protecting users from potential hazards. These policies should mandate safety training before users operate any equipment, especially high-risk tools such as CNC machines, laser cutters, or welding stations. Requirements for personal protective equipment (PPE), such as safety glasses, gloves, or respirators, should be explicitly stated and enforced. Emergency protocols—including fire safety procedures, first-aid station locations, and incident reporting guidelines—must also be clearly communicated to all members.

Policies regarding equipment use and maintenance ensure that tools and machinery are used responsibly and remain in working condition. Some equipment may require users to complete certification programs before gaining access, and policies should outline the training and approval process. For high-demand machines, reservation systems may be necessary to prevent monopolization and ensure fair access. Additionally, users must be aware of reporting procedures for malfunctioning or damaged equipment, as well as their responsibilities for keeping machines clean and operational.

To maintain a positive and collaborative environment, community guidelines and a code of conduct should be clearly defined. These policies set expectations for respectful interactions between members, staff, and visitors, promoting inclusivity and preventing harassment or discrimination. Establishing a structured process for conflict resolution ensures that disputes are handled fairly and efficiently. MakerSpaces thrive on a culture of collaboration, and a well-enforced code of conduct helps sustain a welcoming and productive atmosphere.

Legal and liability policies are also necessary to protect both users and the MakerSpace itself. Many spaces require users to sign liability waivers acknowledging the risks associated with using specialized equipment. Additionally, MakerSpaces should establish protocols for managing insurance coverage, intellectual property concerns, and external partnerships. In cases where the MakerSpace hosts sponsored research or collaborative industry projects, policies regarding ownership of ideas, designs, or prototypes should be clearly outlined to avoid disputes.

Finally, space usage and cleanliness policies help maintain an organized and functional workspace. Users should be required to clean their workstations after use, properly store materials, and follow designated procedures for reserving work areas. Enforcing cleanliness is important; otherwise, a space can quickly become a mess and no one will take responsibility, and it can overly burden the staff. If the MakerSpace allows after-hours access, policies should specify eligibility criteria, security measures, and staff oversight requirements. Additionally, spaces that host private events, classes, or rentals should have clear guidelines on scheduling and usage fees to prevent conflicts.

By establishing and enforcing these policies, MakerSpaces create a structured yet flexible environment where users can safely explore, innovate, and collaborate. Periodic reviews of policies, along with opportunities for user feedback, help ensure that guidelines remain relevant and adaptable to the evolving needs of the MakerSpace community. Clear communication and consistent enforcement are key to maintaining a space that is not only functional but also inspiring and inclusive for all who use it.

Operating Hours

Establishing well-defined operating hours is a critical component of managing a MakerSpace effectively. The right schedule ensures accessibility for users while balancing staff availability, security considerations, and overall resource management. Whether a MakerSpace operates on a fixed schedule, extended hours, or even 24/7 access, careful planning is required to maintain functionality, safety, and financial sustainability.

When determining operating hours, several factors must be considered. User demographics play a major role in shaping the schedule. University-affiliated MakerSpaces often cater to students and faculty, necessitating later evening or weekend hours to accommodate academic schedules. Conversely, community-based or corporate innovation spaces may align more closely with standard business hours. Peak usage times should also be analyzed, as most MakerSpaces experience higher demand in the evenings and on weekends when users have more free time. Staffing availability is another key concern. The space must be open when trained staff or volunteers can provide oversight and technical assistance, particularly for high-risk equipment. Additionally, security and safety considerations should factor into scheduling, especially for spaces that allow late-night or early-morning access. If unstaffed hours are considered, MakerSpaces must implement keycard entry systems, security cameras, or restricted access to hazardous tools.

Different models of operating hours influence staffing and facility management. A fixed business-hour model, such as 9 AM–6 PM, ensures that trained personnel are always present, but it may limit access for students or professionals who prefer to work outside traditional hours.

An extended-hour model, running from early morning to late night (e.g., 7 AM–11 PM), provides greater flexibility but requires staggered staffing shifts or student workers to provide coverage. Some MakerSpaces even adopt a 24/7 access model, allowing pre-approved users to enter the space at any time. However, 24/7 access demands a robust infrastructure of security and liability management, including RFID-based entry, strict user certification, and limitations on the types of equipment available during unstaffed hours.

Beyond regular hours, MakerSpaces often need to reserve specific time blocks for specialized activities. Dedicated training sessions, such as safety certifications or new user orientations, may require scheduled hours outside of general member access. Academic institutions and community spaces frequently block off time for workshops and classes, ensuring structured learning opportunities without interference from general use. Additionally, scheduled maintenance windows are essential to keep machines in good working order while minimizing disruptions.

Regardless of the chosen operating model, clear access policies must be in place to manage entry and usage effectively. Some MakerSpaces require users to check in at the front desk or scan an ID upon entry to track facility usage. In spaces with extended or off-hours access, certain high-risk areas, such as CNC machine bays or laser-cutting stations, may be restricted to staffed hours only. Guest policies should also be established, defining whether visitors are allowed and under what supervision requirements.

As user needs evolve, MakerSpaces must be flexible in adjusting their hours over time. Regular user surveys and feedback can help identify demand for extended hours, while digital check-in data provides insights into peak and underutilized periods. Some MakerSpaces experiment with trial periods of extended access to determine whether expanded hours should become permanent.

Ultimately, operating hours must strike a balance between accessibility, staffing resources, and safety. A well-planned schedule ensures that MakerSpaces remain welcoming and functional while maintaining security and sustainability. Regular evaluations and flexibility in scheduling allow the space to evolve alongside its growing community, ensuring that it continues to meet the needs of makers, students, entrepreneurs, and hobbyists alike.

Managing High-Volume Equipment and Supply Usage

Equipment that is incredibly popular among users is one of the most difficult things to manage in a MakerSpace. It requires careful planning to ensure smooth operation and accessibility for all users. One approach is to grant users direct access to the equipment, fostering a sense of trust and responsibility. However, this requires thorough training and adherence to safety protocols to prevent misuse or damage. Alternatively, implementing a proxy system where users must go through staff to access equipment can provide better oversight and control, ensuring that only qualified individuals use the machines. This approach still requires the end user to be trained, but it does prevent any untrained individuals from accessing equipment.

Implementing reservation systems (see Table 6-6 for a summary), such as Google Calendar or Clustermarket (https://clustermarket.com/), can streamline the process of equipment usage, allowing users to book time slots and avoid conflicts. Using Google Calendar is often straightforward and user-friendly, providing easy integration with existing Google accounts and accessibility across various devices. Its simplicity and widespread familiarity make it an attractive option for many MakerSpaces. However, it may lack some advanced features specifically tailored for equipment booking and management, such as tracking equipment usage history or setting usage limits. On the other hand, Clustermarket offers more specialized tools for managing equipment reservations, including detailed scheduling, user authentication, and usage analytics. While this can lead to more efficient management and better data-driven decision-making, the platform may come with a steeper learning curve and potentially higher costs compared to the free-to-use Google Calendar. Choosing the right reservation system depends on the specific needs and resources of the MakerSpace, balancing ease of use with the need for detailed management capabilities.

More recently, as libraries have moved into MakerSpaces and equipment lending, library software tools have adapted accordingly. Springshare, a company that provides services for libraries, provides great software tools through its LibCal package (`https://www.springshare.com/libcal/`). This one-stop software package can support equipment reservations, room and seat reservations, and event support. The same system can also support scheduling training and even advising support.

Finally, the National Institute of Standards and Technology in the United States has developed an open-source application called NEMO (`https://github.com/usnistgov/NEMO`) which is specific to lab management. This is a powerful tool; however, some programming skills are needed to implement it.

Table 6-6. *Summary of Different Digital Reservation Tools*

Feature	Google calendar	Clustermarket	LibCal	Nemo
Primary focus	General scheduling	Lab equipment and resource management	Room/ equipment booking, event scheduling	Makerspace equipment tracking and usage
Equipment booking	General event booking	Yes, specific to lab equipment	Yes, general equipment	Yes, specific to Makerspaces
Inventory management	No	Yes, for lab consumables	No	No
Reporting and analytics	Basic event analytics	Detailed equipment usage and billing reports	Usage reports for spaces/ equipment	Detailed usage reports
User permissions	Limited	Extensive access control	Basic access control	Extensive control and certifications
Maintenance tracking	No	Yes, for lab equipment	No	Yes, maintenance and safety
Event/ workshop support	Yes	No	Yes	No

(*continued*)

Table 6-6. (*continued*)

Feature	Google calendar	Clustermarket	LibCal	Nemo
Cost recovery/ billing	No	Yes, built-in	No	Yes, based on equipment usage
Support	Standard Google support	Dedicated support for labs	Library or institutional support	Dedicated support for makerspaces
Security and compliance	Standard Google security protocols (2FA, encryption)	Compliance for lab operations, GDPR compliance	Library and academic institutional compliance	Compliance for makerspaces, equipment training verification
Shared calendars	Yes, easy sharing	Yes, can share resources/ equipment	Yes, for spaces and events	Yes, for equipment and teams
API access	Yes, Google API	Yes, for integrations with other tools	Yes, API access for customization	Yes, API for custom Makerspace integration
Mobile app	Yes, available on Android and iOS	No dedicated app, but web-accessible	Yes, mobile-responsive web interface	No dedicated app, but web-accessible

(*continued*)

Table 6-6. (*continued*)

Feature	Google calendar	Clustermarket	LibCal	Nemo
Customization	Limited (color coding, reminders)	Customizable booking systems, time slots, user roles	Configurable space and equipment booking	Customizable based on makerspace needs, certifications, and roles
Integration with other tools	Google Workspace tools (Drive, Gmail, Meet)	Integration with lab management systems, billing software	Integration with institutional systems like Active Directory	Integration with Makerspace systems, safety compliance software

Perhaps the most difficult aspect of these types of systems is tying them directly to the piece of equipment. For example, if you reserve a tool, there is nothing stopping someone from taking the tool or keeping it longer than initially requested. While badging systems and systems that can control power access to devices exist, these can be expensive. While NEMO provides an open-source option, implementation can be complex. Often, the best option is a combination of trust and regular staff check-ins. Unfortunately, at times, consequences have to be defined, such as revoking access to those who do not follow the rules.

Inevitably, in any MakerSpace, some pieces of equipment will be in higher demand than others. For example, for academic MakerSpaces, as deadlines approach, the tools required for the deadline will be in high demand. This is where reservation systems and enforcement will be critical.

The Massachusetts Institute of Technology (MIT) developed a remarkable web portal and app to manage equipment usage and access called Mobius (`https://project-manus.mit.edu/mobius`). This system shows equipment in different locations and its current availability. In effect, it can make a large area, in this case, the entire MIT campus, into a single MakerSpace.

However, managing high-volume equipment requires more than just a simple reservation system. Many successful MakerSpaces employ RFID or barcode tracking systems to monitor tool checkouts and returns, reducing the risk of misplaced or lost equipment. Automated maintenance alerts can also be used to ensure that tools receive regular servicing, preventing unexpected breakdowns. In addition, implementing a user-level certification system, where access to high-risk equipment is granted only after completing training, can prevent accidents and misuse. This system can be further strengthened by integrating badge access or digital logging, which ensures that only qualified users operate certain tools.

Beyond equipment, managing high-use consumables and small tools is equally important. Items such as hand tools, adhesives, screws, sandpaper, and disposable supplies like gloves and masks should be regularly stocked and inventoried. A structured system for tracking supply levels—such as a digital inventory system or a simple sign-out sheet—ensures that materials remain available when needed. Establishing designated tool return areas and providing labeled storage bins can reduce loss and disorganization. The goal of the structured system is to make returning any equipment or supplies as simple as grabbing them. Users of the space should know exactly where to return the supplies and equipment (see Figure 6-7 below for an organized supplies return approach).

Figure 6-7. *Drawer organization to help with returning supplies*

Standard Operating Procedures (SOPs)

A well-organized MakerSpace relies on Standard Operating Procedures (SOPs) to ensure consistency, minimize errors, and create a safe and efficient environment (see Table 6-7 for a sample summary). With a diverse range of equipment—each requiring specialized handling—clear SOPs serve as essential guides for both staff and users. They help prevent misuse, improve safety, and ensure that the space remains accessible and functional, even in the face of staff turnover. This is particularly important in university-affiliated spaces where student workers may only be employed for short periods. By institutionalizing knowledge through documented procedures, MakerSpaces can maintain operational continuity, reducing the burden on experienced staff to constantly retrain new employees.

SOPs cover a wide range of tasks, from basic housekeeping duties to complex equipment maintenance. At the most fundamental level, they help ensure that daily opening and closing procedures are followed, keeping the space clean, organized, and ready for use. These procedures also extend to equipment management, providing clear instructions on how to operate tools like 3D printers, CNC machines, and laser cutters, as well as outlining preventive maintenance schedules to avoid unexpected

267

breakdowns. In addition to operational efficiency, SOPs play a vital role in safety management, detailing emergency shutdown procedures, protective equipment requirements, and response plans for incidents such as fires or injuries.

Another important area covered by SOPs is training and certification. Many MakerSpaces require users to complete safety training before gaining access to specialized equipment. These procedures define the steps for new user orientations, machine certifications, and ongoing skill development. Without well-defined training SOPs, MakerSpaces risk inconsistent enforcement of rules, leading to unsafe working conditions and improper tool usage.

Beyond equipment and safety, inventory and material management is another key area where SOPs contribute to efficiency. Clear guidelines for restocking supplies, tracking tool borrowing, and properly disposing of waste materials ensure that the space remains functional and sustainable. MakerSpaces that work with hazardous materials must also have procedures in place for handling, storing, and disposing of chemicals and electronic waste in compliance with safety regulations.

To be effective, SOPs must be regularly reviewed and updated. As technologies evolve and user needs change, procedures must be refined to reflect the latest best practices. Digital documentation, such as online SOP repositories or QR-code-linked instructions at workstations, can make these guidelines easily accessible to users, reducing confusion and improving adherence. Staff should conduct periodic audits to identify gaps in existing SOPs and gather user feedback to improve clarity and usability.

Table 6-7. *Overview of SOP Types*

SOP category	Function	Key elements
General facility procedures	Ensures the space is clean, organized, and ready for users	Opening/closing procedures, housekeeping, guest policies
Equipment use and maintenance	Prevents misuse and ensures proper functionality of tools and machinery.	Machine operation guides, maintenance schedules, repair reporting
Safety and emergency protocols	Reduces risk and prepares staff and users for emergencies.	PPE requirements, emergency shutdowns, fire and injury response
User training and certification	Standardizes training to ensure users are qualified to operate equipment safely.	New user orientations, machine certifications, skill development
Inventory and material management	Ensures tools and materials are available and used responsibly.	Restocking supplies, tool borrowing, waste disposal policies

Internal Website for Knowledge Management

One of the most effective ways to manage the complexity of a MakerSpace is by developing an internal website that acts as a central repository of information. This digital platform allows staff to easily access and update important documents, SOPs, troubleshooting guides, and maintenance logs. An internal website is particularly valuable in environments where multiple classes, projects, and users converge, each requiring different tools and setups. For example, if a piece of equipment frequently encounters user errors, the internal website can host a dedicated troubleshooting guide to minimize downtime and reduce the need for staff intervention. Additionally, it can serve as a one-stop hub for onboarding new employees, consolidating all the necessary training materials in one place. The internal website can also link to external resources such as equipment manuals, safety data sheets, and supplier websites, making it easier for staff to handle any situation that arises during a shift. With the availability of many free resources, developing these sites are quite straightforward. For example, Google offers "Google Sites" which is free to use; Notion is another tool which is becoming popular as well.

This type of knowledge management is vital in a MakerSpace that serves a broad and dynamic group of users. Because each user may have different needs depending on their project, centralizing knowledge helps staff address questions more efficiently. It also encourages a proactive approach to problem-solving, empowering staff to find solutions independently rather than relying on senior personnel to intervene. Additionally, the website can include task lists, equipment scheduling tools, and forms for tracking user requests, further streamlining operations.

Task Management

Task management software like Asana, Monday.com, and Notion are another critical tool in maintaining a MakerSpace. These tools allow for the centralization of daily, weekly, and monthly tasks, helping staff manage their responsibilities in an organized and time-efficient manner. By using this type of software, MakerSpaces can assign specific tasks to staff members, set deadlines, and track the progress of each job. This level of organization is crucial in environments where many small tasks—like cleaning, restocking, and basic equipment maintenance—can quickly accumulate, if not managed properly. The software can also include checklists that cover daily opening and closing procedures, weekly equipment inspections, and consumable restocking schedules, ensuring that no detail is overlooked. Some of these tools can be expensive, but task management can often be handled through spreadsheets. Notion works well for this, as it can also be used as an internal website.

Interestingly, it can be helpful to have a physical checklist (see Figure 6-8 for a sample). This might seem odd in a high-tech world, especially in a MakerSpace, which is often at the cutting-edge of technology. However, when cleaning and organizing, you don't want your electronics to get dirty. Instead, a sheet of paper can be used. This can, of course, lead to excess waste, so a good solution is a laminated sheet of paper where staff can mark off the completion of tasks using a dry-erase marker. In addition, photos of how an area should look can be placed at each location so staff can easily gauge what needs to be put away.

Morning

- ❏ Turn on all the lights including projects room and the display in the office.

- ❏ Open all the window shades at noon.

- ❏ Arrange each station and remove stuff that does not belong. Make sure trash cans, biohazard bins, kim wipes (1 for every two stations) and paper towels (1 roll near each sink) are evenly distributed. Restock kim wipes when 5 are left.

- ❏ Put away clean and dry glassware on both sides of the lab and both sides of projects room. Check the trough for scoopulas + spoons. Make sure each sink has alcohol, hand soap, dish detergent and DI water.

- ❏ Remove extraneous stuff from the lab entrance and **unlock the main door** by the opening time.

- ❏ Make sure everything looks like the pictures (unless labeled).

- ❏ Check 3D printers for any completed prints + update the 3D print sheet.

Evening

- ❏ Arrange each station and remove stuff that does not belong. Make sure trash cans, biohazard bins, kim wipes (1 for every two stations) and paper towels (1 roll near each sink) are evenly distributed. **Push in chairs and put stools under tables**

- ❏ Make sure each station has a hand sanitizer and isopropanol bottle at each end.

- ❏ Clean white boards AND **turn off projector, even if it seems off**.

- ❏ Straighten up projects room (follow pictures)

- ❏ Remove extraneous stuff from far sides of lab and wipe down scales (follow pictures).

- ❏ Put away clean and dry glassware on both sides of the lab. Make sure each sink has alcohol, hand soap, dish detergent and DI water. If sinks have anything in them, wash and put on racks.

- ❏ Ensure that there is paper towels at 3 poles near sinks (main lab) and 2 above sinks in projects room (restock when 3 are left [435])

- ❏ Ensure S&M glove bins have 2 packs each and L & XL have 1 pack each.

- ❏ Remove extraneous stuff from the lab entrance and lock the main door.

- ❏ **Turn off all the lights** including projects room and the office display and lock the office door.

Weekends

- ❏ **Sat:** Organize green bins in location 265 (ensure **all** materials in **correct** bins).

- ❏ **Sun:** Organize green bins in location 283 (except crimping tools) (ensure **all** materials in **correct** bins)

Figure 6-8. *Sample checklist*

Facilities Management

Facilities management focuses on the ongoing upkeep of the space, covering cleanliness, safety compliance, utilities, and general maintenance. Unlike space organization, which involves planning the layout and structure of a MakerSpace, facilities management is about maintaining the infrastructure and ensuring that everything remains in good working condition for daily operations.

One of the key responsibilities in facilities management is cleanliness and waste management. A MakerSpace can quickly become cluttered with leftover materials, dust, and debris from various fabrication processes, making it essential to implement daily cleaning protocols. Staff and users should be responsible for keeping workstations clean, returning tools to their designated locations, and disposing of materials properly. Trash and recycling systems should be clearly labeled, with separate bins for general waste, recyclables, and hazardous materials such as batteries, solvents, or electronic components. Spaces that involve resins, adhesives, or chemical work must follow proper hazardous waste disposal procedures to comply with environmental and safety regulations.

Beyond cleanliness, safety and compliance play a critical role in facilities management. MakerSpaces must adhere to fire safety regulations, emergency preparedness protocols, and health standards to ensure a safe working environment. Fire extinguishers should be placed in visible, accessible locations, emergency exits must be clearly marked, and evacuation plans should be posted in multiple areas. In spaces where laser cutting, soldering, or chemical work occurs, adequate ventilation systems are necessary to prevent harmful fumes from accumulating. A well-maintained first-aid station and eyewash station should be available, along with clearly posted emergency contact information for staff and first responders.

Infrastructure and utilities maintenance is another ongoing responsibility that ensures the MakerSpace remains fully operational. Electrical systems should be inspected regularly to ensure that outlets, circuit breakers, and surge protectors are functioning correctly and can handle the power demands of high-use equipment. Proper lighting is also crucial, especially for precision workstations, where task lighting may be necessary. Climate control systems, including HVAC and air filtration, help maintain comfortable working conditions and prevent temperature-sensitive materials from degrading. Regular plumbing maintenance ensures that sinks, eye wash stations, and any cooling systems function without issues.

Facilities management is an ongoing process that requires continuous monitoring and proactive maintenance. Regular safety audits, equipment inspections, and cleaning schedules ensure that the space remains welcoming and functional for all users. By focusing on cleanliness, safety, and infrastructure upkeep, MakerSpaces can continue to provide an efficient and safe environment where users can create, experiment, and innovate without disruption.

Low-Cost Automation for MakerSpaces

With the breadth of equipment and opportunities in MakerSpaces, automation of operations can be incredibly useful. Some examples include loaning equipment, reserving equipment, or, in the case of K-12 and University MakerSpaces, purchasing individual supplies from a provided budget. Automation can also include a verification to confirm that the user has been properly trained to borrow a tool or use equipment. The George H. Stephenson Foundation Educational Laboratory & Bio-MakerSpace at the University of Pennsylvania developed a number of custom systems to support its mission to encourage innovation (Figure 6-9). These systems work in tandem with workflows that the university students already use, making user adoption straightforward. In addition, the systems use open-source software and can be quickly customized. These systems, in turn, free up staff time to focus on the user experience.

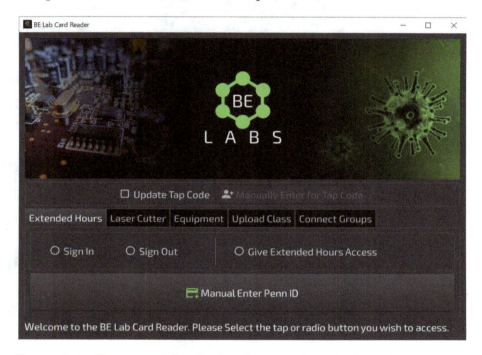

Figure 6-9. *Homepage for the Stephenson Foundation Bio-MakerSpace's access management system*

Access control for various equipment is maintained through ID cards. Users trained in using a piece of equipment are entered into the system, and a script verifies the card tap against the list (Figure 6-10). Staff can see if the user is approved, not approved, or even blacklisted (user is denied access pending review by the MakerSpace's senior staff).

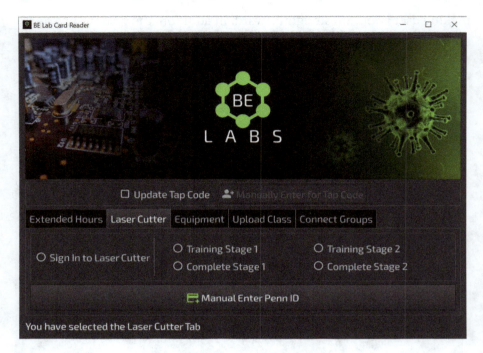

Figure 6-10. *Laser cutter training management*

The same system can also be used to track borrowed equipment and supplies, either as an individual or as a group (Figure 6-11).

Figure 6-11. *Equipment borrowing page*

Another example is with 3D printing. Students submit a print using a Google Form, and a Raspberry Pi monitors the spreadsheet. The Pi can send confirmation emails, update calendar events, and notify users when prints start and finish.

Finally, with supply ordering, students submit the order using a Google Form, and a Raspberry Pi can send automated emails when the order is placed and received.

The beauty of these automation types is that they use the supplies and skills taught in MakerSpaces! Indeed, the cost of the entire system is that of the Raspberry Pi running it. These systems are also customizable depending on the needs of the MakerSpace, rather than trying to force a workflow around a pre-bought system.

Maintaining Equipment and Supplies

Equipment longevity and performance are central to fostering an innovative and sustainable MakerSpace. Just as regular maintenance keeps tools in peak working condition, maintaining an adequate stock of materials ensures that users can complete their projects without unnecessary delays. Neglecting equipment upkeep or failing to replenish essential supplies can lead to inefficiencies, increased costs, and frustration among users.

Without regular maintenance, even the most advanced tools can quickly deteriorate, affecting both the quality and speed of work. Equipment downtime is costly, not only in terms of repairs but also in lost productivity for users who depend on those tools. A well-structured preventive maintenance schedule is essential to avoid these issues. This involves regular inspections, cleaning, calibration, and software updates, all of which should be integrated into the MakerSpace's overall task management system.

Similarly, supply management is a critical aspect of MakerSpace operations. Running out of key consumables—such as 3D printing filament, laser-cutting materials, adhesives, or electronic components—can bring projects to a halt and negatively impact the user experience. A stock tracking system, whether digital or manual, should be in place to monitor inventory levels and trigger timely restocking. Additionally, MakerSpaces must consider material storage solutions, waste management, and supplier relationships to ensure a steady supply of high-quality resources.

This section will outline the best practices for maintaining equipment and managing inventory, including preventive maintenance strategies, warranty considerations, and the consequences of neglecting essential tools and supplies. By integrating structured maintenance routines and efficient supply management, MakerSpaces can create a seamless and reliable environment where users can focus on innovation without unnecessary disruptions.

Regular Equipment Checks

For equipment longevity, weekly checks are not just recommended—they are essential. A regular inspection protocol ensures the equipment remains calibrated and functional, which is especially crucial for high-use machines like 3D printers, laser cutters, and PCR thermocyclers. Whenever you acquire a new piece of equipment, pay attention to the service details, typically listed in the back of the manual. Develop checklists tailored to each piece of equipment that include cleaning, calibration, and testing. This ensures that tools remain in working condition, while also providing a teaching moment for users to understand the importance of preventive care. Each piece of equipment will have maintenance tasks that need to be completed on different timescales, for example, there may be tasks to complete after every use, and there might be tasks to complete after every 100 or so uses. A sample maintenance routine for a 3D printer could look something like Table 6-8 below.

Table 6-8. *Sample Maintenance Routine for a 3D Printer*

Frequency of maintenance	Task
Each use	Clean the print bed after each print to remove any residue or debris
	Check for any filament blockages in the nozzle
	Inspect moving parts such as the extruder gears and guide rails to ensure they are free of dust or obstructions
	Wipe build plate with 90% Isopropanol to ensure proper bed adhesion

(*continued*)

Table 6-8. (*continued*)

Frequency of maintenance	Task
Weekly	Calibrate the print bed to ensure it is level for accurate prints
	Clean the nozzle thoroughly using a wire brush or a cleaning filament
	Lubricate the guide rails and other moving components to reduce friction and wear
Monthly	Check belts for tension and wear, adjusting or replacing them as needed
	Inspect the cooling fan for dust buildup and clean it to ensure optimal airflow
	Update firmware to ensure the printer is running the latest software version, improving performance and adding new features
Quarterly	Perform a deep clean of the printer, including internal components
	Replace any worn parts such as the extruder, belts, or the build plate (if necessary)
	Review print quality and recalibrate if consistent issues are noticed over time

Staying up-to-date with these regular maintenance checks is very important as you cannot control how every user decides to use the equipment. Some users may treat the tools and equipment diligently and with great care, while others may be more laissez-faire in their handling. As such, performing these regular maintenance tasks will ensure that every piece of equipment gets the care it needs to prolong its working life. An additional suggestion to help ensure maintenance tasks are followed, especially ones that must be done after each use of the equipment, is to incorporate visual aids near the piece of equipment. Images of well-maintained machines, alongside tools that have clearly been neglected, can illustrate the direct impact of maintenance on equipment functionality. These can help staff quickly identify when maintenance is needed and what steps are required. Furthermore, creating a culture where users are responsible for minor upkeep—such as cleaning machines after use or replacing consumable items—can reduce the overall workload on staff and prolong the life of the equipment.

Extended Warranties and Calibration Services

In any MakerSpace, where high-end equipment like laser cutters, 3D printers, PCR machines, and CNC machines are shared among multiple users, it can be wise to invest in extended warranties. These warranties can be crucial in minimizing both downtime and unexpected repair costs. Extended warranties offer a safety net for frequently used equipment, particularly in an educational setting where user experience levels vary widely. However, extended warranties should not be the sole strategy for maintaining optimal equipment performance—scheduled calibration and servicing must also be part of the maintenance plan.

Many machines and equipment, especially those used for high-precision tasks, require regular calibration to maintain accuracy. For instance, in mechanical-based MakerSpaces, CNC machines, laser cutters, and Instron Test Systems rely on precise alignment to function effectively. These machines might drift out of alignment without scheduled calibration, potentially invalidating results and disrupting course or project work. In biological and chemical-based MakerSpaces, micropipettes rely on finely tuned pistons to operate, where even a slight misalignment can drastically impact the desired final volume. Regular calibration helps ensure that the equipment continues to perform to specification, reducing project errors and wasted materials risk.

In addition to regular internal maintenance, many types of equipment—particularly those covered by extended warranties—require professional servicing at set intervals. Often offered by the manufacturer or certified technicians, these services go beyond routine cleanings and checks. They typically involve disassembling critical parts, assessing wear on components, and applying specialized tools for recalibration or part replacement that may not be available to general users. Failing to adhere to scheduled professional servicing for machines like PCR thermocyclers or 3D bioprinters can result in voided warranties or long-term operational failures.

Extended warranties and scheduled maintenance should work hand-in-hand. While extended warranties can help cover the cost of unexpected repairs, they are most effective when paired with a proactive approach to maintenance, which includes both user-led calibration routines and manufacturer-recommended servicing. By maintaining a strict schedule for both internal maintenance and professional servicing, MakerSpaces can ensure that equipment not only remains functional but also operates at peak efficiency throughout its life cycle.

Consequences of Poor Maintenance

The success of a MakerSpace relies heavily on the seamless functionality of its equipment. When machines and tools are not properly maintained, the consequences are far-reaching, affecting not only current projects but also future innovation, user safety, and the MakerSpace's reputation as a reliable resource. Poor maintenance can result in costly downtime, inefficient project execution, and potential safety hazards, all of which could be easily avoided with regular upkeep.

One of the immediate and most visible consequences of neglecting maintenance is the decline in equipment performance. Precision instruments like laser cutters, 3D printers, and CNC machines are susceptible to wear and misalignment. For example, a laser cutter with a dirty lens or set of mirrors will produce imprecise or incomplete cuts, wasting material and time. By failing to perform routine checks and cleaning, MakerSpaces expose themselves to the risk of repeated errors and inconsistent output, undermining the quality of student projects and research.

Another consequence of neglecting equipment maintenance is that the likelihood of sudden breakdowns increases, leading to significant downtime. In an environment where tools like PCR machines or laser cutters are shared among dozens of users, any period of downtime can disrupt workflows and cause project delays. This delay causes one of three outcomes for users of the Makerspace: either they have to take their business elsewhere to complete the project on time, or they have to scramble to find alternatives that are less than ideal for the project, or they have to delay their project until the piece of equipment is operational. All of these outcomes degrade the user's trust in the MakerSpace. Moreover, when key equipment is offline, it places a strain on the rest of the MakerSpace's resources. Other machines may become overloaded with increased demand, hastening their wear and amplifying the impact of poor maintenance across the board. This cascading effect can dramatically reduce the MakerSpace's overall efficiency.

Furthermore, neglecting to perform routine maintenance often leads to more severe damage over time, transforming minor repair needs into major expenses. For example, failing to lubricate the rails of a 3D printer or neglecting to replace worn belts can lead to part misalignments or motor strain, which may ultimately require costly repairs or even full replacement of components. The financial implications of deferred maintenance extend beyond immediate repair costs. When equipment is prematurely damaged, it often needs to be replaced sooner than its expected lifespan. MakerSpaces, especially those operating on tight budgets, may struggle to replace expensive tools if maintenance is ignored. Extended warranties, while helpful, typically only cover unforeseen breakdowns, not the result of chronic neglect. This distinction forces the MakerSpace to bear the financial burden of replacing the piece of equipment.

Maintaining Supplies and Inventory Management

In a MakerSpace environment with diverse equipment and consumables, effective management requires a centralized system that tracks both the maintenance schedules of each machine and the inventory levels of materials. It is recommended to develop a master document—a comprehensive, living maintenance and inventory sheet, which not only lists the specific servicing tasks for each piece of equipment but also includes detailed timelines for restocking consumables. By implementing such a system, MakerSpace staff can distribute responsibilities efficiently and ensure that no single person is overburdened. Each staff member can be assigned specific equipment or materials to oversee, ensuring that regular maintenance and inventory management occur without overwhelming any individual. This system also fosters accountability and consistency, as each task is clearly documented and traceable. In addition to manual checks, this sheet can be paired with automated tracking tools, such as barcoding or digital inventory systems, to streamline processes and prevent stockouts or delays in maintenance. Examples can include weekly check on the stock of paper towels or pipette tips. On the other hand, frequently used items, such as resistors might need to be checked more frequently. When supplies run out, items can be refilled from a stock, but the stock's supply also needs to be maintained. In an ideal situation, no user should ever have to find that the supply of something is finished.

An example of this type of document can be seen in Figure 6-12. This example uses a color-coded scheme to assign specific tasks to designated employees. Days of the week are listed on the top, and supply checks are in squares below. Rather than rearranging the squares based on staff changes, tying a staff to a color was easier to do. In addition, staff which have to do more involved tasks can be balanced by giving another staff person for that day many lighter tasks. For example, an involved task might be checking the stock of 50 or more different electrical components which would be represented by one square. Lighter tasks might be to check the stock of calipers. This type of process works well with shift-based staff.

Also, similar to the section on Task Management, here as well, an electronic version may not work as well as a laminated paper copy, since one doesn't want to risk getting a phone or tablet dirty.

Monday	Tuesday	Wednesday	Thursday	Friday
Restock/order stripettes main lab: 2 packs of 10mL and 1 pack of 25 mL [122]; 3 packs each of 10 mL and 25 mL [186/187] Stock in [358]	Refill alcohol bottles (X5), hand soap bottles (X5), and dish soap bottles (X5) next to each sink, regardless of the current level - fill them up	Check/Order gloves: 12 boxes of M, 8 boxes of S, 7 each boxes of L&XL total (1 can be open)	Thoroughly clean scales with 70% Isopropyl [111/161]	Wipe down two side tables with cleaning solution (move equipment first - all equipment except sharker-incubator, instrons, computers, & printer)
Restock/order stripettes in projects room [356]: 1 box of 2mL, 5mL, 10mL, 25mL, & 50mL. Stock should be 1/2 full in [356]	Restock/order bleach bottles under each sink [Stock in 353]	Check/order syringe supply [172]: 1 mL, 3 mL, and 60 ml; 1 bin + unopen box of each	Clean labeling/weighing drawers [112 & 170/171]; at least 5 rolls of tape & 5 markers on each side	Thoroughly Clean inside of microwaves [111/152]
Restock/order mol bio area in projects room [207-222]: lots of everything; 2 aluminum foils, 2 serans, 4 autoclave tapes; fill culture tube drawer with stock on shelf [205] and 96-well plates in [206] - reorder stock when is low	Restock/order 70% isopropyl - make sure there are at least 8 unopened in the flammable cabinet [LOC 226]	Check/order transfer pipettes - 2 boxes [193]; consolidate to one box if possible	Restock/order weighing supplies [112/170]: weighing dishes (both large and small), weigh papers; scopulas; metal spoonulas; metal scoops, aerosol duster; Stock in [430]; order if low	Stock/resupply stationary drawer: 2 scissors, staples in staplers, 2 rulers, some pens and pencils [194/195]
Check/order scalpels (4 FULL boxes), razor blades (2 boxes), biopsy punches (2 boxes each of 0.8 and 0.1 mm) [218]	Check supply of banana cables [272] - inform FT staff if low	check supply of all batteries [433]- order if low	Check/order parafilm on two sides of room above microwave; Stock in [167] - Order if less than 3 in stock	Check supply of Whatmann filter paper [312]- (at least 10) - order if low
Check/order first aid [357]. Stock in [355], order if stock is low	Autoclave Pipette Tips and divide up on two sides of lab if necessary - check for empty or close to empty boxes in drawers. Stock in [204]. Order more tips if necessary: > 3 packs per size should be available.	Restock/order cuvettes in main lab [119/166] - each side should have two boxes of 4ml; Drawer 119 should also contain two 1.5mls. Stock should contain 2x of 1.5 mL and 4.5 mL 500 pk boxes; label all boxes with size ("4.5 mL" or "1.5 mL") on whatever side is visible when stored. Stock in [368]	Wipe down area around all five sinks with cleaning solution	Ensure there are 4 packs of paper next to the printer [More paper can be found in BE office (by 5 pm)]
Check/order TAE buffer [367] (one open and one unopened box)	Organize and Check stock of Mechanical components / small drawers [404]); Restock/reorder if low	Fill/order 15ml & 50 ml tube drawers [121/168]; stock in [361]; Fill regardless of current level	Run eye washes [X2] for 1 minutes	Perform maintenance procedure on both laser cutters
Restock electronic equipment in projects room [273-283]: six small breadboards, six large breadboards; ~50-100 protoboards Stock of breadboards in [409, 278]	Organize and Check stock of electrical components / small drawers [414]); Restock/reorder if low - first look for excess above stock	Refill wires [265] with stock in 405. Order if stock is low	Check full glass disposal bins and prepare for pick-up if full, and replace. Order if new boxes are low	check supply of arduinos [409] - at least 10 - inform FT staff if low
Organize (and make neat) drills and other mech stuff in projects room[251-269]; Make sure location 259 (tape) has four roles of electric tape, four of masking, one duct tape, four roles of surgical tape, and several roles of plumbers tape.	Make sure auto-pipetters and supplies are stocked and organized properly in projects room [376]	Restock/order cuvettes in Projects Room [375] - there should be four 1.5mL and four 4mL boxes, all labeled in front. Stock in [368]. Order if stock is low.	check stock of small & large breadboards - stock in [403] & [282] (minimum of10 of each); inform full time staff if low	Check supply of calipers [257] - at least 7 - inform FT staff if low
Check supply of glues: super glue (x5); epoxy (x3), acrylic glue (x2), regular glue (x2), hot glue sticks (one pack), hot glue guns (x3), rubber cement (x2) [262]; stock in [428] (have the same number of each in stock)	Check supply of strippers (20) and pliers (15), diagonal cutters (15), needle nose pliers (15) [265]. If low inform FT staff.	Check supply of 3d printing material - make sure at least 2 spools of each color available (vanilla, gray, black) [360] - order if low	straighten up and check supply of laser cutting material 1/8" MDF (minimum of about 80 sheets), 1/4" acrylic (20 sheets each of clear and black), 1/8" acrylic (20 sheets each of clear, black, and amber) - reorder if low	Grease the 3D Printer rods (White Lithium Grease [135])
Check electronics waste bins - if HALF full, dispose contents in Levine 166C	If laser cutter waste bin is HALF full, empty; keep resusable pieces	Check supply of EEG/ECG/EMG electrodes [422]- order if 1/2 full	Check stock of 3D printer beds [412], at least 4	Restock jumpers [283] and check stock [402]- order if stock is 1/3 full
Check supply of sandpaper [268]- order if <4 sheets	Run cleaning cycle on Nespresso	Fill isopropynol and hand sanitizer containers at the ends of each station	Clean and organize lab office	Reorganize Lab Coats - Make sure sizing is correct

Figure 6-12. *Sample task management matrix for employees*

In addition to real-time inventory tracking, it can be helpful to maintain a buffer stock of high-demand items in a separate location to ensure immediate availability during busy periods. This reduces the likelihood of project delays caused by out-of-stock items and allows for smoother operations during high-traffic times.

While we never wish to doubt the quality of work of our staff, it is easy to become complacent with supply checks, especially when some supply is not used for months on end. However, space managers need to keep an eye out because suddenly, when the item is needed, the supply might disappear. Consequently, regular spot checks should be planned by the senior staff of different items at different times.

MakerSpace Safety

MakerSpaces are hubs of creativity and exploration—but they also carry inherent risks. From high-speed tools to hazardous chemicals, from fire hazards to biological contamination, the potential for injury or damage is ever-present (Table 6-9 provides a summary). Ensuring a safe environment for all users is not a one-time checklist; it's an ongoing commitment that involves thoughtful design, diligent maintenance, consistent training, and a strong culture of responsibility.

Table 6-9. *MakerSpace Risks and Mitigation Strategies*

Type of risk	Examples	Primary sources	Mitigation strategies
Physical injuries	Cuts, burns, impact injuries	Hand tools, power tools, laser cutters, improper use	PPE (gloves, goggles), proper training, supervision, posted SOPs
Chemical exposure	Skin irritation, inhalation of fumes, toxic reactions	Paints, adhesives, solvents, resins, cleaning agents	MSDS documentation, fume hoods, gloves, respirators, chemical training

(continued)

Table 6-8. (*continued*)

Type of risk	Examples	Primary sources	Mitigation strategies
Biological hazards	Contamination, exposure to pathogens or biohazards	Wet labs, cell cultures, biological samples	Sanitation protocols, PPE (lab coats, gloves), containment practices
Fire hazards	Burns, equipment damage, facility damage	Lithium batteries, soldering irons, Bunsen burners	Fire extinguishers, training, material storage guidelines, electrical safety practices
Equipment failure	Unexpected movement, malfunction, tool breakage	Wear and tear, lack of maintenance, misuse	Scheduled maintenance, inspection logs, user reporting systems
Environmental risks	Slips, falls, respiratory irritation	Slippery floors, poor lighting, dust, fumes	Housekeeping protocols, adequate ventilation, signage, spill kits
User error	Improper tool use, unsafe behaviors	Inadequate training, lack of oversight	Orientation, tiered tool certification, clear consequences for violations

Risks Associated with MakerSpaces

The first step in creating a safe environment is recognizing the variety of risks present in a MakerSpace. Physical injuries—such as cuts, burns, or impact injuries—are the most common, and can result from something as simple as mishandling a pin or operating a laser cutter without proper supervision. Equipment failure, improper use, or lack of training can quickly escalate these risks.

Chemical injuries are also a concern. Even common supplies like glue, paint, or resin can cause harm through skin contact, inhalation of fumes, or accidental mixing of incompatible substances. More advanced spaces may use chemicals that require specific ventilation systems and adherence to Material Safety Data Sheets (MSDS). Similarly, biological MakerSpaces carry their own risks, including the need for sanitation protocols, containment practices, and biohazard disposal. MakerSpaces dealing with chemicals and biologics should have eye washes and safety showers, with appropriate signage (Figure 6-13).

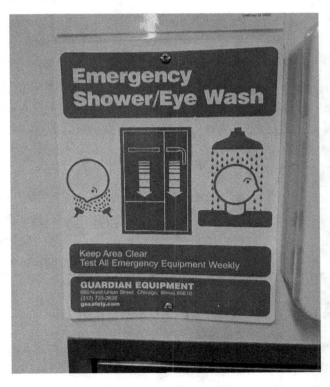

Figure 6-13. *Emergency shower and eye wash station sign*

Fire hazards are a constant threat in spaces that work with electronics, lithium-ion batteries, soldering equipment, and open flames such as Bunsen burners. Laser cutters, improperly ventilated 3D printers, and poorly stored flammable materials can all contribute to dangerous situations if not carefully managed.

Importantly, not all hazards arise from tools or materials—workplace conditions also contribute to risk. Slippery floors, inadequate lighting, poor ventilation, and improper tool storage can lead to preventable accidents. Even the most experienced users are vulnerable when conditions aren't properly maintained.

The Role of PPE and Training

Personal Protective Equipment (PPE) plays a central role in minimizing risk. Safety goggles, hearing protection, gloves, lab coats, and respirators are all common in MakerSpaces—and not just for high-risk zones. Something as routine as soldering or sanding warrants safety glasses and proper attire.

However, PPE only works when used correctly and consistently. Spaces must go beyond merely providing PPE—they must train users on why it matters, how to use it properly, and when it's required. Reinforcing this through signage, orientation, and staff modeling is essential. For example, placing safety glasses and hearing protection at the entrance to a woodworking area, or respirators near chemical workstations, creates physical reminders that build good habits (Figure 6-14).

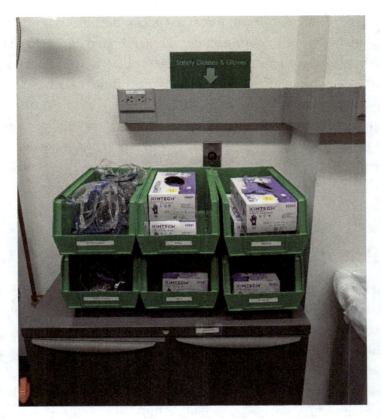

Figure 6-14. *Safety glasses and gloves location. Note that the sign was laser cut*

Training is a cornerstone of safety. All users should receive an introduction to space-wide safety expectations and be taught how to respond in case of fire, chemical exposure, or injury. Tool-specific training, described in detail in an earlier section ensures that users are only allowed to operate equipment when they've demonstrated understanding and competence. Even with training, supervision or buddy systems may be required for higher-risk equipment or for newer users.

Conclusion

As someone using a MakerSpace, you should take time to learn the systems that keep it running, follow safety protocols, use tools respectfully, and contribute to a culture of care since your awareness and participation help make the space better for everyone. As someone creating a new MakerSpace, you need to begin with a vision for how it will operate, recognizing that staffing, funding, safety, and maintenance are just as important as layout and equipment, while starting small, building smart systems early, and prioritizing community and culture from day one. As someone running an existing MakerSpace, you should use operational guidance to evaluate and strengthen your systems by revisiting staff roles, training, task management, maintenance routines, and safety practices while engaging your team and users in building a space that's not just functional but sustainable, inclusive, and inspiring.

Key Takeaways

- *Funding Models Must Reflect Mission and Users*: MakerSpaces can be sustained through subscriptions, one-time use fees, donations, institutional support, and sponsorships. Choosing the right blend depends on your goals and user base.

- *Staff Shape the Culture*: Staff aren't just tool experts— they're culture carriers. Hiring for curiosity, safety awareness, and community orientation ensures the space remains welcoming, functional, and resilient.

- *Structured Training Builds Trust*: Begin staff and user training with safety and operations, then layer in technical skill-building and specialization. Use a combination of in-person, self-paced, and hybrid formats to scale training efficiently.

- *Track Skills Across the Team*: Maintain a central record of who is trained on what, and to what depth. Balance your team so no expertise area is left unsupported.

- *Orient Users to Culture, Not Just Tools*: User onboarding is a chance to reinforce values like shared responsibility, respect for tools and others, and an inclusive environment. It sets the tone for everything that follows.

- *Enforce Training with Systems, Not Just Rules*: Make training enforcement visible—through signage, color-coded zones, or digital access control. Certification or peer mentorship ensures users are truly ready.

- *Create Resilient Operations with SOPs and Checklists*: Documented procedures—from daily opening to emergency shutdowns—help maintain continuity across staff shifts and high turnover, especially in university spaces.

- *Use Internal Websites and Task Management Tools*: Centralize operations with digital systems (e.g., Notion or Google Sites) that hold SOPs, training guides, checklists, and maintenance logs. It saves time and builds transparency.

- *Leverage Automation to Save Time*: Raspberry Pi-based systems or Google Form workflows can automate access, 3D print approvals, and supply requests, freeing up staff for high-value interactions.

- *Be Strategic with Operating Hours*: Align hours with user needs while managing staffing and safety. Off-hour access may require RFID controls, security cameras, and restricted equipment usage.

- *Manage High-Demand Tools with Reservations and Policies*: Equipment scheduling, user tracking, and badge-level access are key to ensuring fair use, preventing monopolization, and avoiding burnout—for tools and staff alike.

- *Maintain Equipment Like It's Part of the Team*: Preventive maintenance schedules, calibration, and even extended warranties protect against downtime. Clear visual guides can reinforce good habits after each use.

- *Inventory Systems Must Be Proactive, Not Reactive*: Use checklists, staff assignments, and color-coded tracking sheets to ensure consumables are stocked and tools are returned. Trust systems, not memory.

- *Safety Is a Daily Practice, Not a Poster on the Wall*: From PPE placement to emergency drills, safety must be woven into space design, culture, and expectations. Everyone owns it.

- *A Culture of Care Sustains the Space*: MakerSpaces thrive when users feel empowered and accountable—when they contribute not only ideas but also to cleanliness, tool upkeep, and mutual respect.

CHAPTER 7

Building a Maker Community

A MakerSpace is a hub of creativity, innovation, and learning. While having state-of-the-art machinery like 3D printers, laser cutters, or sewing machines is exciting, and as seen in the previous chapter, having a strong operational system is important, MakerSpaces' true potential lies in the hands of those who use them. The key to unlocking this potential is fostering a vibrant, engaged community around the space.

Creating a thriving MakerSpace community means bridging disciplines, forging connections, and empowering users. It's about offering programming and classes that make technology approachable, sparking curiosity across fields from engineering to art. It requires effective marketing to reach new audiences and virtual opportunities that extend the MakerSpace's impact beyond its physical walls. By encouraging entrepreneurship, the space can serve as a launchpad for ideas and innovation, while actively seeking user feedback ensures the MakerSpace evolves to meet the needs of its community.

This chapter explores strategies for building that community, highlighting the importance of collaboration, visibility, inclusivity, and user-centric design. After all, the tools in a MakerSpace are only as valuable as the ideas, projects, and people they support.

© Sevile G. Mannickarottu, Michael G. Patterson, and Carolyne Godon 2025
S. G. Mannickarottu et al., *Creating MakerSpaces*, Maker Innovations Series,
https://doi.org/10.1007/979-8-8688-1309-2_7

Building Community Through Collaboration

Encouraging collaboration is fundamental to building a strong community in a MakerSpace. Collaboration fosters innovation and problem-solving by bringing together diverse perspectives and ideas. When people from different backgrounds and disciplines come together, the potential for creative breakthroughs multiplies. Frequently, solutions to challenges in one area can be found by borrowing techniques or insights from another, and the cross-pollination of ideas often leads to unexpected and innovative outcomes.

One way to nurture both general and interdisciplinary collaboration is by organizing events and activities that encourage users to work together. Group workshops, creative challenges, or community projects can bring people with different skill sets and experiences into the same space, fostering connections and enabling them to learn from one another. For example, a woodworking enthusiast might discover new approaches by collaborating with someone experienced in electronics, or a textile artist might find inspiration in digital fabrication techniques.

These interactions create more than just innovative projects; they build a culture of openness and mutual support where users feel empowered to experiment and explore. By promoting communication, teamwork, and the blending of diverse talents, a MakerSpace can transform into a vibrant hub where innovation thrives—not just through the tools it provides but through the dynamic and interdisciplinary community it cultivates.

Programming and Classes

Creating an active, vibrant community within your MakerSpace is about fostering enthusiasm and curiosity through hands-on programs, classes, and events that bring people together to learn, create, and collaborate (Figure 7-1). The best way to get users excited about your MakerSpace is by offering interactive, hands-on experiences that cater to a wide range of interests and skill levels.

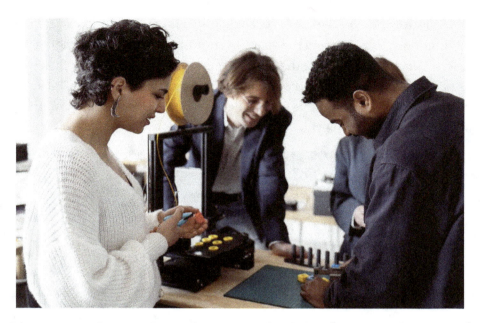

Figure 7-1. *Community event at a MakerSpace (Designed by Freepik)*

Classes and workshops are an effective means of creating community, can be geared toward beginners or advanced users, and cover a variety of Maker fields. Beginners, for instance, may enjoy a low-cost or free class that introduces them to using basic equipment like a sewing machine or completing a creative project, such as designing custom stickers. For those with more experience, consider offering a series of advanced classes, like a multi-part workshop on programming a Raspberry Pi to create a custom home-monitoring system for pets. This project might walk users through programming basics, connecting a camera module, and configuring software—all in a fun, collaborative environment. Depending on the structure of the MakerSpace, this could either be a free to low-cost event for the user where the MakerSpace supplies the necessary equipment for the user to borrow. All of the work for the project could be done in the MakerSpace. Alternatively this could be an event where users pay a fee to be able to take the final device home.

Offering themed classes or seasonal projects can help build a calendar of rotating events, keeping the space lively and continuously engaging new users. For example, during the holiday season, a series of candle making (see Figure 7-2) workshops could not only draw in participants of all ages but also create a memorable experience that encourages them to return and explore other projects.

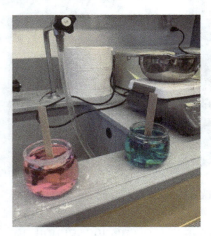 

Figure 7-2. *Photos from a candle-making event by the Stephenson Foundation Bio-MakerSpace at the University of Pennsylvania*

Hosting Events to Engage New Audiences

Events are a fantastic way to showcase the MakerSpace and attract people who may not have previously considered visiting. Hosting events like birthday parties, family Maker Days, or adult craft nights can make the MakerSpace feel like an accessible, inviting place. For instance, you might host a children's birthday event centered around building simple robotics or assembling crafts using the MakerSpace's tools, sparking a lifelong interest in STEM. Meanwhile, adults may enjoy a "DIY Night" where they can experiment with resin casting or woodworking furniture, socializing while they learn.

Regularly scheduled open houses or "Maker Mondays" give users a chance to explore the space, meet the staff, and ask questions, reducing any intimidation they may feel about using unfamiliar tools. These events also foster community interaction and generate excitement around what's possible within the MakerSpace. This could include events, such as making personalized stickers for your laptop (Figure 7-3).

Figure 7-3. *Custom sticker (top left) made for a laptop*

To enhance these events further, consider integrating themed workshops or collaborative projects. For example, during a family "Maker Day," you could organize a group activity like building a community art piece or designing a simple mechanical device that participants can contribute to and take pride in. For adult craft nights, introducing friendly competitions, such as who can design the most creative resin piece or construct the sturdiest mini furniture, can add an element of fun and engagement.

In addition, inviting local experts or artists to lead sessions can add credibility and variety to your events. These collaborations not only bring fresh perspectives but also build partnerships that extend the MakerSpace's reach into the community. Capturing highlights from these events—through photos, videos, or testimonials—and sharing them online or within the space can help sustain interest and encourage more people to participate in the future.

Showcasing User Projects and Success Stories

Highlighting the projects and achievements of users can go a long way in building a strong, engaged community. Sharing user stories—either through an online gallery, social media posts, or a dedicated area in the MakerSpace itself—gives recognition to the innovative work being done and inspires others to get involved (see Figure 7-4 for a sample of displayed work). For instance, a showcase of past projects might include photos of the user's Minimal Viable Products or first Ugly Working Prototype.

Figure 7-4. *Device created and now showcased, with a "Sponge Bob" theme, in a MakerSpace*

To further amplify the impact of these success stories, consider inviting users to give presentations or host workshops at the MakerSpace. These sessions can serve as inspiration and practical learning opportunities for others. Highlighting their journey—from ideation to execution—can provide invaluable insights and encouragement. Additionally, offering these individuals speaking points to share their challenges, breakthroughs, and lessons learned will make their stories even more relatable and motivating.

Marketing

Marketing your MakerSpace is a great way to both attract new users and keep the current user community strongly engaged. Marketing a MakerSpace can take many forms and reach users through many different channels. It can be as simple as branding a MakerSpace consistently and encouraging users to show off their completed projects within the facility on a "wall of fame" display or as complex as creating a full social media strategy and carefully monitoring engagement analytics. Ultimately, the best marketing approach for a MakerSpace will depend on your budget and what you want to achieve. Table 7-1 provides various marketing channels and corresponding examples.

Table 7-1. *MakerSpace Marketing Channels*

MakerSpace marketing channel	Example
Social media	Instagram, Facebook, TikTok, YouTube, LinkedIn
Content marketing	Blog, email newsletter, podcast
Local partnerships and collaboration	Schools, businesses, local events
Search engine optimization (SEO)	Local search optimization, blogging
Paid advertising	Google Ads, Facebook/Instagram Ads, local publications
Community engagement and events	Open houses, workshops, maker fairs
Referral and loyalty programs	Referral discounts, member rewards
Public relations and media outreach	Press releases, media coverage
Word-of-mouth and testimonials	Member stories, community events

(continued)

Table 7-1. (*continued*)

MakerSpace marketing channel	Example
Influencer and blogger partnerships	Maker influencers, local bloggers
Local advertising	Flyers, posters, direct mail
Website and online booking	Online reservations, user-generated content
Community boards and forums	Reddit, Meetup

Marketing Within the MakerSpace

To effectively market your Makerspace, it's important to not only reach people outside the space but also create a compelling experience within it. By fostering a sense of community, celebrating creativity, and showcasing the work being done in your space, you can build a strong internal culture that naturally attracts attention.

One of the most powerful ways to market your Makerspace is by highlighting the incredible work being done by your members (see earlier section). Consider dedicating a "Wall of Fame" where you feature completed projects, whether it is a 3D-printed sculpture, a custom-built piece of furniture, or a hand-crafted gadget. Rotate the displayed works regularly to keep it fresh and exciting. You can also use display cases to showcase smaller or more intricate projects. This not only celebrates your members' creativity but also demonstrates the variety and potential of the tools and resources available in your space.

Everyone loves a freebie, and offering small, branded gifts can help leave a lasting impression. Instead of traditional promotional items like pens or notebooks, think about fun, creative alternatives. For example, you could give away small items made directly in your Makerspace, like keychains, custom-engraved wooden items, or 3D-printed trinkets (see Figure 7-5 for an example). These gifts not only serve as a reminder of the space but also showcase the capabilities of your equipment.

Figure 7-5. *Laser cut branded keychains given out at an event*

Another simple yet effective option is branded snacks, like M&Ms in custom packaging or stickers that visitors can slap on their laptops or water bottles (see Figure 7-6). These little touches reinforce your Makerspace's identity and make visitors feel appreciated.

Figure 7-6. *Various branding options. The left image are custom M&M candy; the right image is a sticker. Both represent the Stephenson Foundation Bio-MakerSpace at Penn Engineering*

A Makerspace isn't just for scheduled classes and workshops—it should also be a place where people feel comfortable hanging out and interacting outside of formal programming. Encourage members to visit casually, whether it's to brainstorm, socialize, or simply work on personal projects. Design the space with comfortable seating, a cozy lounge area, or even a café corner, if possible. Offering a laid-back, creative environment will help people feel more connected to the space and foster organic word-of-mouth marketing. A place where people want to spend time is a place they'll talk about to others.

Marketing Within the Broader Community

Building awareness and attracting new members to your Makerspace goes beyond just reaching your immediate audience—it's about embedding your space into the broader community. By leveraging word of mouth, advertising your offerings, and creating relationships with local institutions, you can expand your Makerspace's reach and impact.

Part of this is creating a strong digital presence, such as a website, as outlined in Chapter 5. This is the place to highlight events and activities, and all other advertising and marketing should direct to this site. Emotionally engaging photos or a video would be an effective tool on the front page of the site.

One of the most powerful and cost-effective marketing tools is word of mouth. When your members are passionate about the space, they become natural ambassadors. Encourage members to share their experiences with friends, family, and colleagues. Consider implementing a referral program that rewards members who bring in new people. Word-of-mouth thrives when people feel a personal connection to a place—so foster a welcoming, creative atmosphere where members feel inspired and excited to tell others.

To attract new users to your space, consistently advertise your programming and classes. Make sure your schedule is easily accessible both online and offline. Use local newspapers, newsletters, and community bulletin boards to spread the word about upcoming workshops and events. Additionally, social media ads targeting local community members can help increase visibility. Highlight the diverse range of classes offered—everything from 3D printing to woodworking to coding—to appeal to a broad audience. Offering "beginner-friendly" courses can also help attract people who may not yet be familiar with the idea of a Makerspace but are curious about getting started in a creative, hands-on environment.

Building relationships with local institutions—like libraries, schools, and townships—can help solidify your Makerspace as a valuable community resource. One effective way to engage administrators is by offering free workshops for local government or institutional staff. For example, invite township or university administrators to attend a workshop that showcases what your Makerspace has to offer. This not only familiarizes them with your space but also helps build allies who can advocate for your Makerspace when it comes to securing funding, partnerships, or other community initiatives. Providing hands-on demonstrations for local officials can show them the potential for collaboration, such as integrating your Makerspace into local education programs or community outreach projects.

Expand your presence by building partnerships with local schools, universities, and nonprofit organizations. Offer discounted or sponsored memberships to students or educational staff to encourage them to explore the space. You can also organize community-focused events or hackathons that bring together local talent from diverse sectors (education, technology, art). Partnering with local organizations for volunteer-driven projects or community outreach programs can also serve as a mutually beneficial marketing tool—while promoting your space, you're simultaneously giving back to the community.

Get involved in local community events by either sponsoring or participating. Whether it's a local fair, art show, or innovation expo, being present at these events allows you to network with a broader audience. Set up a booth or table to showcase the projects being worked on in your Makerspace. Engage directly with people, handing out informational flyers, free branded items, and offering a "join now" discount for new members. You can also host live demonstrations or short workshops at these events, giving people a taste of the creative work happening at your Makerspace.

Building connections with local media outlets, such as newspapers, radio stations, or TV networks, is another keyway to market your Makerspace. Reach out to local reporters to pitch stories about exciting events, notable projects, or special community initiatives happening at your space. A feature in a local newspaper or a segment on a local news show can bring significant visibility to your Makerspace, especially if you're hosting a high-profile event or collaborating with other community organizations. Local publications are often interested in covering stories about community-driven initiatives and can be valuable allies in spreading the word about your space.

Social Media and Online Marketing

In today's digital age, a strong online presence is crucial for attracting new members and engaging with your community. Social media, in particular, offers a powerful way to showcase the creativity and energy of your Makerspace while fostering a sense of connection among members. By maintaining a consistent online presence and encouraging active participation, you can build a vibrant digital community that mirrors the spirit of your physical space.

A consistent and active social media presence is a must. Platforms like Instagram, Facebook, TikTok, and YouTube provide an opportunity to reach diverse audiences and share the work being done in your Makerspace. To make it easy for people to find and engage with your space, ensure your handles are identical across all platforms (e.g., @ YourMakerspaceName). This consistency reinforces your brand identity and makes it easy for people to tag you when they share their work.

Encourage members to post pictures or videos of their projects, tagging your Makerspace in the process. People love showing off their creations, and by encouraging them to share and tag your space, you create organic, community-driven marketing. Rewarding posts that tag your space with likes, reposts, or shout-outs can increase member engagement and promote your Makerspace as a hub of creativity.

Brand consistency is key in online marketing. From your logo to your tone of voice, ensure your Makerspace's branding is consistent across all social media platforms. Your profile pictures, banners, and even the way you caption posts should reflect the same look and feel you've developed for your physical space.

This consistent identity helps make your Makerspace recognizable, whether someone sees your social media posts or walks into your physical space. Additionally, use brand colors, fonts, and messaging in your posts, stories, and ads to strengthen your identity and keep everything cohesive.

Social media offers a fantastic opportunity to showcase what happens behind the scenes in your Makerspace. Post photos or videos of members working on projects, tool demonstrations, or new equipment being installed. These posts humanize your space, showing it as a dynamic, creative environment that's more than just a place to work—it's a community. Also, by tagging the user, the user's broader community will be able to learn about the space.

Member spotlights are also a great way to highlight the diverse talents in your space. Share success stories, interviews, or time-lapse videos of a member's project coming to life. This not only gives recognition to your members but also shows potential users the kinds of projects they could work on when they join.

A thoughtful way to stay connected with your online community is by acknowledging special moments in the year. Holiday cards sent out via email or posted on social media are a personal touch that shows your Makerspace cares about its community. These cards can feature photos of members' projects, highlights of the year, or even behind-the-scenes shots of staff and members at work.

At the end of the year, consider posting a year-in-review recap. Showcase the best moments from the past year—highlighting your most popular workshops, major milestones, new equipment, or community events. This helps members reflect on the space's growth while also inspiring potential members to join. A well-designed year-in-review post can also be repurposed in your email newsletter or as a promotional piece for the following year.

For social media platforms which allow users to vote can be a fun method to engage with users. For example, the Stephenson Foundation Bio-MakerSpace (@PennBElabs) uses Instagram to have followers vote on fun things. For example, they have the staff rank candy, and based on the ranks, have users vote at the same time as the NCAA March Madness competition, to identity the most popular candy. The Bio-MakerSpace has done this for cookies, Disney movies, pasta, and all sorts of other things.

User-generated content is one of the most authentic and impactful forms of marketing. When people share their own experiences and projects, they're not just promoting your space—they're building trust and credibility. Encourage members to post their work, ideas, or projects with a branded hashtag (e.g., #MadeAt[YourMakerspaceName]) so you can easily track and repost their content. Feature the best content on your page to inspire others and build a sense of community.

You can also host social media challenges or contests that incentivize members to create and share content. For example, a 30-day DIY challenge, a themed project contest, or a "before and after" project transformation competition can generate excitement and foster engagement.

Video is one of the most engaging types of content online. Use platforms like YouTube, Instagram Reels, or TikTok to share quick tutorials, tips, and tool demonstrations. These videos don't need to be high-budget productions; even simple, well-shot content can be very effective. Show your members how to use specific tools, create basic projects, or introduce new features of your Makerspace. This type of video tool training can be part of the MakerSpace's repertoire which can provide users skills and in turn, also help advertise the space.

Live-streaming events, workshops, or Q&A sessions is another great way to engage your online audience in real time, making them feel like part of the action. This can also help promote upcoming in-person classes or events by creating buzz.

Don't limit your social media activity to just posting content—engage directly with your followers! Respond to comments, share user content, and interact with members of the community in real time. Social media is a two-way street, and the more you engage, the more you build a loyal following.

Consider using platforms like Reddit or Facebook Groups to join local or relevant Maker communities, where you can offer advice, answer questions, and share your space's offerings. You can also use Twitter to engage in real-time conversations or trending topics related to creativity, DIY, technology, and innovation.

While organic content is essential, paid social media ads can help you reach a wider audience. Facebook and Instagram ads can target specific demographics (e.g., age, location, interests) to bring in new members or promote events and classes. These ads can be highly effective when combined with visually appealing content, such as videos of projects or images of your Makerspace in action.

Virtual Opportunities

In an increasingly digital world, MakerSpaces can extend their reach and engage members through virtual opportunities. By embracing online platforms, MakerSpaces can offer diverse learning experiences, foster collaboration, and maintain a strong sense of community, even from a distance. Here are several strategies for creating impactful virtual MakerSpaces.

Virtual Classes for Teaching Software

Virtual classes are an excellent way to teach software skills, especially for tools commonly used in MakerSpaces. Platforms like Google Meet, Zoom, or Microsoft Teams can be utilized to host interactive sessions on CAD software such as OnShape, photo editing, and video editing tools. These classes can cater to various skill levels, ensuring that both beginners and advanced users can benefit. Consider incorporating screen sharing, step-by-step demonstrations, and live Q&A sessions to enhance engagement and learning outcomes.

Teaching Coding

Coding is a fundamental skill in the Maker community, and virtual platforms provide an ideal medium for teaching it. Classes can cover programming languages like Python, JavaScript, or Scratch, depending on the target audience. Hands-on coding projects, such as building simple games or automating tasks, can keep learners motivated. Tools like Replit, Google Colab, and GitHub allow for real-time collaboration and sharing of code, making virtual coding classes interactive and effective.

GatherTown and Virtual MakerSpaces

During the COVID-19 pandemic, platforms like GatherTown became popular for creating virtual spaces that simulate real-world environments. GatherTown allows users to interact in a virtual MakerSpace, complete with customizable rooms, shared screens, and collaborative whiteboards. While GatherTown is one example, the concept can be adapted to other platforms, serving as a template for creating an immersive virtual MakerSpace experience. These environments can host workshops, casual meetups, or even virtual Maker fairs. Figure 7-7 is an example of the George H. Stephenson Bio-MakerSpace digitally deployed in order to engage its users during the height of the COVID-19 pandemic.

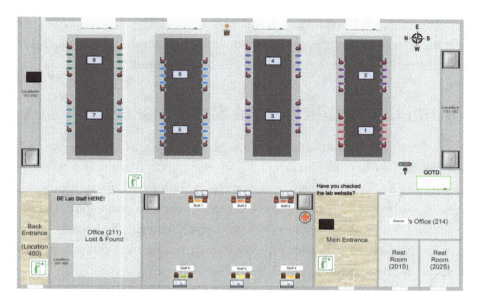

Figure 7-7. *Virtual representation of the George H. Stephenson Foundation Bio-MakerSpace during the COVID pandemic. This was created through GatherTown*

Zoom Support and Office Hours

Providing virtual office hours through platforms like Zoom can help members receive one-on-one support or troubleshooting assistance. This service can be invaluable for answering questions about projects, providing guidance on equipment use, or troubleshooting software issues. Scheduling regular office hours ensures members have access to expert help when needed, maintaining a high level of support and engagement.

Instant Messaging for Community Building

Instant messaging platforms like Slack or Discord can be used to foster ongoing communication and collaboration among members. These platforms allow for the creation of topic-specific channels, such as

#coding-help, #3D-printing, or #project-showcase. By encouraging members to share their projects, ask questions, and provide feedback, you can cultivate a vibrant and supportive online community.

Virtual Competitions and Showcases

Hosting virtual competitions and showcases can inspire creativity and innovation within your MakerSpace community. Challenges like a virtual hackathon, a CAD design contest, or a coding competition can motivate members to push their boundaries. Virtual showcases allow participants to present their projects to a broader audience, fostering a sense of accomplishment and community pride. Incorporate live voting or awards to increase engagement.

Resource Libraries and Tutorials

Create and maintain an online resource library with tutorials, project guides, and recorded webinars. This repository can be a valuable tool for members to access learning materials at their own pace. Platforms like YouTube or a dedicated section on your MakerSpace's website can host these resources. Regularly updating the library ensures it remains relevant and useful.

Maintain Branding on Virtual Platforms

Consistency in branding across all virtual platforms is crucial for reinforcing your MakerSpace's identity. Ensure your logo, color scheme, and tone of voice are reflected in all online materials, including your website, virtual class presentations, and social media channels. This consistency helps build trust and recognition, making your MakerSpace stand out in the digital landscape.

By leveraging these virtual opportunities, MakerSpaces can broaden their reach, support diverse learning styles, and create a thriving online community that complements their physical offerings. Whether teaching software, coding, or hosting virtual events, the key is to stay adaptable and responsive to the needs of your members.

MakerSpaces As Catalysts for Entrepreneurship

MakerSpaces have become integral to the entrepreneurial ecosystem, acting as incubators for innovation and community-driven progress. These dynamic environments provide entrepreneurs with access to state-of-the-art tools, collaborative spaces, and valuable networks. Through these resources, MakerSpaces enable individuals and teams to transform ideas into impactful ventures.

A Launchpad for Startups

MakerSpaces often serve as the birthplace for successful startups, demonstrating their role in enabling groundbreaking innovations. For example, Brianna Wronko, founder of HueDx (formerly GroupK Diagnostics), a venture focused on healthcare diagnostics, leveraged the George H. Stephenson Foundation Bio-MakerSpace's resources to prototype and test her product. Through experimentation and prototype development, she was able to secure funding to help her open her own office and laboratory. In the same manner, Strella Biotechnology, which developed technology for monitoring produce ripeness, took advantage of the same space. By offering access to advanced fabrication tools, 3D printers, and rapid prototyping equipment, MakerSpaces allow entrepreneurs to test and iterate their ideas without the prohibitive costs associated with traditional manufacturing.

These spaces also foster a culture of problem-solving and experimentation. Unlike conventional workspaces, MakerSpaces encourage iterative learning, where failures are seen as steps toward progress. This supportive atmosphere empowers startups to take calculated risks and explore innovative solutions. In the case of Strella Biotechnology, the founder, Katherine Sizov was able to leverage the educational tools and resources to learn the engineering skills needed to develop her product.

IP-Neutral Environments

A key feature of many MakerSpaces is their commitment to being intellectual property (IP)-neutral. This policy ensures that entrepreneurs and makers retain ownership of their creations, fostering a sense of trust and openness. The IP-neutral model eliminates barriers to collaboration, encouraging individuals to share knowledge, skills, and ideas freely. This exchange often leads to serendipitous breakthroughs, as diverse perspectives converge to tackle challenges. Rather than fighting to gain ownership or equity with a startup or new technology, the MakerSpace relinquishes this in order to encourage innovation and engagement.

For startups, this neutrality simplifies the path from concept to commercialization. Entrepreneurs can focus on building their ventures without concerns about ownership conflicts, allowing for smoother innovation and collaboration.

Regardless of the official "IP-neutrality" of the space, it would be in the interest of the MakerSpace to add a clause that entrepreneurs should consult their own attorney.

Building Community and Connections

One of the most significant benefits of MakerSpaces is their ability to build communities. These spaces attract a diverse group of individuals, including designers, engineers, artists, and entrepreneurs, creating an ecosystem rich in talent and ideas. For startups, this means access to potential co-founders, advisors, and collaborators who can help bring their visions to life.

MakerSpaces also serve as networking hubs. Entrepreneurs can meet investors, industry experts, and community leaders through events, workshops, and hackathons hosted by the MakerSpace. For example, partnerships with organizations like NextFab amplify these opportunities, providing additional resources and exposure. In fact, NextFab, which originated as a MakerSpace, developed and then spun off its own Venture Fund. These connections often lead to funding, mentorship, and strategic partnerships that are critical for scaling a venture.

Giving Back: Donations from Startups

Many startups that originate in MakerSpaces choose to give back, creating a virtuous cycle of support and growth. These contributions often come in the form of financial donations or volunteering time to mentor and train the next generation of makers and entrepreneurs. By sharing their experiences and insights, these alumni startups enrich the MakerSpace community and inspire new ventures.

Additionally, these success stories help build the MakerSpace's reputation, attracting more entrepreneurs and resources. This reciprocal relationship strengthens the ecosystem, ensuring its sustainability and continued impact.

Talent Recruitment and Development

For startups, MakerSpaces are ideal environments for recruiting talent. The diverse pool of skilled individuals within these spaces includes engineers, designers, fabricators, and creative thinkers who are deeply engaged in hands-on problem-solving. Entrepreneurs can identify and hire team members who are not only technically proficient but also aligned with the innovative and collaborative culture of their startup.

Furthermore, MakerSpaces provide opportunities for skill development through workshops, training sessions, and collaborative projects. These programs equip members with the tools and knowledge needed to excel in entrepreneurial ventures, creating a pipeline of talent ready to contribute to startup success.

A Platform for Branding and Community Engagement

Beyond tangible resources, MakerSpaces help startups build their brands and connect with the local community. By participating in MakerSpace activities and showcasing their projects, entrepreneurs position themselves as innovators committed to solving real-world problems. This visibility not only attracts customers and investors but also strengthens ties with the community.

MakerSpaces themselves benefit from these success stories. Each startup that emerges from a MakerSpace becomes a testament to the space's impact, enhancing its reputation and appeal. This mutual branding effort reinforces the MakerSpace's role as a hub for innovation and entrepreneurship.

Expanding Networks Through Partnerships

MakerSpaces often form strategic partnerships with external organizations, expanding the resources available to their members. Collaborations with groups like NextFab exemplify how these networks can benefit entrepreneurs, providing access to additional tools, specialized expertise, and funding opportunities. These partnerships also expose entrepreneurs to new markets and audiences, increasing their chances of success.

Driving Local Economic Development

The impact of MakerSpaces extends beyond individual startups to the broader community. By fostering entrepreneurship, MakerSpaces contribute to job creation, economic growth, and technological advancement in their local areas. They serve as engines of innovation, attracting talent and investment that benefit the entire region.

User Feedback

A thriving MakerSpace community depends on understanding and responding to the needs of its members. Gathering user feedback is an essential part of this process. Feedback not only helps improve the physical space and available tools but also ensures that the community's activities align with its members' interests and goals. Table 7-2 shows how to effectively gather and utilize feedback in your makerspace.

Table 7-2. *Summary Table on User Feedback*

Method	Description	Purpose	Notes
Surveys	Online or paper-based questionnaires	Broad input on tools, programming, and services	Include open-ended questions for deeper insights
Suggestion box	Physical or digital place for anonymous feedback	Continuous input and privacy	Regularly review and display notable suggestions
Community meetings	In-person or virtual group discussions	Open dialogue and consensus-building	Schedule regularly; consider breakout groups

(*continued*)

Table 7-2. (*continued*)

Method	Description	Purpose	Notes
Informal conversations	Casual interactions with staff	Real-time feedback, often more candid	Train staff to listen and report themes
Feedback wall	Visible space for sticky notes with ideas or comments	Transparent and community-driven suggestions	Rotate prompts to keep it engaging
Interviews	One-on-one conversations with members	Deep insights from diverse perspectives	Use for targeted improvement or programming ideas
Follow-up communication	Updates to users about changes made based on feedback	Build trust and demonstrate responsiveness	Use newsletters, posters, or social media
Pilot programs	Test small-scale implementations of new ideas	Gather more feedback before full rollout	Useful for evaluating new tools or classes

Why Feedback Matters

Feedback serves multiple purposes. It provides vital information for decision-making by highlighting what is working well and what requires improvement. This guidance helps in making informed decisions about tools, resources, and programming. Additionally, feedback fosters trust and engagement within the community. When members see their input leading to meaningful changes, they feel valued and more connected. Moreover, feedback promotes inclusivity by ensuring diverse perspectives are considered, making the makerspace relevant to a broader audience.

Methods for Collecting Feedback

There are many ways to collect feedback effectively. Surveys, either online or on paper, offer a structured method to gather insights from a large number of members. Including open-ended questions allows participants to share unique ideas, such as suggestions for new tools or equipment. Suggestion boxes, whether physical or digital, provide an anonymous way for members to express their thoughts. Community meetings, held in person or virtually, offer a platform for open discussions about members' experiences and ideas, fostering a collaborative atmosphere.

Informal conversations between staff and members can yield valuable insights through casual exchanges, often uncovering nuanced feedback. A feedback wall within the makerspace provides a visible space for members to post suggestions, complaints, or praise using sticky notes, creating a transparent feedback loop. Additionally, conducting one-on-one interviews with a diverse range of members offers deeper insights into their specific needs and experiences, adding a personal touch to the feedback process.

Turning Feedback into Action

Once feedback is collected, it is essential to turn it into actionable steps. Reviewing and categorizing feedback regularly helps identify patterns and prioritize areas for improvement. Communicating the resulting changes to members reinforces the value of their input and builds a stronger connection between the community and the makerspace. Posting updates about new initiatives or enhancements inspired by user feedback demonstrates that contributions are being taken seriously. Implementing changes on a trial basis and gathering further feedback allows for refinement and ensures successful adoption. Recognizing members whose ideas lead to significant improvements further fosters a culture of collaboration and innovation.

Tips for Effective Feedback Processes

To make feedback processes effective, it is crucial to keep them simple and accessible to all members. Regular feedback collection should become an integral part of the makerspace's operations, ensuring that the community remains responsive and adaptive. Maintaining an open-minded attitude toward constructive criticism encourages meaningful growth and development, strengthening the community as a whole.

Conclusion

As someone using MakerSpaces, you should take advantage of diverse opportunities by attending events, trying new tools, and sharing your experiences to contribute to community growth while providing feedback to help improve the space and support its continued evolution. As someone thinking of starting a MakerSpace, you need to remember that community-building is as important as setting up the physical environment, requiring you to develop engaging programming, inclusive marketing, and accessible virtual opportunities since the combination of these three pillars will attract and retain a diverse user base. As someone running an existing MakerSpace, you should focus on fostering a culture of collaboration and innovation by routinely evaluating your events, marketing, and user feedback to ensure that the MakerSpace remains a dynamic and welcoming environment.

Key Takeaways

- *Collaboration and Inclusivity*: Foster a culture where users from all backgrounds and disciplines feel encouraged to share ideas and work together.

- *Engaging Programming*: Offer diverse, hands-on classes and events that cater to a variety of skill levels and interests to attract and retain users.

- *Community Engagement*: Host events and build partnerships with local organizations to establish the MakerSpace as a valuable community resource.

- *Showcase Achievements*: Highlight user projects and success stories to inspire others and build a sense of community pride in the MakerSpace.

- *Effective Marketing*: Use both online and offline strategies to promote your MakerSpace, leveraging user success stories and community partnerships.

- *Virtual Opportunities*: Expand your reach through online classes, virtual events, and collaborative platforms to ensure accessibility to your MakerSpace to all.

- *Support for Entrepreneurs*: Provide resources, mentorship, and networking opportunities to help innovators turn their ideas into tangible outcomes.

- *User Feedback*: Actively gather and act on feedback from your MakerSpace members to align your offerings with the needs of the community.

- *Continuous Improvement*: Regularly update tools, programming, and policies based on evolving user needs and emerging technologies.

CHAPTER 8

Final Thoughts

As we conclude our exploration of MakerSpaces, we will now reflect on the lessons learned from the previous chapters. The journey through the previous chapters has revealed MakerSpaces as not just physical spaces equipped with tools but as dynamic ecosystems where ideas flourish, communities grow, and transformative projects are born. This chapter ties together these insights, emphasizing the key principles and practical strategies to ensure MakerSpaces thrive as hubs of innovation, learning, designing, and inventing.

The Essence of MakerSpaces

From their origins as shared spaces for crafting and learning to their modern incarnations as we know them, MakerSpaces have evolved immensely to meet the diverse needs of their communities. Chapter 1 introduced MakerSpaces as places that democratize access to resources and inspire creativity. Whether in libraries, schools, universities, or community centers, these spaces provide a platform where all individuals can explore, create, and learn without the barriers of cost or access to specialized equipment. The core philosophy of MakerSpaces revolves around inclusivity, collaboration, and sharing the joy of making.

The history of MakerSpaces, as discussed in Chapter 2, showcases their deep-rooted connection to human ingenuity and collaboration. From Renaissance guilds to modern co-working labs, the spirit of communal

S. G. Mannickarottu et al., *Creating MakerSpaces*, Maker Innovations Series, https://doi.org/10.1007/979-8-8688-1309-2_8

learning and skill-sharing remains a cornerstone of these spaces.
By embracing this heritage, MakerSpaces continue to serve as melting
pots for ideas, fostering interdisciplinary innovation. These spaces are
particularly effective in breaking down barriers between traditional
disciplines, creating environments where engineers, artists, scientists, and
entrepreneurs can work together side by side.

In many academic settings, MakerSpaces also serve as bridges
between education and innovation. They enable learners to apply
theoretical knowledge in practical settings, making learning both engaging
and impactful. By fostering a hands-on approach to learning, MakerSpaces
cultivate problem-solving skills and encourage users to think critically
about their projects and objectives.

Diverse Fields of Making

Chapter 3 highlighted the breadth of Maker fields, encompassing arts
and crafts, electronics, mechanical design, and emerging areas like
bioengineering and culinary arts. Each of these fields brings unique
tools, techniques, and cultural elements to MakerSpaces, enriching their
diversity and appeal. For instance, arts and crafts spaces often serve as
gateways for beginner Makers, offering a tactile introduction to making
with tools, equipment and techniques that are often more familiar
to members of the broader community. Culinary MakerSpaces are
another type of gateway MakerSpaces that may be appealing to a wider
audience. These spaces can be platforms for experimenting with new
flavors, techniques, and sustainable food practices. Conversely, high-tech
Maker fields like robotics or molecular biology push the boundaries of
innovation, enabling users to tackle complex challenges with cutting-
edge tools that are traditionally restricted to specialized academic or
industrial spaces.

This diversity of Maker fields is not merely a feature but a strength. It allows MakerSpaces to cater to users from various backgrounds, encouraging the cross-pollination of ideas. In such a MakerSpace, a woodworking enthusiast might collaborate with an electronics expert to create a smart furniture prototype, blending traditional craftsmanship with modern technology. Such interdisciplinary projects are the hallmark of successful MakerSpaces, showcasing the potential for creativity when diverse perspectives converge. Additionally, the inclusion of emerging fields like augmented reality (AR) and virtual reality (VR) opens new horizons for experiential learning and creative innovation.

MakerSpaces are particularly effective at fostering innovation in niche fields. For instance, bioengineering-focused MakerSpaces provide opportunities for exploring genetic engineering or molecular sensing. By offering access to specialized tools and fostering a collaborative culture, MakerSpaces create ecosystems where niche fields can thrive alongside more traditional disciplines.

Infrastructure and Tools

The physical setup of MakerSpaces plays a critical role in their functionality and success. Chapter 4 delved into the importance of selecting and maintaining the right tools and equipment. From 3D printers and laser cutters to sewing machines and pottery wheels, the inventory of tools available in MakerSpaces determines the scope of projects users can undertake in that space.

Strategic planning is crucial when designing the layout of a MakerSpace and selecting equipment. Factors such as user demand, budget constraints, and future scalability usually guide decisions. Additionally, maintaining equipment through regular checks and preventive maintenance helps to ensure their longevity and reliability.

As highlighted in Chapter 6, a well-maintained MakerSpace not only enhances user experience but also fosters a culture of responsibility and respect for shared resources.

Effective space utilization is another cornerstone of successful MakerSpaces. Often, those who run MakerSpaces want to include lots of different equipment and the availability of physical space quickly becomes a limiting factor. Selecting furnishings with modular designs, such as adjustable workspace tables and rolling storage units, can help provide flexibility and adaptability to meet changing needs of the MakerSpace. Incorporating features like soundproof rooms for noisy equipment, dedicated zones for specific maker fields, and communal areas for brainstorming can further enhance the user experience. Careful planning of the physical space is essential.

Additionally, the integration of technology into the infrastructure of a MakerSpace is becoming increasingly important. Smart tools and IoT-enabled devices can help streamline operations, while digital dashboards can help monitor equipment usage and maintenance schedules. These innovations not only improve efficiency but also demonstrate the MakerSpace's commitment to staying at the forefront of technological advancements.

Organizing and Operating MakerSpaces

Chapters 5 and 6 provided insights into organizing and operating MakerSpaces effectively.

Operational strategies such as implementing reservation systems, providing training programs, and maintaining an inventory of supplies are essential for smooth functioning. Software tools like Google Calendar or Clustermarket can streamline equipment booking and prevent conflicts, while comprehensive training programs empower users to utilize tools safely and effectively.

Organizational efficiency extends beyond keeping a tidy physical space. Establishing clear policies and guidelines for equipment usage, safety protocols, and community behavior is also important for creating a respectful and productive environment. Regular staff training and user orientation sessions can further reinforce these principles among all users of the MakerSpace.

Funding and sustainability are also important considerations. MakerSpaces often operate on tight budgets, requiring creative approaches to resource management. Partnerships with local businesses, grants, and sponsorships may provide financial support, while user fees or membership models can contribute to offsetting ongoing operational costs. Diversifying revenue streams for the MakerSpace can help long-term stability and reduce dependence on any single funding source.

Building a Vibrant Community

The true value of a MakerSpace lies in its community. Chapter 7 emphasized the importance of fostering a sense of belonging and collaboration among users. By organizing workshops, hosting events, and showcasing projects previously completed by users, MakerSpaces can create an environment that inspires creativity and encourages participation.

Collaboration is a powerful driver of innovation. When individuals from different disciplines come together, their diverse skills and perspectives can lead to creative solutions. MakerSpaces can strive to actively promote interdisciplinary interactions through group projects, challenges, and community initiatives. These interactions not only enhance individual projects but also contribute to a collective sense of achievement and camaraderie.

Overcoming Challenges

While MakerSpaces offer immense potential, they also face challenges that can hinder their operations. Among the most significant issues are funding constraints, equipment maintenance, user engagement, fostering inclusivity, and adapting to future needs.

Funding Constraints: Securing sufficient funding to operate and expand is a persistent challenge for many MakerSpaces. The cost of high-quality equipment, supplies, staffing, and facility maintenance can quickly add up. Many MakerSpaces address this issue through a combination of membership fees, grant applications, and partnerships with local businesses or educational institutions. Sponsorships from technology companies or community organizations can also provide financial support, while hosting revenue-generating events like workshops or classes may also help offset costs. Diversifying funding sources is important to ensure long-term stability.

Equipment Maintenance: MakerSpaces heavily rely on their tools and equipment to deliver value to users. However, frequent usage can lead to wear and tear, making regular maintenance essential. Neglecting maintenance can result in costly repairs or replacements and disrupt operations. A systematic approach that includes routine inspections, cleaning schedules, and preventive maintenance can help mitigate these issues. Investing in durable, high-quality equipment and training users in proper handling may also reduce the likelihood of damage. Additionally, some MakerSpaces choose to incorporate maintenance fees into membership costs to help cover repair expenses.

Maintaining User Engagement: Attracting and retaining users is vital for a MakerSpace's success. Offering a dynamic programming schedule that includes workshops, challenges, and collaborative events is one way of engaging users. Hosting themed activities, such as seasonal crafting sessions or hackathons, can also pique interest and encourage participation in the MakerSpace. Regularly updating tools and offering advanced training sessions for returning users can help ensure that long-time members remain invested and interested. Creating a welcoming environment where users feel valued and supported fosters a loyal community.

Fostering Inclusivity: Inclusivity is a cornerstone of MakerSpaces, but achieving it requires deliberate effort. This involves hiring diverse staff, offering scholarships or reduced membership fees for underrepresented groups, and ensuring the space is accessible to individuals with disabilities. Partnering with community organizations that serve marginalized populations can also broaden the MakerSpace's reach. Inclusive programming—such as events tailored to specific demographics or beginner-friendly workshops—helps create an environment where everyone feels welcome.

Keeping an Eye on the Future: The rapidly changing landscape of technology and innovation means that MakerSpaces must continually adapt to stay relevant. Regularly gathering user feedback through surveys or town hall meetings provides valuable insights into evolving needs. Planning for future growth, such as allocating space for new equipment or emerging Maker fields, ensures that the MakerSpace remains a cutting-edge resource. Collaborating with educational institutions and industry leaders can also keep MakerSpaces aligned with the latest trends and technologies.

A summary table of the biggest challenges facing MakerSpaces can be seen below in Table 8-1.

Table 8-1. *Summary Table of MakerSpace Challenges*

Challenge	Solution
Funding constraints	Diversify funding sources, apply for grants, and seek sponsorships.
Equipment maintenance	Implement routine checks, train users in proper handling, and invest in durable tools.
Maintaining engagement	Offer dynamic programming, introduce new tools, and create an inclusive space.
Fostering inclusivity	Hire diverse staff, provide scholarships, and partner with community organizations.
Keeping an eye on the future	Gather user feedback, embrace emerging technologies, and plan for future expansion.

The Future of MakerSpaces

As we look ahead, MakerSpaces are poised to play an even more critical role in shaping the future of creativity and innovation. The rapid pace of technological advancement, the growing emphasis on interdisciplinary collaboration, and the increasing need for accessible innovation hubs will drive the evolution of MakerSpaces in several key directions.

Future MakerSpaces will increasingly adopt advanced technologies such as artificial intelligence (AI), blockchain, and extended reality (XR), including Augmented and Virtual Reality. These tools will enhance users' ability to prototype, simulate, and refine their projects. For example, XR could enable virtual prototyping, where Makers can test and tweak designs in a virtual environment before committing to physical fabrication. AI could provide real-time design suggestions or troubleshooting advice, empowering users with smarter, more intuitive tools.

With the global push toward sustainability, MakerSpaces will evolve to prioritize eco-friendly practices and tools. Incorporating sustainable materials, offering equipment for recycling and upcycling, and hosting workshops on green innovation will become common. MakerSpaces may also become hubs for researching and developing solutions to pressing environmental challenges, fostering innovation in renewable energy, waste management, and sustainable product design.

As MakerSpaces strive to become more inclusive, there will be a stronger emphasis on making these spaces accessible to diverse populations. This includes providing resources and training for individuals with disabilities, offering multilingual programming, and addressing digital divides through remote access to Maker tools via cloud-based platforms. Mobile MakerSpaces—equipped vehicles that bring tools and workshops to underserved communities—may also see increased adoption.

The future of MakerSpaces will likely involve deeper partnerships with industries, startups, and educational institutions. These collaborations can provide access to advanced tools, mentorship opportunities, and real-world challenges that inspire innovation. For instance, universities might integrate MakerSpaces more fully into their curricula, while companies could sponsor Maker challenges or co-develop prototypes with Makers.

With the advent of smart tools and IoT-enabled devices, future MakerSpaces will leverage data to enhance operations and user experiences. Analytics can provide insights into equipment usage patterns, popular projects, and user preferences, enabling space managers to optimize resources and offer personalized support. Additionally, digital platforms could allow users to share their progress, collaborate remotely, and access resources tailored to their specific interests.

As the boundaries of innovation expand, so too will the scope of Maker fields. Emerging areas like synthetic biology, quantum computing, and space technology may find dedicated MakerSpaces where enthusiasts and professionals can experiment and innovate. This diversification will not only attract new users but also inspire groundbreaking interdisciplinary projects.

Future MakerSpaces will likely place greater emphasis on their role as community anchors. By addressing local challenges, offering programs that align with regional needs, and fostering entrepreneurial initiatives, MakerSpaces can drive meaningful social and economic impact. Partnerships with community organizations, schools, and local governments will ensure these spaces remain vibrant, relevant, and impactful.

A summary table of the Future of MakerSpaces can be seen below in Table 8-2.

Table 8-2. *Summary of Future Trends of MakerSpaces*

Trend	Description
Integration of emerging technologies	Adoption of AI, blockchain, and extended reality (XR) to enhance prototyping, simulation, and project development
Focus on sustainability and green innovation	Emphasizing eco-friendly materials, recycling, and upcycling; fostering innovation in renewable energy and sustainable design
Broadening accessibility	Enhancing inclusivity through multilingual programming, disability-friendly resources, and mobile MakerSpaces for underserved communities
Collaboration with industry and academia	Strengthening ties with universities, startups, and corporations for mentorship, funding, and access to advanced tools
Data-driven operations and personalization	Utilizing IoT and analytics to optimize resource allocation, track user preferences, and provide personalized support
Expanding the scope of Maker fields	Inclusion of fields like synthetic biology, quantum computing, and space technology to push the boundaries of innovation
Strengthening community impact	Addressing local challenges, fostering entrepreneurship, and collaborating with community organizations to maximize social and economic benefits.

Conclusion

MakerSpaces are more than just workshops—they are ecosystems of innovation, collaboration, and growth. As they continue to evolve and adapt to the changing needs of their users and communities, their potential to inspire creativity and drive meaningful progress remains limitless. MakerSpaces are not simply physical spaces filled with tools, equipment, and supplies. Instead, they are a haven for creativity, innovation, and design, a home for continual learning and collaboration, and most importantly an incubator for the revolutionary power of a person with an idea and the tools to make it a reality. By embracing the challenges and opportunities of the future, MakerSpaces can cement their place as cornerstones of innovation in the years to come.

As you embark on your journey in creating a MakerSpace or as you continue to nurture an existing space, remember that the secret formula to success lies in the journey itself. Always remember to celebrate the successes, embrace challenges, and above all else cherish the small moments of accomplishment because these moments are what make these remarkable spaces possible. With all of this said, we bid you farewell. Happy making!

References

Chapter 1

- What is a MakerSpace, Fort Worth Library—`https://youtu.be/lwvaNyuZcfU`

- What is the MakerSpace, The MakerSpace—`https://youtu.be/wti6FMvDAE4`

- Makerspace: Make Community, TEDx Talks—`https://youtu.be/CQnXaShzuHw`

Chapter 2

- I Like To Make Stuff—`https://www.youtube.com/@Iliketomakestuff`

- Totally Handy—`https://www.youtube.com/@TotallyHandy`

- DIY Perks -- `https://www.youtube.com/c/DIYPerks`

- This Old House—`https://www.youtube.com/thisoldhouse`

Chapter 3

- An Open-Source Plate Reader: `https://pubs.acs.org/doi/10.1021/acs.biochem.8b00952`

- Fablab: `https://www.fablabs.io/`

- Nature article on DIY lab automation: `https://www.nature.com/articles/d41586-019-01590-z`

- Yale Center for Engineering Innovation and Design: `https://ceid.yale.edu/`

- Makerspaces, SparkFun Electronics—`https://youtu.be/tzHue3yMEkk`

- Makerspace Project ideas, Your Shop Mitchell SD—`https://youtu.be/dQNyAiIXnJc`

- The Nuts and Bolts of Makerspaces, indianapublicmedia—`https://youtu.be/u7_uSsvE5EI`

Chapter 4

- Arts and Crafts:
  - Knitting Machine: `https://youtu.be/9N1NB-ewyJY`
  - Using a pottery wheel: `https://youtu.be/PUAwDPUNyrs`

- Biology and Chemistry
  - How to stock a biology lab: `https://youtu.be/zqQ4x9rmkKg`
  - Using a micropipette: `https://youtu.be/uEy_NGDfo_8`

- How to use a microscope: `https://youtu.be/bERaLwrVwCk`

- Lab Tools and equipment: `https://youtu.be/chODOKSPJS4`

- Electronics

  - Setting up an electronics lab: `https://youtu.be/dR8nqJzrnSg`

  - How to solder: `https://youtu.be/f95i88OSWB4`

  - How to use an oscilloscope: `https://youtu.be/u4zyptPLlJI`

  - How to use a multimeter: `https://youtu.be/SLkPtmnglOI`

- Mechanical

  - How 3D Printers Work: `https://youtu.be/HlvK6DLwCz4`

  - Introduction to the Lathe: `https://youtu.be/UjPc5CewLsA`

  - Various wood working tools: `https://youtu.be/2eFeB2fTiQY`

Chapter 5

- Makerspace Organization and Management for Elementary Schools: `https://youtu.be/LeieRdmFZbw`

- Some MakerSpace organization tips: `https://youtu.be/7hJEuWAfSPY`

REFERENCES

- Artisan's Asylum: https://www.artisansasylum.com/
- Chattanooga Public Library MakerSpace: https://chattlibrary.org/4th-floor/
- George H. Stephenson Foundation Educational Laboratory and Bio-MakerSpace: http://belabs.seas.upenn.edu
- Paper on digital organization of a MakerSpace: https://monolith.asee.org/public/conferences/140/papers/25721/view
- Yale Center for Engineering Innovation & Design: https://ceid.yale.edu/
- Waste Management and Sustainability
  - https://www.mygreenlab.org/
  - https://sustainability.mit.edu/green-labs
  - https://sustainable.harvard.edu/schools-units/sustainable-labs/
  - https://makerspace.engineering.nyu.edu/sustainability/
  - https://blogs.lawrence.edu/makerspace/2022/06/21/reducing-waste-in-a-makerspace/

Chapter 6

- Videos:

  - Budgeting for your MakerSpace: `https://youtu.be/cSGVNsCOXJQ`

  - Streamlining Makerspace Training with Hybrid and Online Delivery: `https://youtu.be/A1ZISeTyvDo`

  - MakerSpace NFC Part Management System: `https://youtu.be/oevHEGISBhA`

  - Clustermarket Software Demonstration: `https://youtu.be/ufUm5L5B1ZU`

  - General Makerspace Safety: `https://youtu.be/DOhpBLz6sLk`

- Other references:

  - Paper on MakerSpace operations: `https://monolith.asee.org/public/conferences/172/papers/29661/view`

  - Clustermarket: `https://clustermarket.com/`

  - NEMO: `https://github.com/usnistgov/NEMO`

  - MIT Mobius: `https://project-manus.mit.edu/mobius`

Chapter 7

- Sample overview video: `https://youtu.be/cI g-PGmOWJY`

- NextFab in Philadelphia: `https://nextfab.com/`

Index

A

Accessibility, 9–11, 95
Agar-based microbial art, 88
AR, *see* Augmented reality (AR)
Arduino, 94, 136, 142
Artisanal handicrafts, 76
Artisan's Asylum, 193
Arts and crafts MakerSpaces, 74,
    79, 80, 82, 115, 116
Arts and crafts projects
    as artisanal handicrafts, 76
    Community Quilt, 83
    Digital illustration, 78
    digital knitting machine, 76
    environmental conditions, 82
    furniture and accessories, 81
    hand-sewn sketchbook, 77
    mixed media, 78, 79
    paper arts, 78, 79
    sculpture, 78, 79
    space
        power outlets, 80
        sewing machines, 80, 81
    technological innovation, 82
    textile arts, 78, 79
    ventilation and fresh air, 82
    working with sewing pattern, 84

Augmented reality (AR), 109, 327
Autoclaves, 127, 128, 132
Automation
    access control, 275
    access management system,
        274, 275
    equipment borrowing page,
        276, 277
    laser cutter training
        management, 275, 276
    supply ordering, 277
    3D printing, 277

B

Balances and scales, 128, 134
Bioethics, 90
Biological/chemical
    MakerSpaces, 85
    artistic biology, 86
    bio-inspired sensing devices, 86
    chemical synthesis, 85, 86
    edible chemistry, 86
    ethical considerations, 89, 90
    expensive biology testing
        tool, 90
    scientific equipment
        development, 85, 86

© Sevile G. Mannickarottu, Michael G. Patterson, and Carolyne Godon 2025
S. G. Mannickarottu et al., *Creating MakerSpaces*, Maker Innovations Series,
https://doi.org/10.1007/979-8-8688-1309-2

GPSR Compliance
The European Union's (EU) General Product Safety Regulation (GPSR) is a set
of rules that requires consumer products to be safe and our obligations to
ensure this.

If you have any concerns about our products, you can contact us on

ProductSafety@springernature.com

In case Publisher is established outside the EU, the EU authorized
representative is:

Springer Nature Customer Service Center GmbH
Europaplatz 3
69115 Heidelberg, Germany